Angular Projects
Second Edition

Build modern web apps by exploring Angular 12 with
10 different projects and cutting-edge technologies

Aristeidis Bampakos

BIRMINGHAM—MUMBAI

Angular Projects
Second Edition

Copyright © 2021 Packt Publishing

Associate Group Product Manager: Pavan Ramchandani
Publishing Product Manager: Ashitosh Gupta
Senior Editor: Keagan Carneiro
Content Development Editor: Rakhi Patel
Technical Editor: Deepesh Patel
Copy Editor: Safis Editing
Project Coordinator: Manthan Patel
Proofreader: Safis Editing
Indexer: Manju Arsan
Production Designer: Nilesh Mohite

First published: September 2019
Second edition: June 2021
Production reference: 1020721

Published by Packt Publishing Ltd.
Livery Place
35 Livery Street
Birmingham
B3 2PB, UK.

ISBN 978-1-80020-526-0

www.packt.com

To my parents, Konstantinos and Anastasia, who taught me the real values and principles in life.

– Aristeidis Bampakos

Foreword

Angular is a powerful web framework that helps teams build robust scalable applications. Angular continues to evolve but the core values remain the same: build a platform developers love to use, enable developers to build applications that users love to use, and have a community where everyone feels welcomed

Angular Projects is a book that embraces these values and takes a unique approach to empower new and experienced developers to build great applications using Angular. Aristeidis uses a project-driven approach to help learners understand modern Angular techniques in an intriguing and accessible way.

This guide will help learners to build their first application with the powerful Angular CLI, take advantage of Angular's strong PWA integration, build performant static applications with Scully, and more. This book will add significant value to developers looking to get the most out of their Angular experience

As Angular continues to power incredible experiences inside Google and across the web this book will serve as an excellent learning resource for developers looking to build great apps.

Mark Thompson

Angular Team at Google

Contributors

About the author

Aristeidis Bampakos is an experienced frontend web developer and a Google Developer Expert for the Angular framework. From 2011, he has mainly focused on developing applications with AngularJS and Angular frameworks, TypeScript, and Angular Material. He is currently working at Plex-Earth, where he specializes in Angular development and also works as an Angular Senior Tech Instructor for Code.Hub, where he teaches the Angular framework to other developers and individuals

I am grateful to all people who have supported and believed in me, especially my wife, Ria, and my good friend, Jeffrey Bosch, for encouraging me and never letting me give up.

I also want to thank Sander Elias from the Scully team and Mike Hartington from the Ionic team for their help throughout the book.

Here's what they had to say:

Everything looks good to me. Job well done!

- Sander Elias

Overall, it's really good. Everything was clearly explained. Great job!

- Mike Hartington

About the reviewer

Fabio Biondi is a frontend instructor, a community leader, and a frequent contributor in many Italian JavaScript user groups.

He's a Google Developer Expert in Angular and a Microsoft MVP with more than 15 years of experience in developing enterprise-level applications, interactive experiences, UIKit, and components in several web technologies.

He is a Twitch Partner and also runs a YouTube channel on which he frequently publishes technical content.

Table of Contents

3

Building an Issue Tracking System using Reactive Forms

4

Building a PWA Weather Application Using Angular Service Worker

5

Building a WYSIWYG Editor for the Desktop using Electron

6

Building a Mobile Photo Geotagging Application Using Capacitor and 3D Maps

7

Building an SSR Application for a GitHub Portfolio Using Angular

8
Building an Enterprise Portal Using Nx Monorepo Tools and NgRx

9
Building a Component UI Library Using Angular CLI and Angular CDK

10

Customizing Angular CLI Commands Using Schematics

Other Books You May Enjoy

Index

Preface

Angular is a popular JavaScript framework that can run on a broad range of platforms, including web, desktop, and mobile. It has an array of rich features right out of the box and a wide range of tools that makes it popular among developers. This updated second edition of *Angular Projects* will teach you how to build efficient and optimized web applications using Angular.

You will start by exploring the essential features of the framework by creating 10 different real-world web applications. Each application will demonstrate how to integrate Angular with a different library and tool. As you advance, you will learn how to implement popular technologies such as Angular Router, Scully, Electron, Angular's service worker, Nx's monorepo tools, NgRx, and more while building an issue tracking system, a PWA weather application, a mobile photo geotagging application, a component UI library, and many other exciting projects. In the concluding chapters, you'll get to grips with customizing Angular CLI commands using schematics.

By the end of this book, you will have the skills you need to build Angular apps using a variety of different technologies according to you or your client's needs.

Who this book is for

If you are a developer who has beginner-level experience with Angular and you're looking to become well versed in the essential tools for dealing with the various use cases you may encounter with Angular, then this Angular development book is for you. Beginner-level knowledge of web application development and basic experience of working with ES6 or TypeScript are assumed.

What this book covers

Chapter 1, *Creating Your First Web Application in Angular*, explores the main features of the Angular framework and teaches you about the basic building blocks that comprise a typical Angular application. You will investigate the different tools and IDE extensions that are available in the Angular ecosystem to enhance the developer's workflow and experience.

Chapter 2, Building an SPA Application with Scully and Angular Router, looks at how an Angular application is based on the **Single Page Application (SPA)** architecture, where typically we have multiple pages that are served by different URLs or routes. On the other hand, Jamstack is a hot technology that is emerging and allows you to build fast, static websites and serve them directly from a CDN.

In this chapter, we will use the Angular Router to implement routing functionality in an Angular application. We will also use Scully, the best static site generator for Angular, to create a personal blog that embraces the Jamstack architecture.

Chapter 3, Building an Issue Tracking System Using Reactive Forms, is where we build an issue tracking management system and use Angular reactive forms to add new issues to the system. We will design our forms using Clarity Components from VMware, and we will incorporate built-in and custom validations. We will also react to value changes in the forms and take actions accordingly.

Chapter 4, Building a PWA Weather Application Using Angular Service Worker, covers how the user experience of a web application is not the same for all users, especially in places with poor network coverage and connectivity. When we build a web application, we should take into account all sorts of network types.

In this chapter, we will create an application that uses the OpenWeather API to display the weather of a specified region. We will learn how to deploy the application to Firebase Hosting. We will also explore PWA techniques using the Angular service worker to provide a seamless user experience when offline.

Chapter 5, Building a WYSIWYG Editor for the Desktop Using Electron, explores Electron, a cross-platform JavaScript framework for building desktop applications using web technologies. When combined with Angular, it can yield really performant apps.

In this chapter, we will create a WYSIWYG editor that can run on the desktop. We will build an Angular application and integrate it with ngx-wig, a popular WYSIWYG Angular library, and we will use Electron to package it as a desktop application. Data is persisted locally in the filesystem using a Node.js API.

Chapter 6, Building a Mobile Photo Geotagging Application Using Capacitor and 3D Maps, covers Capacitor, a service provided by the Ionic framework that turns any web application, such as one created with Angular, into a native one. Its main advantage is that we can build a native mobile application and a web app using the same code base. Cesium is a popular JavaScript framework for building 3D maps.

In this chapter, we will use Capacitor to build a geotagging mobile application for our photos. We will use various Ionic plugins to take a photo in a specified location and persist it to Cloud Firestore. We will then display a list of all photos taken inside the Cesium 3D viewer.

Chapter 7, Building an SSR Application for a GitHub Portfolio Using Angular, dives into **Search Engine Optimization (SEO)**, a critical aspect for any website nowadays. Who doesn't want their website to look good when sharing it via social media? The real challenge for client web applications is to optimize it, which can be accomplished by rendering content on the server.

In this chapter, we will learn how to create a GitHub portfolio application using the GitHub API. We will then render it on the server and learn how to transfer the state to the browser. We will also see how to set the page title and additional metadata dynamically and use preboot to manage page transitions.

Chapter 8, Building an Enterprise Portal Using Nx Monorepo Tools and NgRx, covers monorepo architecture, which is a popular technique for when working with multiple applications under a single repository, giving speed and flexibility to the development process.

In this chapter, we will use Nx monorepo development tools to create two portals: one for the end user, in which they will be able to select a **Point of Interest (POI)** and visit it on a map, and another for admins to check on visit statistics for a given POI. Application state is managed using NgRx.

Chapter 9, Building a Component UI Library Using Angular CLI and Angular CDK, addresses how enterprise organizations usually need custom UI libraries that can be used across different web applications. The Angular CDK provides a broad range of functionalities for creating accessible and high-performing UI components.

In this chapter, we will create two different components using the Angular CDK and the Bulma CSS framework. We will also package them as a single Angular library and learn how to publish them on npm, so that they can be re-used in different apps. We will also investigate how we can use each component as an Angular element.

Chapter 10, Customizing Angular CLI Commands Using Schematics, covers how organizations usually follow different guidelines when it comes to creating Angular entities such as components or services. Angular schematics can assist them by extending Angular CLI commands and providing custom automation.

In this chapter, we will learn how to use the Angular schematics API to build our own set of commands for generating components and services. We will build a schematic for creating an Angular component that contains the Tailwind CSS framework. We will also build an Angular service that uses the built-in HTTP client by default.

To get the most out of this book

You will need a version of Angular 12 installed on your computer, preferably the latest minor one. All code examples have been tested using Angular 12.0.0 on Windows but they should work with any future release of Angular 12 as well.

Software/hardware covered in the book	Operating system requirements
Angular 12	Windows, macOS, or Linux
Visual Studio Code	Windows, macOS, or Linux
Scully	Windows, macOS, or Linux
Clarity Design	Windows, macOS, or Linux
Angular PWA	Windows, macOS, or Linux
Electron	Windows, macOS, or Linux
Ionic	Windows, macOS, or Linux
CesiumJS	Windows, macOS, or Linux
Firebase	Windows, macOS, or Linux
GitHub API	Windows, macOS, or Linux
Nx monorepo tools	Windows, macOS, or Linux
NgRx	Windows, macOS, or Linux
Angular Material	Windows, macOS, or Linux (Any)
Angular CDK	Windows, macOS, or Linux (Any)
Angular schematics	Windows, macOS, or Linux (Any)

If you are using the digital version of this book, we advise you to type the code yourself or access the code from the book's GitHub repository (a link is available in the next section). Doing so will help you avoid any potential errors related to the copying and pasting of code.

Download the example code files

You can download the example code files for this book from GitHub at `https://github.com/PacktPublishing/Angular-Projects-Second-Edition`. If there's an update to the code, it will be updated in the GitHub repository.

We also have other code bundles from our rich catalog of books and videos available at `https://github.com/PacktPublishing/`. Check them out!

Download the color images

We also provide a PDF file that has color images of the screenshots and diagrams used in this book. You can download it here: `https://static.packt-cdn.com/downloads/9781800205260_ColorImages.pdf`.

Conventions used

There are a number of text conventions used throughout this book.

`Code in text`: Indicates code words in text, database table names, folder names, filenames, file extensions, pathnames, dummy URLs, user input, and Twitter handles. Here is an example: "It will add all the necessary npm packages of the Clarity library to the `dependencies` section of the `package.json` file."

A block of code is set as follows:

```
<div class="main-container">
  <div class="content-container">
    <div class="content-area">
      <app-issue-list></app-issue-list>
    </div>
  </div>
</div>
```

When we wish to draw your attention to a particular part of a code block, the relevant lines or items are set in bold:

```
"styles": [
    "node_modules/@clr/ui/clr-ui.min.css",
    "src/styles.css"
]
```

Any command-line input or output is written as follows:

```
ng add @angular/material --theme=indigo-pink --typography=true
--animations=true
```

Bold: Indicates a new term, an important word, or words that you see onscreen. For instance, words in menus or dialog boxes appear in **bold**. Here is an example: "Click on the **ADD NEW ISSUE** button and enter the details of a new issue."

Tips or important notes

Appear like this.

Get in touch

Feedback from our readers is always welcome.

General feedback: If you have questions about any aspect of this book, email us at customercare@packtpub.com and mention the book title in the subject of your message.

Errata: Although we have taken every care to ensure the accuracy of our content, mistakes do happen. If you have found a mistake in this book, we would be grateful if you would report this to us. Please visit www.packtpub.com/support/errata and fill in the form.

Piracy: If you come across any illegal copies of our works in any form on the internet, we would be grateful if you would provide us with the location address or website name. Please contact us at copyright@packt.com with a link to the material.

If you are interested in becoming an author: If there is a topic that you have expertise in and you are interested in either writing or contributing to a book, please visit authors.packtpub.com.

Share Your Thoughts

Once you've read *Angular Projects Second Edition*, we'd love to hear your thoughts! Scan the QR code below to go straight to the Amazon review page for this book and share your feedback.

https://packt.link/r/1800205260

Your review is important to us and the tech community and will help us make sure we're delivering excellent quality content.

1
Creating Your First Web Application in Angular

Angular is a popular and modern **JavaScript** framework that can run on different platforms additional to the web, such as desktop and mobile. Angular applications are written in **TypeScript**, a superset of JavaScript that provides syntactic sugar such as strong typing and object-oriented techniques.

Angular applications are created and developed using a command-line tool made by the Angular team called the **Angular CLI**. It automates many development tasks, such as scaffolding, testing, and deploying an Angular application, which would take a lot of time to configure manually.

The popularity of the Angular framework is considerably reflected in its broad support of tooling. The **Visual Studio Code** (**VSCode**) editor contains various extensions that enhance the development experience when working with Angular.

In this chapter, we will cover the following topics:

- Introduction to Angular
- Introduction to the Angular CLI
- Exploring the rich ecosystem of Angular tooling in VSCode
- How to create our first Angular application
- How to use **Nx Console** for automating Angular CLI commands

Essential background theory and context

The Angular framework is a cross-platform JavaScript framework that can run on a wide range of environments, including the web, servers, mobile, and desktop. It consists of a collection of JavaScript libraries that we can use for building highly performant and scalable web applications. The architecture of an Angular application is based on a hierarchical representation of components. Components are the fundamental building blocks of an Angular application. They represent and control a particular portion of a web page called the *view*. Some examples of components are as follows:

- A list of blog posts
- An issue reporting form
- A weather display widget

Components of an Angular application can be logically organized as a tree:

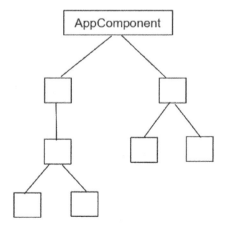

Figure 1.1 – Component tree

An Angular application typically has one main component, called **AppComponent**, by convention. Each component in the tree can communicate and interact with its siblings using an application programming interface defined by each one.

An Angular application can have many features that are called modules. Each module serves a block of single functionality that corresponds to a particular application domain or workflow. Angular modules are used to group Angular components that share similar functionality:

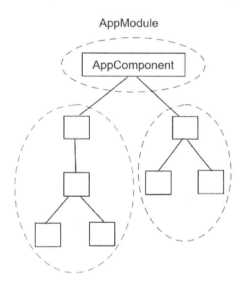

Figure 1.2 – Module hierarchy

In the previous diagram, the dashed line circles represent Angular modules. An Angular application typically has one main module, called **AppModule**, by convention. Each module can import other modules in an Angular application if they wish to use part of their functionality.

The functionality of a module can be further analyzed in the presentational and business logic of a feature. Angular components should only be responsible for handling the presentational logic and delegating business logic tasks to services. The Angular framework provides Angular services to components using a built-in **dependency injection (DI)** mechanism.

The Angular DI framework uses special-purpose objects, called injectors, to hide much of the complexity of providing dependencies to an Angular application. Components are not required to know any of the actual implementation of an Angular service. They only need to ask for it from an injector.

An Angular service should follow the single responsibility principle, and it should not cross boundaries between different Angular modules. Some examples of services are as follows:

- Access data from a backend API using the HTTP protocol.
- Interact with the local storage of the browser.
- Error logging.
- Data transformations.

An Angular developer does not need to remember how to create components, modules, and services off by heart while building an Angular application. Luckily, the Angular CLI can assist us by providing a command-line interface to accomplish these tasks.

Introduction to the Angular CLI

The Angular CLI is a tool created by the Angular team that improves the developer experience while building Angular applications. It hides much of the complexity of scaffolding and configuring an Angular application while allowing the developer to concentrate on what they do best – coding! Before we can start using the Angular CLI, we need to set up the following prerequisites in our system:

- **Node.js**: A JavaScript runtime that is built on the v8 engine of Chrome. You can download any **Long-Term Support** (**LTS**) version from https://nodejs.org/en.
- **npm**: A package manager for the Node.js runtime.

We can then install the Angular CLI using npm from the command line:

```
npm install -g @angular/cli
```

We can use the -g option to install the Angular CLI globally since we want to create Angular applications from any path of our operating system.

> **Important note**
> Installing the Angular CLI may require administrative privileges in some operating systems.

To verify that the Angular CLI has been installed correctly, we can run the following from the command line:

```
ng version
```

The previous command will report the version of the Angular CLI that has been installed in our system. The Angular CLI provides a command-line interface through the `ng` command, which is the binary executable of the Angular CLI. It can accept various options, including the following:

- **serve**: Build and serve an Angular application.
- **build**: Build an Angular application.
- **test**: Run the unit tests of an Angular application.
- **generate**: Generate a new Angular artifact, such as a component or module.
- **add**: Install a third-party library that is compatible with the Angular framework.
- **new**: Create a new Angular application.

The previous options are the most common ones. If you want to view all the available commands, execute the following in the command line:

```
ng help
```

The previous command will display a list of all the supported commands from the Angular CLI.

The Angular tooling ecosystem is full of extensions and utilities that can help us when developing Angular applications. In the next section, we will overview some of them that work with VSCode.

Angular tooling in VSCode

There are many extensions available in the VSCode Marketplace that enhance the Angular tooling ecosystem. In this section, we will learn about the most popular ones that can significantly help us in Angular development:

- Nx Console
- Angular Language Service
- Angular Snippets
- Angular Evergreen
- Material Icon Theme

The preceding list is not exhaustive, and some of the extensions are already included in the **Angular Essentials pack**. However, you can browse more Angular extensions for VSCode at `https://marketplace.visualstudio.com/search?term=angular&target=VSCode`.

Nx Console

The Nx Console is a VSCode extension developed by the Nrwl team that provides a graphical user interface over the Angular CLI. It contains most of the Angular CLI commands, and it uses the Angular CLI internally to execute each one. We will learn more about this extension in the *Building our application with Nx Console* section.

Angular Language Service

The Angular Language Service extension provides various enhancements while editing HTML templates in an Angular application, including the following:

- Code autocompletion
- Compile error messages
- Go-to definition techniques

Code autocompletion is a feature that helps us find the right property or method to use while typing. It works by displaying a list of suggestions while we start typing in HTML content:

```
<span>{{ ti }} app is running!</span>
            title            (property) AppComponent.title: stri...
            title
            title
```

Figure 1.3 – Code completion

In the previous screenshot, when we start typing the word `ti`, the Angular Language Service suggests the `title` component property. Notice that code completion only works for the public properties and methods in a component.

One of the most common issues when developing web applications is detecting errors before the application reaches production. This problem can be solved partially by the Angular compiler, which is bootstrapped upon building an Angular application for production. Moreover, the Angular Language Service can take this further by displaying compilation error messages far before our application reaches the compilation process:

> any
>
> Property 'tile' does not exist on type 'AppComponent'. Did you mean 'title'? ngtsc(2551)
>
> View Problem (Alt+F8)   No quick fixes available

```
<span>{{ tile }} app is running!</span>
```

Figure 1.4 – Compile error message

For example, if we accidentally misspell the name of a property or method of the component, the Angular Language Service will display an appropriate error message.

Angular Snippets

The Angular Snippets extension contains a collection of Angular code snippets for TypeScript and HTML. In TypeScript, we can use it to create components, modules, or services in a blank TypeScript file:

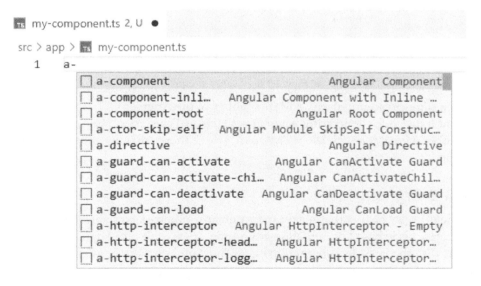

Figure 1.5 – New Angular component snippet

In an HTML template, we can use the extension to create useful Angular artifacts, such as the *ngFor directive, to loop through a list in HTML:

🖪 my-component.html U ●

src > app > 🖪 my-component.html

!!MISSING: command!!

```
1    a-
```
☐ a-formGroupName
☐ a-ng-container   ng-container
☐ a-ng-container
☐ a-ng-content   ng-content
☐ a-ng-content
☐ a-ng-template   ng-template
☐ a-ng-template
☐ a-ngClass   ngClass
☐ a-ngClass
☐ a-ngFor   ngFor
☐ a-ngFor   Angular *ngFor (Angular Snippets (V...
☐ a-ngFor-trackBy   ngFor with trackBy

Figure 1.6 – *ngFor snippet

Due to the widespread popularity and capabilities of the Angular CLI, it looks more convenient to use it for generating Angular artifacts in TypeScript. However, Angular Snippets does a great job with the HTML part, where there are more things to remember off by heart.

Angular Evergreen

One of the primary factors that makes the Angular framework so stable is that it follows a regular release cycle based on semantic versioning. If we want our Angular applications to be packed with the latest features and fixes, we must update them regularly. But how can we stay up to date in the most efficient way? We can use the Angular Evergreen extension for that!

It compares the Angular and Angular CLI versions of an Angular CLI project with the latest ones and alerts you about whether you need to update it:

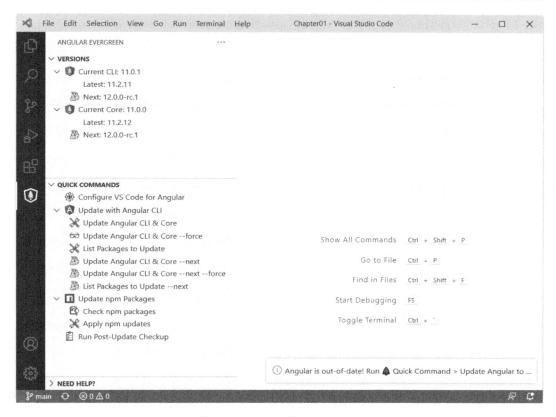

Figure 1.7 – Angular Evergreen

It provides an easy-to-use user interface for executing the following commands:

- Upgrading Angular dependencies to the *latest* version

- Upgrading Angular dependencies to the *next* version

- Upgrading all npm dependencies

Angular Evergreen is the perfect extension for never staying out of date with your Angular projects.

Material Icon Theme

The last extension in the list does not add much value regarding the productivity of the developer. Instead, it focuses on the discoverability and aesthetic point of view by modifying the icon theme of VSCode.

The Material Icon Theme contains a ton of icons that are based on Material Design. It can understand the type of each file in your project and display the related icon automatically. For example, Angular modules are displayed with a red Angular icon, whereas components are displayed with a blue Angular icon.

VSCode has a default file icon theme called **Seti**. Once you've installed Material Icon Theme, it will prompt you to select which one you would like to activate:

Figure 1.8 – Selecting a file icon theme

Selecting **Material Icon Theme** will update the icons of your current Angular project automatically.

> **Important note**
> Material Icon Theme is installed and applied globally to VSCode, so you do not need to activate it separately for each Angular CLI project.

Now, when you open your Angular project, you will understand the type of each file at a glance, even if its name is not displayed as a whole on the screen.

Project overview

In this project, we will use the Angular CLI to create a new Angular application from scratch. Then, we will interact with the core functionality of the Angular framework to make a simple change to our application. Finally, we will learn how to use the Nx Console extension to build and serve our application.

Build time: 15 minutes.

Getting started

The following software tools are required to complete this project:

- **Git**: A free and open source distributed version control system. You can download it from https://git-scm.com.

- **VSCode**: A code editor that you can download from `https://code.visualstudio.com/Download`.

- **Angular CLI**: The command-line interface for Angular that we introduced in the *Essential background theory and context* section.

- **GitHub material**: The related code for this chapter can be found in the `Chapter01` folder at `https://github.com/PacktPublishing/Angular-Projects-Second-Edition`.

Creating our first Angular application

To create a fresh new Angular application, we must execute the `ng new` command of the Angular CLI, passing the name of the application as an option:

```
ng new my-angular
```

The new command is used to create a new Angular application or a new Angular workspace. An Angular workspace is an Angular CLI project that contains one or more Angular applications, where some of them can be Angular libraries. So, when we execute the `ng new` command, we create an Angular workspace with an Angular application by default.

In the previous command, the name of our Angular application is `my-angular`. Upon executing the command, the Angular CLI will ask some questions to collect as much information as possible regarding the nature of the application that we want to create. Let's take a look:

1. Initially, it will ask whether we want to enable routing in our Angular application:

    ```
    ? Would you like to add Angular routing? (y/N)
    ```

    Figure 1.9 – Angular routing

    Routing in Angular is all about navigating between the components of an Angular application using a URL. In this project, we are not concerned with routing, so press *Enter* to accept the default value.

2. Then, the Angular CLI prompts us to select the style format that we want to use throughout the Angular application:

```
? Which stylesheet format would you like to use? (Use arrow keys)
> CSS
  SCSS   [ https://sass-lang.com/documentation/syntax#scss              ]
  Sass   [ https://sass-lang.com/documentation/syntax#the-indented-syntax ]
  Less   [ http://lesscss.org                                           ]
```

Figure 1.10 – Stylesheet format

3. Select a format from the list of available stylesheets and press *Enter*.

> **Tip**
> You can use the arrow keys of your keyboard to navigate between the available stylesheet options.

The Angular CLI initiates the creation process of your Angular application, which consists of the following:

- Scaffolding the necessary folder structure of a typical Angular CLI project
- Installing the required npm dependencies and Angular packages
- Initializing Git in the Angular CLI project

This process may take some time, depending on the speed of your network. Once it has finished, you should have a new folder named my-angular in the path where you ran the ng new Angular CLI command.

Now, the time has finally come to run our Angular application and see it in action:

1. Open a Terminal window and navigate to the my-angular folder.

2. Run the following Angular CLI command:

```
ng serve
```

This will build the Angular application and start a built-in web server that we can use to preview it. The web server is started in watch mode; that is, it automatically rebuilds the Angular application whenever we make a change in the code. The first time an Angular application is built, it takes a considerable amount of time to complete, so we must be patient. You will know when the process has finished with no errors when you see the following message in the Terminal window:

```
** Angular Live Development Server is listening on localhost:4200, open your browser on http://localhost:4200/ **

√ Compiled successfully.
```

Figure 1.11 – Angular build output

3. Fire up your favorite browser and navigate to `http://localhost:4200` to get a preview of your brand-new Angular application:

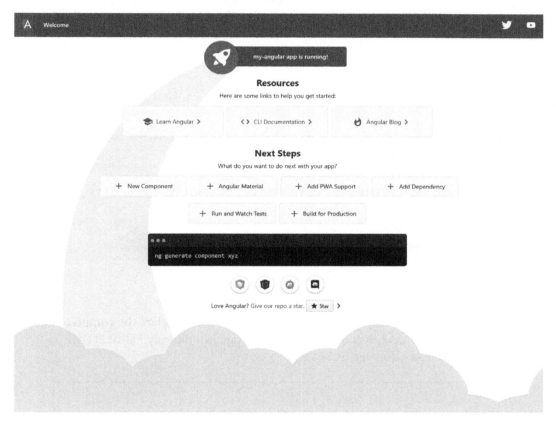

Figure 1.12 – Minimal Angular application

The Angular CLI creates a minimal Angular application by default to provide us with a starting point for our Angular project. It contains some ready-made CSS styles and HTML content, which we will learn how to change according to our specifications in the following section.

Interacting with the Angular framework

When working with Angular, the real fun starts when we get our hands dirty with the framework itself. Understanding how Angular works and writing the application code is what matters, after all.

The application source code resides inside the `src\app` folder, in the root of our Angular CLI project. It contains all the files needed to build and test our Angular application, including a component and a module. The component is the main component of the Angular application:

app.component.ts

```
import { Component } from '@angular/core';


@Component({
  selector: 'app-root',
  templateUrl: './app.component.html',
  styleUrls: ['./app.component.css']
})
export class AppComponent {
  title = 'my-angular';
}
```

The following properties characterize an Angular component:

- `selector`: A unique name that is used to identify and declare the component inside HTML content. It is used as an HTML tag, just like any native HTML element, such as `<app-root></app-root>`.

> **Tip**
>
> The Angular CLI provides the `app` prefix by default in component selectors. We can use a custom one using the `--prefix` option when creating a new Angular CLI application from scratch. A custom prefix can be based on the name of an organization or a particular product, and it helps avoid collisions with other libraries or modules.

- `templateUrl`: The path pointing to an HTML file that contains the HTML content of the component, which is called the template of the component.

- `styleUrls`: A list of paths where each one points to a stylesheet file containing the CSS styles of the component.

The preceding properties are defined using the @Component decorator. It is a function that decorates the TypeScript class of the component and recognizes it as an Angular component. The title property of the AppComponent class is a public property that contains a string value and can be used in the template of the component.

The main module of our Angular application uses a similar decorator called @NgModule to define its properties:

app.module.ts

```typescript
import { NgModule } from '@angular/core';
import { BrowserModule } from '@angular/platform-browser';

import { AppComponent } from './app.component';

@NgModule({
  declarations: [
    AppComponent
  ],
  imports: [
    BrowserModule
  ],
  providers: [],
  bootstrap: [AppComponent]
})
export class AppModule { }
```

The decorator of an Angular module defines a set of properties that can be used to configure the module. The most common ones are as follows:

- declarations: Defines Angular components that are part of the Angular module. Every component that exists in the Angular module *must* be added to the declarations array.

- imports: Defines other Angular modules that contain functionality the Angular module needs.

Let's get our feet wet now by modifying the code of our Angular application. We will change the following greeting message, which is displayed at application startup, to something more meaningful:

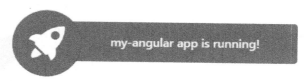

Figure 1.13 – Greeting message

First, we need to find the location where the message in the previous screenshot is declared. The main component of an Angular application is the component that is loaded at application startup by default.

> **Tip**
>
> The component that is displayed when an Angular application is bootstrapped is indicated by the bootstrap property of the main module of the application. We rarely need to change this property. The selector of that component is used in the index.html file by default.

So, the message should be declared inside the app.component.ts file. Let's take a look:

1. Open the VSCode editor and select **Open folder...** from the **Start** section of the **Welcome** screen.

2. Find the my-angular folder of the Angular application that we created and select it.

3. Navigate to the src\app folder from the **EXPLORER** pane and select the app.component.ts file.

4. Locate the title property in the AppComponent class and change its value to Angular Projects:

```
title = 'Angular Projects';
```

5. Run ng serve from the Terminal window, if the application is not running, and navigate to http://localhost:4200 using your browser. Our Angular application should now display the following greeting message:

Figure 1.14 – Greeting message

The `title` property is bound to the template of the main component. If we open the `app.component.html` file and go to line 346, we will see the following HTML code:

```
<span>{{ title }} app is running!</span>
```

The `{{}}` syntax that surrounds the `title` property is called **interpolation**. During interpolation, the Angular framework reads the enclosed component property value, converts it into text, and prints it on the screen.

The Angular CLI provides a rich collection of commands that can assist us during our daily development routine. Running these commands from a Terminal window may look simple, but it could quickly turn into a nightmare.

Building our application with Nx Console

The Angular CLI is a command-line tool with a variety of commands. Each command can accept a wide range of options and parameters according to the task that we want to accomplish. The process of remembering these commands and their options off by heart is daunting and time-consuming. In such cases, the ecosystem of Angular tooling can come in handy. VSCode Marketplace contains many useful extensions that we can install to help us during Angular development. One of these extensions is the Nx Console, which provides a user interface over the Angular CLI. To install the Nx Console in your environment, follow these steps:

1. Open VSCode and click on the **Extensions** menu in the sidebar:

Figure 1.15 – VSCode Extensions

2. In the **EXTENSIONS** pane that appears, type `Nx Console`.

3. Click the **Install** button on the first item to install the Nx Console extension.

The Nx Console extension is now installed globally in our environment, which means we can use it in any Angular project. It is a graphical representation of the most common Angular CLI commands. Currently, it supports the following commands (the related Angular CLI command is shown in parentheses):

*   **Generate**: Generate new Angular artifacts, such as components and modules (`ng generate`).

*   **Run**: Run an architect target, as defined in the `angular.json` configuration file of the Angular CLI workspace (`ng run`).

*   **Build**: Build an Angular application (`ng build`).

*   **Serve**: Build and serve an Angular application (`ng serve`).

*   **Test**: Run the unit tests of an Angular application (`ng test`).

*   **E2E**: Run the end-to-end or integration tests of an Angular application (`ng e2e`).

*   **Lint**: Check an Angular application according to a set of linting rules (`ng lint`).

*   **Change workspace**: Load a different Angular CLI workspace in VSCode.

Whatever we can do with the Angular CLI can almost be achieved using the Nx Console. The real benefit is that the developer does not need to remember all the Angular CLI command options as they are all represented in a graphical interface. Let's see how:

1. Open the `my-angular` folder using VSCode and click on the **Nx Console** menu in the sidebar:

Figure 1.16 – Nx Console

2. Click on the **Serve** command from the **NX CONSOLE** pane:

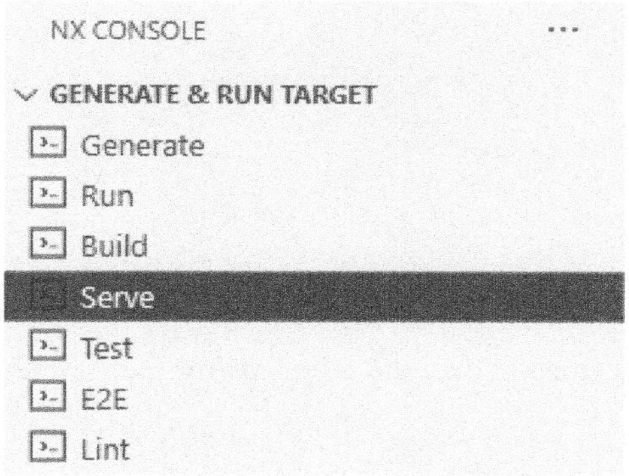

Figure 1.17 – Serve command

3. Select the **my-angular** project in the dialog that appears:

Figure 1.18 – Selecting a project

The Nx Console will open the **Serve** tab, where you can optionally set additional options supported by the `serve` command of the Angular CLI. Each option contains a title with a short description that explains what it does.

> **Important note**
>
> Some options may contain the word **(deprecated)** in their title. This indicates that the option has been deprecated in the current version of Angular CLI, and that it will finally be removed in a later version.

4. Click on the **Run** button to start the Angular application:

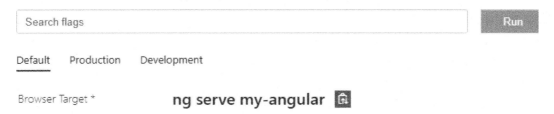

Figure 1.19 – Serve tab

VSCode opens an integrated Terminal at the bottom of the editor and executes the ng serve command:

Figure 1.20 – VSCode integrated Terminal

This is the same command that we execute when using the Angular CLI from a Terminal window.

The Nx Console uses tasks internally to run Angular CLI commands. Tasks are a built-in mechanism of VSCode that allow us to run scripts or start external processes without interacting directly with the command line.

The Nx Console extension does a fantastic job of removing the burden of remembering Angular CLI commands off by heart. The VSCode Marketplace contains many more extensions for Angular developers that supplement the job of the Nx Console.

Summary

In this chapter, we learned about the basic principles of the Angular framework and provided a brief overview of the Angular architecture. We saw some popular extensions for VSCode that we can use to enhance our development experience while working with Angular.

Then, we learned how to use the Angular CLI, a powerful tool of the Angular ecosystem, to scaffold and build a new Angular application from scratch. We also made our first interaction with Angular code by modifying the Angular component of a typical Angular CLI application. Finally, we installed the Nx Console extension and learned how to build our application with it.

In the next chapter, we will look at the Angular Router and learn how to use it to create a personal blog using the Scully static website generator.

Practice questions

Let's take a look at a few practice questions:

1. What is the basic building block of an Angular application?

2. How do we group components of similar functionality?

3. Who is responsible for handling business logic tasks in an Angular application?

4. Which Angular CLI command can we use to create a new Angular application?

5. Which Angular CLI command can we use to serve an Angular application?

6. How do we declare an Angular component in HTML?

7. How do we declare Angular components in a module?

8. What syntax do we use for text binding on HTML templates?

9. What is the benefit of using the Nx Console?

10. Which extension do we use to perform static analysis in our Angular code?

Further reading

Here are some links to build upon what we learned in the chapter:

- Introduction to Basic Concepts: `https://angular.io/guide/architecture`
- Interpolation: `https://angular.io/guide/interpolation`
- Nx Console: `https://nx.dev/latest/angular/cli/console`
- Angular Essentials: `https://marketplace.visualstudio.com/items?itemName=johnpapa.angular-essentials`
- Angular Evergreen: `https://expertlysimple.io/get-evergreen`

2

Building an SPA Application with Scully and Angular Router

Angular applications follow the **Single Page Application (SPA)** architecture, where different views of the web page can be activated according to the browser URL. Any changes to that URL can be intercepted by the Angular router and translated to routes that can activate a particular Angular component.

Scully is a popular static website generator that is based on the **Jamstack** architecture. It can cooperate nicely with the Angular router to prerender the content of an Angular application according to each route.

In this chapter, we are going to combine Angular and Scully to create a personal blog. The following topics are going to be covered:

- Setting up routing in an Angular application
- Creating the basic layout of our blog
- Configuring routing for our application
- Adding blog capabilities with Scully
- Displaying blog posts on the home page

Essential background theory and context

In the old days of web development, client-side applications were highly coupled with the underlying server infrastructure. Much machinery was involved when we wanted to visit the page of a website using a URL. The browser would send the requested URL to the server, and the server should respond with a matching HTML file for that URL. This was a complicated process that would result in delays and varying round-trip times.

Modern web applications eliminate these problems using the SPA architecture. A client needs to request a single HTML file only once from the server. Any subsequent changes to the URL of the browser are handled internally from the client infrastructure. In Angular, the router is responsible for intercepting in-app URL requests and handling them according to a defined route configuration.

Jamstack is a hot, emerging technology that allows us to create fast and secure web applications. It can be used for any application type, ranging from an e-commerce website to a **Software as a Service (SaaS)** web application or even a personal blog. The architecture of Jamstack is based on the following pillars:

- **Performance**: Pages are generated and prerendered during production, eliminating the need to wait for content to load.
- **Scaling**: Content is static files that can be served from anywhere, even from a **Content Delivery Network (CDN)** provider that improves the performance of the application.
- **Security**: The serverless nature of server-side processes and the fact that content is already static eliminates potential attacks that target server infrastructures.

Scully is the first static website generator for Angular that embraces the Jamstack approach. It essentially generates pages of the Angular application during build time to be immediately available when requested.

Project overview

In this project, we will build a personal blog using the Angular framework and enhance it with Jamstack characteristics using the Scully site generator. Initially, we will scaffold a new Angular application and enable it for routing. We will then create the basic layout of our application by adding some barebone components. As soon as we have a working Angular application, we will add blog support to it using Scully. We will then create some blog posts using Markdown files and display them on the home page of our application.

Build time: 1 hour.

Getting started

The following software tools are required to complete this project:

- Angular CLI: A command-line interface for Angular that you can find at `https://angular.io/cli`

- GitHub material: The related code for this chapter, which you can find in the `Chapter02` folder at `https://github.com/PacktPublishing/Angular-Projects-Second-Edition`.

Setting up routing in an Angular application

We will kick off our project by creating a new Angular application from scratch. Execute the following command of the Angular CLI in a terminal window to create a new Angular application:

```
ng new my-blog --routing --style=scss
```

We use the `ng new` command to create a new Angular application, passing the following options:

- `my-blog`: The name of the Angular application that we want to create. The Angular CLI will create a `my-blog` folder in the path where we execute the command.

  > **Important Note**
  > Every command that we run in the terminal window should be run inside this folder.

- `--routing`: Enables routing in the Angular application.

- `--style=scss`: Configures the Angular application to use the SCSS stylesheet format when working with CSS styles.

When we enable routing in an Angular application, the Angular CLI imports several artifacts from the @angular/router npm package in our application:

- It creates the app-routing.module.ts file, which is the main routing module of our application:

```
import { NgModule } from '@angular/core';
import { RouterModule, Routes } from '@angular/router';

const routes: Routes = [];

@NgModule({
  imports: [RouterModule.forRoot(routes)],
  exports: [RouterModule]
})
export class AppRoutingModule { }
```

- It imports AppRoutingModule into the main module of our application, app.module.ts:

```
import { NgModule } from '@angular/core';
import { BrowserModule } from '@angular/platform-browser';

import { AppRoutingModule } from './app-routing.module';
import { AppComponent } from './app.component';

@NgModule({
  declarations: [
    AppComponent
  ],
  imports: [
    BrowserModule,
    AppRoutingModule
  ],
  providers: [],
  bootstrap: [AppComponent]
})
export class AppModule { }
```

We configured our application to use the SCSS stylesheet format. Instead of creating the styles of our application manually, we will use the **Bootstrap CSS** library:

1. Execute the following command in a terminal window to install Bootstrap:

    ```
    npm install bootstrap
    ```

    We use the npm executable to install the bootstrap package from the npm registry in the previous command.

2. Add the following import statement at the top of the styles.scss file that exists in the src folder of our Angular application:

    ```
    @import "~bootstrap/scss/bootstrap";
    ```

    The styles.scss file contains CSS styles that are applied globally in our application. In the previous snippet, we import all the styles from the Bootstrap library into our application. The @import CSS rule accepts the absolute path of the bootstrap.scss file as an option, without adding the .scss extension. The ~ character represents the node_modules folder of our Angular application.

    > **Important Note**
    >
    > The node_modules folder contains all the npm packages and libraries that our application needs, either during development or runtime.

In the following section, we will learn how to create the basic layout of our blog by creating components, such as the header and the footer.

Creating the basic layout of our blog

A blog typically has a header containing all the primary website links and a footer containing copyright information and other useful links. In the world of Angular, both can be represented as separate components.

The header component is used only once since it is added when our application starts up, and it is always rendered as the main menu of the website. In Angular, we typically create a module, named **core** by convention, to keep such components or services central to our application. To create the module, we use the generate command of the Angular CLI:

```
ng generate module core
```

The preceding command will create the module in the `src\app\core` folder of our application. To create the header component, we will use the same command, passing a different set of options:

```
ng generate component header --path=src/app/core --module=core
--export
```

The previous command will create all necessary component files inside the `src\app\core\header` folder:

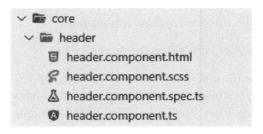

Figure 2.1 – Header component

It will also declare `HeaderComponent` in the `core` module and add it to its `exports` property so that other modules can use it:

---

core.module.ts

```typescript
import { NgModule } from '@angular/core';
import { CommonModule } from '@angular/common';
import { HeaderComponent } from './header/header.component';

@NgModule({
  declarations: [
    HeaderComponent
  ],
  imports: [
    CommonModule
  ],
  exports: [
    HeaderComponent
  ]
})
export class CoreModule { }
```

The header component should display the main links of our blog. Open the header. component.html template file of the header component and replace its content with the following snippet:

header.component.html

```
<nav class="navbar navbar-expand navbar-light bg-light">
  <div class="container-fluid">
    <a class="navbar-brand">Angular Projects</a>
    <ul class="navbar-nav me-auto">
      <li class="nav-item">
        <a class="nav-link">Articles</a>
      </li>
      <li class="nav-item">
        <a class="nav-link">Contact</a>
      </li>
    </ul>
  </div>
</nav>
```

The footer component can be used more than once in an Angular application. Currently, we want to display it on the main page of our application. In the future, we may want to have it also on a login page that will be available for blog visitors. In such a case, the footer component should be reusable. When we want to group components that will be reused throughout our application, we typically create a module named **shared** by convention. Use the Angular CLI generate command to create the shared module:

```
ng generate module shared
```

The previous command will create the shared module in the src\app\shared folder. The footer component can now be created using the following command:

```
ng generate component footer --path=src/app/shared
--module=shared --export
```

The previous command will create all necessary files of the footer component inside the src\app\shared\footer folder. It will also add FooterComponent in the declarations and exports properties of the shared module:

shared.module.ts

```
import { NgModule } from '@angular/core';
import { CommonModule } from '@angular/common';
import { FooterComponent } from './footer/footer.component';

@NgModule({
  declarations: [
    FooterComponent
  ],
  imports: [
    CommonModule
  ],
  exports: [
    FooterComponent
  ]
})
export class SharedModule { }
```

The content of the footer component should contain copyright information about our blog. Let's see how to add this information to our component:

1. Open the footer.component.ts TypeScript class file of the footer component. Add a currentDate property in the FooterComponent class and initialize it to a new Date object:

```
export class FooterComponent implements OnInit {

  currentDate = new Date();

  constructor() { }

  ngOnInit(): void {
  }

}
```

2. Open the `footer.component.html` template file of the footer component and replace its content with the following:

```
<nav class="navbar fixed-bottom navbar-light bg-light">
  <div class="container-fluid">
    <p>Copyright @{{currentDate | date: 'y'}}. All
      Rights Reserved</p>
  </div>
</nav>
```

The preceding code uses interpolation to display the value of the `currentDate` property on the screen. It also uses the built-in `date` pipe to display only the year of the current date.

> **Important Note**
>
> Pipes are a built-in feature of the Angular framework that apply transformations on the view representation of a component property. The underlying value of the property remains intact.

We have already created the essential components of our blog. Now it is time to display them on the screen:

1. Open the main module of the application, the `app.module.ts` file, and add `CoreModule` and `SharedModule` into the `imports` property of the `@NgModule` decorator:

```
@NgModule({
  declarations: [
    AppComponent
  ],
  imports: [
    BrowserModule,
    AppRoutingModule,
    CoreModule,
    SharedModule
  ],
  providers: [],
  bootstrap: [AppComponent]
})
```

2. Add the appropriate `import` statements at the top of the file for each module:

```
import { NgModule } from '@angular/core';
import { BrowserModule } from '@angular/platform-
browser';


import { AppRoutingModule } from './app-routing.module';
import { AppComponent } from './app.component';
import { CoreModule } from './core/core.module';
import { SharedModule } from './shared/shared.module';
```

3. Open the `app.component.html` template file of the main component and replace its content with the following HTML snippet:

```
<app-header></app-header>
<app-footer></app-footer>
```

We added the header and the footer component in the preceding snippet by using their CSS selectors.

If we run the `serve` command of the Angular CLI to preview the application, we should get the following:

Figure 2.2 – Basic layout

We have already completed the basic layout of our blog application, and it looks great! But the header contains two additional links that we have not covered yet. We will learn how to use routing for activating those links in the following section.

Configuring routing for our application

The header component that we created in the previous section contains two links:

- **Articles**: Displays a list of blog articles
- **Contact**: Displays personal information about the blog owner

The previous links will also become the main features of our application. So, we need to create an Angular module for each one.

> **Tip**
> When you design your website and need to decide upon the Angular modules that you will use, check out the main menu of the website. Each link of the menu should be a different feature and, thus, a different Angular module.

By convention, Angular modules that contain functionality for a specific feature are called **feature modules**.

Creating the contact page

Let's begin by creating our contact feature first:

1. Create a module that will be the home for our contact feature:

   ```
   ng generate module contact
   ```

2. Create a component that will be the main component of the contact module:

   ```
   ng generate component contact --path=src/app/contact
   --module=contact --export --flat
   ```

   We pass the --flat option to the generate command so that the Angular CLI will not create a separate folder for our component, as in previous cases. The contact component will be the only component in our module, so there is no point in having it separately.

3. Open the `contact.component.html` file and add the following HTML content:

```html
<div class="card mx-auto text-center border-light"
style="width: 18rem;">
    <img src="assets/angular.png" class="card-img-top"
    alt="Angular logo">
    <div class="card-body">
        <h5 class="card-title">Angular Projects</h5>
        <p class="card-text">
        A personal blog created with the Angular
        framework and the Scully static site generator
        </p>
        <a href="https://angular.io/" target="_blank"
        class="card-link">Angular</a>
        <a href="https://scully.io/" target="_blank"
        class="card-link">Scully</a>
    </div>
</div>
```

In the preceding code, we used the `angular.png` image, which you can find in the `src\assets` folder of the project from the accompanying GitHub repository.

> **Tip**
> The `assets` folder in an Angular CLI project is used for static content such as images, fonts, or JSON files.

We have already created our contact feature. The next step is to add it to the main page of our Angular application:

1. Open the `app-routing.module.ts` file and add a new route configuration object in the `routes` property:

```typescript
import { ContactComponent } from './contact/contact.
component';

const routes: Routes = [
    { path: 'contact', component: ContactComponent }
];
```

The preceding code indicates that when the URL of the browser points to the contact path, our application will activate and display ContactComponent on the screen. The routes property of a routing module contains the routing configuration of the respective feature module. It is an array of route configuration objects where each one defines the component class and the URL path that activates it.

2. Add ContactModule in the imports array of the @NgModule decorator of AppModule to be able to use it:

```
@NgModule({
  declarations: [
    AppComponent
  ],
  imports: [
    BrowserModule,
    AppRoutingModule,
    CoreModule,
    SharedModule,
    ContactModule
  ],
  providers: [],
  bootstrap: [AppComponent]
})
```

Do not forget to add the respective import statement for ContactModule at the top of the file.

3. Routed components, just like ContactComponent, need a place where they can be loaded. Open the app.component.html file and add the router-outlet directive:

```
<app-header></app-header>
<div class="container">
  <router-outlet></router-outlet>
</div>
<app-footer></app-footer>
```

Now, we need to wire up the route configuration that we created with the actual link on the header component:

1. Open the `header.component.html` file and add the `routerLink` directive to the respective anchor HTML element:

    ```html
    <li class="nav-item">
      <a routerLink="/contact" routerLinkActive="active"
        class="nav-link">Contact</a>
    </li>
    ```

    In the preceding snippet, the `routerLink` directive points to the `path` property of the route configuration object. We have also added the `routerLinkActive` directive, which sets the `active` class on the anchor element when the specific route is activated.

    > **Important Note**
    >
    > Notice that the value of the `routerLink` directive contains a leading `/`, whereas the `path` property of the route configuration object that we defined does not. According to the case, omitting the `/` would give a different meaning to the route.

2. The `routerLink` and `routerLinkActive` directives are part of the Angular router package. We need to import `RouterModule` in the core module to use them:

    ```typescript
    import { NgModule } from '@angular/core';
    import { CommonModule } from '@angular/common';
    import { HeaderComponent } from './header/header.
    component';
    import { RouterModule } from '@angular/router';

    @NgModule({
      declarations: [
        HeaderComponent
      ],
      imports: [
        CommonModule,
        RouterModule
      ],
      exports: [
    ```

```
        HeaderComponent
    ]
})
export class CoreModule { }
```

We are now ready to preview our new contact page! If we run the application using `ng serve` and click on the **Contact** link, we should see the following output:

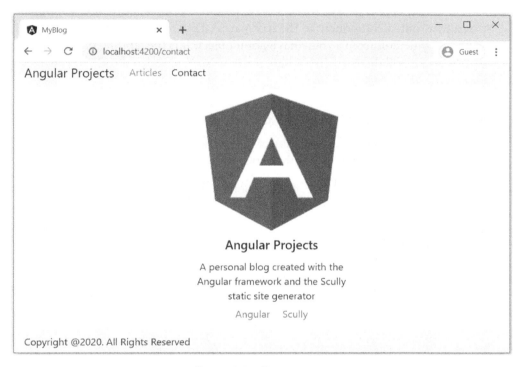

Figure 2.3 – Contact page

In the following section, we will build the functionality for the **Articles** link of the header in our blog.

Adding the articles page

The feature that is responsible for displaying articles in our blog will be the articles module. It will also be the module that connects the dots between Angular and Scully. We will use the `generate` command of the Angular CLI to create that module:

```
ng generate module articles --route=articles --module=app-
routing
```

In the previous command, we pass some additional routing options:

- --route: Defines the URL path of our feature
- --module: Indicates the routing module that will define the route configuration object that activates our feature

The Angular CLI performs additional actions, instead of just creating the module, upon executing the command:

- It creates a routed component in the src\app\articles folder that will be activated by default from a route navigation object. It is the landing page of our feature, and it will display a list of blog posts, as we will see in the *Displaying blog data on the home page* section.

- It creates a routing module, named articles-routing.module.ts, that contains the routing configuration of the articles module.

- It adds a new route configuration object in the route configuration of the main application module that activates the articles module.

The articles-routing.module.ts file contains the routing configuration for the articles module:

articles-routing.module.ts

```
import { NgModule } from '@angular/core';
import { RouterModule, Routes } from '@angular/router';
import { ArticlesComponent } from './articles.component';


const routes: Routes = [{ path: '', component:
ArticlesComponent }];


@NgModule({
  imports: [RouterModule.forChild(routes)],
  exports: [RouterModule]
})
export class ArticlesRoutingModule { }
```

It imports `RouterModule` using the `forChild` method to pass the routing configuration to the Angular router. If we take a look at the main routing module of the application, we will see that it follows a slightly different approach:

app-routing.module.ts

```
import { NgModule } from '@angular/core';
import { RouterModule, Routes } from '@angular/router';
import { ContactComponent } from './contact/contact.component';
const routes: Routes = [
    { path: 'contact', component: ContactComponent },
    { path: 'articles', loadChildren: () =>
      import('./articles/articles.module').then(m =>
      m.ArticlesModule) }
];

@NgModule({
    imports: [RouterModule.forRoot(routes)],
    exports: [RouterModule]
})
export class AppRoutingModule { }
```

The `forChild` method is used in feature modules, whereas the `forRoot` method should be used *only* in the main application module.

The route configuration of the articles module contains only one route that activates `ArticlesComponent`. The path of the route is set to an empty string to indicate that it is the default route of the routing module. It essentially means that `ArticlesComponent` will be activated whenever that module is loaded. But how is the articles module loaded in our application?

The second route of the main routing module contains a route configuration object that does not activate a component but rather a module. It uses the `loadChildren` method to load `ArticlesModule` dynamically when navigation triggers the `articles` path.

> **Important Note**
>
> The `import` function in the `loadChildren` property accepts the relative path of the TypeScript module file without the extension.

The previous approach is called **lazy loading** and improves the startup and the overall performance of an Angular application. It creates a separate bundle for each lazy-loaded module, which is loaded upon request, reducing the final bundle size and the memory consumption of your application. Let's wire up the new route to our header component:

1. Open the `header.component.html` file and add the following `routerLink` and `routerLinkActive` directives to the `Articles` anchor HTML element:

```
<li class="nav-item">
    <a routerLink="/articles" routerLinkActive="active"
       class="nav-link">Articles</a>
</li>
```

2. Run `ng serve` and use your favorite browser to preview your application.

3. Open the developer tools of your browser, click on the **Articles** link and inspect the **Network** tab:

Name	Status	Type	Initiator	Size	Time	Waterfall
localhost	304	document	Other	233 B	3 ms	
styles.css	304	stylesheet	(index)	235 B	8 ms	
runtime.js	304	script	(index)	234 B	10 ms	
polyfills.js	304	script	(index)	235 B	13 ms	
styles.js	304	script	(index)	235 B	18 ms	
vendor.js	304	script	(index)	236 B	25 ms	
main.js	304	script	(index)	234 B	26 ms	
info?t=1605360309087	200	xhr	zone-evergreen.js:...	391 B	2 ms	
favicon.ico	304	vnd.micro...	Other	233 B	3 ms	
websocket	101	websocket	sockjs.js:1684	0 B	Pending	
articles-articles-module.js	304	script	bootstrap:149	234 B	3 ms	
favicon.ico	304	vnd.micro...	Other	233 B	3 ms	

Figure 2.4 – Lazy loading Angular module

Among other requests, you should see one named **articles-articles-module.js**. It is the bundle of the lazy-loaded articles module that was loaded when you clicked on the **Articles** link.

We are now ready to convert our amazing Angular application into a professional blog website. Before we move on, let's add some additional routes to the `app-routing.module.ts` file:

```
const routes: Routes = [
  { path: 'contact', component: ContactComponent },
  { path: 'articles', loadChildren: () =>
    import('./articles/articles.module').then(m =>
    m.ArticlesModule) },
  { path: '', pathMatch: 'full', redirectTo: 'articles' },
  { path: '**', redirectTo: 'articles' }
];
```

We added a default route to automatically redirect our blog users to the `articles` path upon visiting the blog. Additionally, we created a new route configuration object with its path set to `**` that also navigates to the `articles` path. The `**` syntax is called the **wildcard** route, and it is triggered when the router cannot match a requested URL with a defined route.

> **Tip**
> Define the most specific routes first and then add any generic ones such as the default and the wildcard routes. The Angular router parses the route configuration in the order that we define and follows a *first match wins* strategy to select one.

We have already enabled and configured routing in our Angular application. In the following section, we will establish the infrastructure needed to add blogging capabilities to our application.

Adding blog capabilities with Scully

Our application currently does not have any specific logic regarding blog posts. It is a typical Angular application that uses routing. However, by adding a routing configuration, we have established the foundation for adding blog support using Scully.

> **Important Note**
> Scully needs *at least* one route defined in an Angular application to work correctly.

First, we need to install Scully in our application.

Installing the Scully library

We will use the `add` command of the Angular CLI to install Scully in our Angular application:

```
ng add @scullyio/init
```

The preceding command downloads and installs all the necessary npm packages for Scully to work correctly in our Angular application. It also modifies the structure of the Angular project to accommodate its specific needs.

It imports `ScullyLibModule` in our main application module:

app.module.ts

```typescript
import { NgModule } from '@angular/core';
import { BrowserModule } from '@angular/platform-browser';

import { AppRoutingModule } from './app-routing.module';
import { AppComponent } from './app.component';
import { ContactModule } from './contact/contact.module';
import { CoreModule } from './core/core.module';
import { SharedModule } from './shared/shared.module';
import { ScullyLibModule } from '@scullyio/ng-lib';

@NgModule({
  declarations: [
    AppComponent
  ],
  imports: [
    BrowserModule,
    AppRoutingModule,
    CoreModule,
    SharedModule,
    ContactModule,
    ScullyLibModule
  ],
  providers: [],
```

```
  bootstrap: [AppComponent]
})
export class AppModule { }
```

`ScullyLibModule` is the main module of the Scully library that contains various Angular services and directives that Scully will need.

It also creates a configuration file for the Scully library in the root folder of the Angular CLI workspace:

scully.my-blog.config.ts

```
import { ScullyConfig } from '@scullyio/scully';
export const config: ScullyConfig = {
  projectRoot: "./src",
  projectName: "my-blog",
  outDir: './dist/static',
  routes: {
  }
};
```

The configuration file contains information about our Angular application that Scully will need along the way:

- `projectRoot`: The path containing the source code of the Angular application
- `projectName`: The name of the Angular application
- `outDir`: The output path of the Scully generated files

> **Important Note**
> The Scully output path must be different from the path that the Angular CLI outputs the bundle of your Angular application. The latter can be configured from the `angular.json` file.

- `routes`: It contains the route configuration that will be used for accessing our blog posts. Scully will populate it automatically, as we will see in the following section.

Since we have installed Scully successfully in our Angular application, we can now configure it to initialize our blog.

Initializing our blog page

Scully provides a specific Angular CLI schematic for initializing an Angular application, such as a blog, by using Markdown (.md) files:

```
ng generate @scullyio/init:markdown
```

The previous command will start the configuration process of our blog by going through a list of questions (default values are shown inside parentheses):

1. Type posts as the name of the blog module:

   ```
   ? What name do you want to use for the module? (blog)
   ```

   Figure 2.5 – Blog module name

   This will create a new Angular module named **posts**.

2. Leave the slug choice empty, and press *Enter* to accept the default value:

   ```
   ? What slug do you want for the markdown file? (id)
   ```

   Figure 2.6 – Markdown slug

   The slug is a unique identifier for each post, and it is defined in the route configuration object of the module.

3. Enter mdfiles as the path that Scully will use to store our actual blog post files:

   ```
   ? Where do you want to store your markdown files?
   ```

   Figure 2.7 – Markdown files path

   This will create an mdfiles folder inside the root path of our Angular CLI project. By default, it will also create a blog post for our convenience. We will learn how to create our own in the *Displaying blog data on the home page* section.

4. Type posts as the name of the route for accessing our blog posts:

   ```
   ? Under which route do you want your files to be requested?
   ```

   Figure 2.8 – Blog route name

   The name of the route is the path property of the route configuration object that will be created.

Scully performs various actions upon executing the preceding commands, including the creation of the routing configuration of the posts module:

posts-routing.module.ts

```
import {NgModule} from '@angular/core';
import {Routes, RouterModule} from '@angular/router';

import {PostsComponent} from './posts.component';

const routes: Routes = [
  {
    path: ':id',
    component: PostsComponent,
  },
  {
    path: '**',
    component: PostsComponent,
  }
];

@NgModule({
  imports: [RouterModule.forChild(routes)],
  exports: [RouterModule],
})
export class PostsRoutingModule {}
```

path for the first route is set to :id and activates PostsComponent. The colon character indicates that id is a route parameter. The id parameter is related to the slug property defined earlier in the Scully configuration. Scully works by creating one route for each blog post that we create. It uses the route configuration of the posts module and the main application module to construct the routes property in the Scully configuration file:

```
routes: {
  '/posts/:id': {
    type: 'contentFolder',
    id: {
      folder: "./mdfiles"
```

```
        }
    },
}
```

`PostsComponent` is the Angular component that is used to render the details of each blog post. The template file of the component can be further customized according to your needs:

posts.component.html

```
<h3>ScullyIo content</h3>
<hr>

<!-- This is where Scully will inject the static HTML -->
<scully-content></scully-content>
<hr>
<h4>End of content</h4>
```

You can customize all content in the previous template file except the `<scully-content></scully-content>` line, which is used internally by Scully.

At this point, we have completed the installation and configuration of Scully in our Angular application. It is now time for the final part of the project! In the next section, we will put Angular and Scully to cooperate and display blog posts in our Angular application.

Displaying blog posts on the home page

We would like our users to see the list of available blog posts as soon as they land on our blog website. According to the default route path that we have defined, `ArticlesComponent` is the landing page of our blog. Scully provides `ScullyRoutesService`, an Angular service that we can use in our components to get information about the routes that it will create according to the blog posts. Let's put this service in action on our landing page:

1. Navigate to the `articles.component.ts` TypeScript class file.

2. Import `ScullyRoute` and `ScullyRoutesService` from the `@scullyio/ng-lib` package:

   ```
   import { ScullyRoute, ScullyRoutesService } from '@
   scullyio/ng-lib';
   ```

3. Inject `ScullyRoutesService` in the constructor of the `ArticlesComponent` class:

```
constructor(private scullyService: ScullyRoutesService) {
}
```

4. Create a component property of `ScullyRoute` array type:

```
posts: ScullyRoute[] = [];
```

5. Edit the `ngOnInit` method of the component and add the following code:

```
ngOnInit(): void {
  this.scullyService.available$.subscribe(posts => {
    this.posts = posts.filter(post => post.title);
  });
}
```

6. Open the `articles.component.html` file and add the following HTML code:

```
<div class="list-group mt-3">
  <a *ngFor="let post of posts"
    [routerLink]="post.route" class="list-group-item
      list-group-item-action">
    <div class="d-flex w-100 justify-content-between">
      <h5 class="mb-1">{{post.title}}</h5>
    </div>
    <p class="mb-1">{{post.description}}</p>
  </a>
</div>
```

There are many Angular techniques involved in the previous steps, so let's break them down piece by piece.

When we want to use an Angular service in a component, we just need to ask for it from the Angular framework. How? By adding it as a property in the constructor of the component. The component does not need to know anything about how the service is implemented.

The `ngOnInit` method is part of the `OnInit` interface, which is implemented by our component. It is called by the Angular framework when a component is initialized and provides us with a hook to add custom logic to be executed.

> **Tip**
> Angular services that provide initialization logic to a component should be called inside the ngOnInit method and *not* in the constructor because it is easier to provide mocks about those services when unit testing the component.

The available$ property of ScullyRoutesService is called an **observable**. To retrieve its value, we need to subscribe to it. The returned posts variable will contain all the available routes that were generated from Scully. Scully is run against all routes of our Angular application. To avoid displaying routes other than those related to blog posts, such as the contact route, we filter out the results from the available$ property.

When we subscribe to an observable, we need to unsubscribe from it when our component no longer exists. Otherwise, we may experience memory leaks in our Angular application. Let's see how we can accomplish this task using another life cycle hook of the component called ngOnDestroy:

1. Declare a private routeSub property of the Subscription type in the ArticlesComponent class. Subscription can be imported from the rxjs npm package.

2. Set the returned value of the available$ observable to the routeSub property.

3. Add the OnDestroy interface to the list of implemented interfaces of the component. OnDestroy can be imported from the @angular/core npm package. It is executed when the component is destroyed, and it is not rendered on the screen anymore.

4. Implement the ngOnDestroy method and call the unsubscribe method of the routeSub property in the body of the method.

The resulting TypeScript file of the component should look like the following:

articles.component.ts

```typescript
import { Component, OnInit, OnDestroy } from '@angular/core';
import { ScullyRoute, ScullyRoutesService } from '@scullyio/ng-lib';
import { Subscription } from 'rxjs';

@Component({
  selector: 'app-articles',
  templateUrl: './articles.component.html',
```

```
    styleUrls: ['./articles.component.scss']
})
export class ArticlesComponent implements OnInit, OnDestroy {

    posts: ScullyRoute[] = [];
    private routeSub: Subscription | undefined;

    constructor(private scullyService: ScullyRoutesService) { }

    ngOnInit(): void {
        this.routeSub =
            this.scullyService.available$.subscribe(posts => {
            this.posts = posts.filter(post => post.title);
        });
    }

    ngOnDestroy(): void {
        this.routeSub?.unsubscribe();
    }

}
```

In the template of our component, we use the *ngFor Angular built-in directive to iterate over the posts array inside HTML. We can then access each item of the array using the post **template reference variable** and use interpolation to display title and description.

Finally, we add a routerLink directive to each anchor element to navigate to the respective blog post when clicked. Notice that routerLink is surrounded by []. The [] syntax is called **property binding**, and we use it when we want to bind the property of an HTML element to a variable. In our case, we bind the routerLink directive to the route property of the post template reference variable.

Now that we have finally completed all the pieces of the puzzle, we can see our blog website in action:

1. Run the build command of the Angular CLI to build our Angular application:

    ```
    ng build
    ```

2. Execute the following npm command to build Scully and generate our blog routes:

```
npm run scully
```

The preceding command will create a `scully-routes.json` file inside the `src\assets` folder. It contains the routes of our Angular application and is needed from the Scully runtime.

> **Tip**
> Running the Scully executable for the first time will prompt you to collect anonymous errors to improve its services.

3. Run the following npm command to serve our blog:

```
npm run scully:serve
```

The preceding command will start two web servers: one that contains the static prerendered version of our website built using Scully and another that is the Angular live version of our application:

```
using plugins from folder "./scully"
": starting static server
Angular distribution server started on "http://localhost:1864/"
Scully static server started on "http://localhost:1668/"
":
```

Figure 2.9 – Serving our application

If we open our browser and navigate to `http://localhost:1668`, we will not see any blog posts. Why is that?

A blog post created with Scully is not returned in the `available$` property of `ScullyRoutesService` *unless* we publish it. To publish a blog post, we do the following:

1. Navigate to the `mdfiles` folder that Scully created and open the only `.md` file that you will find. The name and contents may vary from your file because it is based on the creation date from Scully:

```
---
title: 2020-11-15-posts
description: 'blog description'
published: false
```

```
slugs:
   - ___UNPUBLISHED___khm71wkh_
hIzSmrBDHceuWrDrqqTnY8qCwvurkxdT
---


# 2020-11-15-posts
```

Scully has defined a set of properties between the closing and ending - - - lines at the top of the file representing metadata about the blog post. You can also add your own as key-value pairs.

2. Delete the `slugs` property and set the `published` property to `true`:

```
---
title: 2020-11-15-posts
description: 'blog description'
published: true
---


# 2020-11-15-posts
```

> **Tip**
> If you do not want to publish a post manually, Scully supports the automatic publishing of blog posts. You can use the reserved `publishDate` property in the metadata to define the date you want to publish the blog post, and Scully will do the rest.

3. Run the following command to force Scully to regenerate the routes of our application:

```
npm run scully
```

We need to execute the previous command *every time* we make a change in our blog-related files.

4. Execute the `npm run scully:serve` command and navigate to preview the generated website.

We can now see one blog post, the default one that was created when we installed Scully. Let's create another one:

1. Run the following `generate` command of the Angular CLI:

    ```
    ng generate @scullyio/init:post --name="Angular and
    Scully"
    ```

    In the preceding command, we use the `@scullyio/init:post` schematic, passing the name of the post that we want to create as an option.

2. Set the target folder for the new blog post to `mdfiles`:

    ```
    ? What's the target folder for this post? (blog)
    ```

    Figure 2.10 – New blog post target folder

3. Scully will create a Markdown file named `angular-and-scully.md` inside the specified folder. Open that file and update its content to be the same as the following:

    ```
    ---
    title: 'Angular and Scully'
    description: 'How to build a blog with Angular and
    Scully'
    published: true
    ---


    # Angular and Scully
    Angular is a robust JavaScript framework that we can use
    to build excellent and performant web applications.
    Scully is a popular static website generator that
    empowers the Angular framework with Jamstack
    characteristics.
    You can find more about them in the following links:

     - https://angular.io
     - https://scully.io
     - https://www.jamstack.org
    ```

4. Run `npm run scully` to create a route for the newly created blog post. Scully will also update the `scully-routes.json` file with the new route.

If we preview our application now, it should look like the following:

Figure 2.11 – List of blog posts

If we click on one of the blog items, we will navigate to the selected blog post. The content that is currently shown on the screen is a prerendered version of the blog post route:

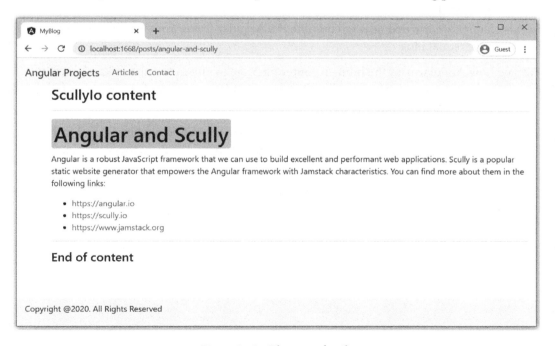

Figure 2.12 – Blog post details

To verify that, navigate to the `dist` folder of your Angular project, where you will find two folders:

- `my-blog`: This contains the Angular live version of our application. When we execute the `ng build` Angular CLI command, it builds our application and outputs bundle files in this folder.

- `static`: This contains a prerendered version of our Angular application generated from Scully when we run the `npm run scully` command.

If we navigate to the `static` folder, we will see that Scully has created one folder for each route of our Angular application. Each folder contains an `index.html` file, which represents the component that is activated from that route. The contents of the `index.html` file are auto-generated from Scully, and it is the result as if we run our application live and navigate to that component.

Now you can take your Angular application, upload it to the CDN or web server of your choice, and you will have your blog ready in no time! All you will have to do then will be to exercise your writing skills to create excellent blog content.

Summary

In this chapter, we learned how to combine the Angular framework with the Scully library to create a personal blog.

We saw how Angular uses the built-in router package to enhance web applications with in-app navigation. We also learned how to organize an Angular application into modules and how to navigate through these.

We introduced Jamstack to our Angular application using the Scully library and saw how easy it is to convert our application into a prerendered blog. We used the Scully interface to create some blog posts and display them on the screen.

In the following chapter, we will investigate another exciting feature of the Angular framework, forms. We are going to learn how to use them and build an issue-tracking system.

Practice questions

Let's take a look at a few practice questions:

1. Which library do we use for routing in an Angular application?
2. How do we add routing capabilities in an HTML anchor element?
3. Which Angular pipe do we use for date formatting?
4. What is the purpose of the `assets` folder in an Angular CLI application?
5. Which route property do we use for lazily loading a module?
6. Which Angular CLI command we use for installing Scully?
7. Which service do we use for fetching Scully routes?
8. What is the property binding?
9. Which Angular directive do we use for iterating over an array in HTML?
10. What is the difference between a standard Angular application and a Scully one?

Further reading

Here are some links to build upon what we learned in this chapter:

- Angular routing: `https://angular.io/guide/router`
- Angular feature modules: `https://angular.io/guide/module-types`
- Lazy loading modules: `https://angular.io/guide/lazy-loading-ngmodules`
- Angular built-in pipes: `https://angular.io/api?type=pipe`
- Bootstrap CSS: `https://getbootstrap.com/`
- Jamstack: `https://jamstack.org/`
- Scully: `https://scully.io/`
- Mastering Markdown: `https://guides.github.com/features/mastering-markdown/`

3

Building an Issue Tracking System using Reactive Forms

Web applications use HTML forms to collect data from users and validate them, such as when logging in to an application, performing a search, or completing an online payment. The Angular framework provides two types of forms, reactive and template-driven, that we can use in an Angular application.

In this chapter, we will build a system for managing and tracking issues. We will use Angular reactive forms for reporting new issues. We will also use **Clarity Design System** from VMware for designing our forms and displaying our issues.

We will cover the following topics:

- Installing the Clarity Design System to an Angular application
- Displaying an overview of issues
- Reporting new issues

- Marking an issue as resolved

- Turning on suggestions for new issues

Essential background theory and context

The Angular framework provides two types of forms that we can use:

- **Template-driven**: They are easy and straightforward to set up in an Angular application. Template-driven forms do not scale well and are difficult to test because they are defined in the template of the component.

- **Reactive**: They are based on a reactive programming approach. Reactive forms operate in the TypeScript class of the component, and they are easier to test and scale better than template-driven forms.

In this chapter, we will get hands-on with the reactive forms approach, which is the most popular in the Angular community.

Angular components can get data either from external sources such as HTTP or from other Angular components. In the latter case, they interact with components that have data using a public API:

- `@Input()`: This is used to pass data into a component.

- `@Output()`: This is used to get notified about changes or get data back from a component.

Clarity is a design system that contains a set of UX and UI guidelines for building web applications. It also consists of a proprietary HTML and CSS framework packed with these guidelines. Luckily, we do not have to use this framework since Clarity already provides a wide variety of Angular-based UI components that we can use in our Angular applications.

Project overview

In this project, we will build an Angular application for managing and tracking issues using reactive forms and Clarity. Initially, we will display a list of issues in a table that we can sort and filter. We will then create a form for allowing users to report new issues. Finally, we will create a modal dialog for resolving an issue. We will also go the extra mile and turn on suggestions when reporting an issue to help users avoid duplicate entries.

Build time: 1 hour

Getting started

The following software tools are required for completing this project:

- **Angular CLI**: A command-line interface for Angular that you can find at `https://angular.io/cli`
- **GitHub material**: The related code for this chapter that you can find in the `Chapter03` folder at `https://github.com/PacktPublishing/Angular-Projects-Second-Edition`.

Installing Clarity to an Angular application

Let's start creating our issue tracking system by scaffolding a new Angular application:

```
ng new issue-tracker --defaults
```

We use the `ng new` command of the Angular CLI to create a new Angular application with the following characteristics:

- `issue-tracker`: The name of the Angular application.
- `--defaults`: This disables Angular routing for the application and sets the stylesheet format to be CSS.

We now need to install the Clarity library in our Angular application. The VMware team has created an Angular CLI schematic that we can use. Navigate to the `issue-tracker` folder that was created with the preceding command and run the following `add` command of the Angular CLI:

```
ng add @clr/angular
```

The previous command will perform the following modifications in our Angular CLI workspace:

1. It will add all the necessary npm packages of the Clarity library to the `dependencies` section of the `package.json` file.
2. It will add the necessary styles in the configuration file of the Angular CLI workspace, `angular.json`:

```
"styles": [
    "node_modules/@clr/ui/clr-ui.min.css",
    "src/styles.css"
]
```

3. Finally, it will import `ClarityModule` in the main application module, `app.module.ts`:

```
import { NgModule } from '@angular/core';
import { BrowserModule } from '@angular/platform-browser';

import { AppComponent } from './app.component';
import { ClarityModule } from '@clr/angular';
import { BrowserAnimationsModule } from
  '@angular/platform-browser/animations';

@NgModule({
  declarations: [
    AppComponent
  ],
  imports: [
    BrowserModule,
    ClarityModule,
    BrowserAnimationsModule
  ],
  providers: [],
  bootstrap: [AppComponent]
})
export class AppModule { }
```

It will also import `BrowserAnimationsModule` from the `@angular/platform-browser/animations` npm package. `BrowserAnimationsModule` is used to display animations when specific actions happen in our application, such as clicking a button.

Now that we have completed installing Clarity in our application, we can start building beautiful designs with it. In the following section, we will begin by creating a list for displaying our issues.

Displaying an overview of issues

Our Angular application will be responsible for managing and tracking issues. When the application starts up, we should display a list of all pending issues in the system. Pending issues are defined as those issues that have not been resolved. The process that we will follow can be further analyzed into the following:

- Fetching pending issues
- Visualizing issues using a data grid

Fetching pending issues

First, we need to create a mechanism for fetching all pending issues:

1. Use the `generate` command of the Angular CLI to create an Angular service named `issues`:

```
ng generate service issues
```

   The preceding command will create an `issues.service.ts` file in the `src\app` folder of our Angular CLI project.

2. Every issue will have specific properties of a defined type. We need to create a TypeScript interface for that with the following Angular CLI command:

```
ng generate interface issue
```

   The previous command will create an `issue.ts` file in the `src\app` folder of the project.

3. Open the `issue.ts` file and add the following properties in the `Issue` interface:

```
export interface Issue {
    issueNo: number;
    title: string;
    description: string;
    priority: 'low' | 'high';
    type: 'Feature' | 'Bug' | 'Documentation';
    completed?: Date;
}
```

   The `completed` property is the date that an issue is resolved. We define it as optional because new issues will not have this property set.

4. Open the Angular service that we created in *step 1* and add an `issues` property to hold our issue data. Also create a `getPendingIssues` method that will return all issues that have not been completed:

```typescript
import { Injectable } from '@angular/core';
import { Issue } from './issue';

@Injectable({
  providedIn: 'root'
})
export class IssuesService {

  private issues: Issue[] = [];

  constructor() { }

  getPendingIssues(): Issue[] {
    return this.issues.filter(issue =>
      !issue.completed);
  }

}
```

5. We initialize the `issues` property to an empty array. If you want to get started with sample data, you can use the `mock-issues.ts` file from the `src\assets` folder that exists in the GitHub material of this chapter and import it as follows:

```typescript
import { issues } from '../assets/mock-issues';
```

In the following section, we will create a component for displaying those issues.

Visualizing issues in a data grid

We are going to use the **data grid** UI component of the Clarity library to display data in a tabular format. A data grid also provides mechanisms for filtering and sorting out of the box. Let's create the Angular component that will host the data grid first:

1. Use the `generate` command of the Angular CLI to create the component:

```
ng generate component issue-list
```

2. Open the template of the main component of our application, `app.component.html`, and replace its content with the following HTML code:

```
<div class="main-container">
  <div class="content-container">
    <div class="content-area">
      <app-issue-list></app-issue-list>
    </div>
  </div>
</div>
```

The list of issues will be displayed in the main component of the Angular application, as soon as it starts up.

3. Currently, the `app-issue-list` component does not display any issue data. We need to connect it with the Angular service that we created in the *Fetching pending issues* section. Open the `issue-list.component.ts` file and inject `IssuesService` in the constructor of the `IssueListComponent` class:

```
import { Component, OnInit } from '@angular/core';
import { IssuesService } from '../issues.service';

@Component({
  selector: 'app-issue-list',
  templateUrl: './issue-list.component.html',
  styleUrls: ['./issue-list.component.css']
})
export class IssueListComponent implements OnInit {

  constructor(private issueService: IssuesService) { }

  ngOnInit(): void {
  }

}
```

4. Create a method named get Issues that will call the getPendingIssues method of the injected service and keep its returned value in the issues component property:

```
import { Component, OnInit } from '@angular/core';
import { Issue } from '../issue';
import { IssuesService } from '../issues.service';


@Component({
  selector: 'app-issue-list',
  templateUrl: './issue-list.component.html',
  styleUrls: ['./issue-list.component.css']
})
export class IssueListComponent implements OnInit {

  issues: Issue[] = [];

  constructor(private issueService: IssuesService) { }

  ngOnInit(): void {
  }

  private getIssues() {
    this.issues =
      this.issueService.getPendingIssues();
  }
}
```

5. Finally, call the get Issues method in the ngOnInit component method to get all pending issues upon component initialization:

```
ngOnInit(): void {
  this.getIssues();
}
```

We have already implemented the process for getting issue data in our component. All we have to do now is display it in the template. Open the `issue-list.component.html` file and replace its content with the following HTML code:

issue-list.component.html

```
<clr-datagrid>
  <clr-dg-column [clrDgField]="'issueNo'"
    [clrDgColType]="'number'">Issue No</clr-dg-column>
  <clr-dg-column [clrDgField]="'type'">Type</clr-dg-column>
  <clr-dg-column [clrDgField]="'title'">Title</clr-dg-
    column>
  <clr-dg-column [clrDgField]="'description'">Description
    </clr-dg-column>
  <clr-dg-column [clrDgField]="'priority'">Priority
    </clr-dg-column>

  <clr-dg-row *clrDgItems="let issue of issues">
    <clr-dg-cell>{{issue.issueNo}}</clr-dg-cell>
    <clr-dg-cell>{{issue.type}}</clr-dg-cell>
    <clr-dg-cell>{{issue.title}}</clr-dg-cell>
    <clr-dg-cell>{{issue.description}}</clr-dg-cell>
    <clr-dg-cell>
     <span class="label" [class.label-danger]=
      "issue.priority === 'high'">{{issue.priority}}</span>
    </clr-dg-cell>
  </clr-dg-row>

  <clr-dg-footer>{{issues.length}} issues</clr-dg-footer>
</clr-datagrid>
```

In the preceding snippet, we use several Angular components of the Clarity library:

- `clr-datagrid`: Defines a table.

- `clr-dg-column`: Defines a column of a table. Each column uses the `clrDgField` directive to bind to the property name of the issue represented by that column. The `clrDgField` directive provides us with sorting and filtering capabilities without writing even a single line of code in the TypeScript class file. Sorting works automatically only with string-based content. If we want to sort by a different primitive type, we must use the `clrDgColType` directive and specify the particular type.

- `clr-dg-row`: Defines a row of a table. It uses the `clrDgItems` directive to iterate over the issues and create one row for each issue.

- `clr-dg-cell`: Each row contains a collection of `clr-dg-cell` components to display the value of each column using interpolation. In the last cell, we add the `label-danger` class when an issue has a high priority to indicate its importance.

- `clr-dg-footer`: Defines the footer of a table. In this case, it displays the total number of issues.

If we run our Angular application using `ng serve`, the output will look like the following:

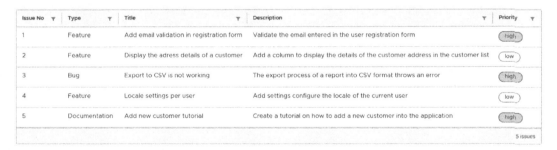

Figure 3.1 – Overview of pending issues

> **Important Note**
> In the previous screenshot, the application uses sample data from the `mock-issues.ts` file.

The data grid component of the Clarity library has a rich set of capabilities that we can use in our Angular applications. In the following section, we will learn how to use reactive forms to report a new issue.

Reporting new issues

One of the main features of our issue tracking system is the ability to report new issues. We will use Angular reactive forms to create a form for adding new issues. The feature can be further subdivided into the following tasks:

- Setting up reactive forms in an Angular application
- Creating the report issue form
- Displaying a new issue in the list
- Validating the details of an issue

Let's begin by introducing reactive forms in our Angular application.

Setting up reactive forms in an Angular application

Reactive forms are defined in the @angular/forms npm package of the Angular framework:

1. Open the app.module.ts file and import ReactiveFormsModule:

```
import { ReactiveFormsModule } from '@angular/forms';
```

2. Add ReactiveFormsModule into the imports array of the @NgModule decorator:

```
@NgModule({
  declarations: [
    AppComponent,
    IssueListComponent
  ],
  imports: [
    BrowserModule,
    ClarityModule,
    BrowserAnimationsModule,
    ReactiveFormsModule
  ],
  providers: [],
  bootstrap: [AppComponent]
})
```

`ReactiveFormsModule` contains all necessary Angular directives and services that we will need to work with forms, as we will see in the following section.

Creating the report issue form

Now that we have introduced reactive forms in our Angular application, we can start building our form:

1. Create a new Angular component named `issue-report`:

    ```
    ng generate component issue-report
    ```

2. Open the `issue-report.component.ts` file and inject `FormBuilder` in the constructor of the `IssueReportComponent` class:

    ```typescript
    import { Component, OnInit } from '@angular/core';
    import { FormBuilder } from '@angular/forms';

    @Component({
      selector: 'app-issue-report',
      templateUrl: './issue-report.component.html',
      styleUrls: ['./issue-report.component.css']
    })
    export class IssueReportComponent implements OnInit {

      constructor(private builder: FormBuilder) { }

      ngOnInit(): void {
      }

    }
    ```

    `FormBuilder` is an Angular service that we use to build a reactive form in an easy and convenient way.

3. Declare an `issueForm` property of the `FormGroup` type and initialize it inside the `ngOnInit` method:

    ```typescript
    import { Component, OnInit } from '@angular/core';
    import { FormBuilder, FormGroup } from
    ```

```
    '@angular/forms';

@Component({
  selector: 'app-issue-report',
  templateUrl: './issue-report.component.html',
  styleUrls: ['./issue-report.component.css']
})
export class IssueReportComponent implements OnInit {

  issueForm: FormGroup | undefined;

  constructor(private builder: FormBuilder) { }

  ngOnInit(): void {
    this.issueForm = this.builder.group({
      title: [''],
      description: [''],
      priority: [''],
      type: ['']
    });
  }

}
```

FormGroup is used to group individual controls into a logical representation of a form. The group method of the FormBuilder class is used to build the form. It accepts an object as a parameter where each key is the unique name of a form control and each value an array that contains its default value. In this case, we initialize all controls to empty strings because the form will be used to create a new issue from scratch.

4. We now need to associate the FormGroup object that we created with the respective HTML elements. Open the issue-report.component.html file and replace its content with the following HTML code:

```
<h3>Report an issue</h3>
<form clrForm *ngIf="issueForm" [formGroup]="issueForm">
  <clr-input-container>
    <label>Title</label>
```

```
    <input clrInput formControlName="title" />
  </clr-input-container>
  <clr-textarea-container>
    <label>Description</label>
    <textarea clrTextarea
      formControlName="description"></textarea>
  </clr-textarea-container>
  <clr-radio-container clrInline>
    <label>Priority</label>
    <clr-radio-wrapper>
      <input type="radio" value="low" clrRadio
        formControlName="priority" />
      <label>Low</label>
    </clr-radio-wrapper>
    <clr-radio-wrapper>
      <input type="radio" value="high" clrRadio
        formControlName="priority" />
      <label>High</label>
    </clr-radio-wrapper>
  </clr-radio-container>
  <clr-select-container>
    <label>Type</label>
    <select clrSelect formControlName="type">
    <option value="Feature">Feature</option>
    <option value="Bug">Bug</option>
    <option value="Documentation">Documentation
      </option>
    </select>
  </clr-select-container>
</form>
```

The formGroup and clrForm directives are used to associate the HTML form element with the issueForm property and identify it as a Clarity form.

The formControlName directive is used to associate HTML elements with form controls using their name. Each control is also defined using a Clarity container element. For example, the title input control is a clr-input-container component that contains an input HTML element.

Each native HTML element has a Clarity directive attached to it according to its type. For example, the `input` HTML element contains a `clrInput` directive.

5. Finally, add some styles to our `issue-report.component.css` file:

```
.clr-input, .clr-textarea {
  width: 30%;
}


button {
  margin-top: 25px;
}
```

Now that we have created the basics of our form, we will learn how to submit its details:

1. Add an HTML `button` element *before* the closing tag of the HTML form element:

```
<button class="btn btn-primary" type="submit">
  Create</button>
```

We set its type to `submit` to trigger form submission upon clicking the button.

2. Open the `issues.service.ts` file and add a `createIssue` method that inserts a new issue into the `issues` array:

```
createIssue(issue: Issue) {
  issue.issueNo = this.issues.length + 1;
  this.issues.push(issue);
}
```

We automatically assign a new `issueNo` to the issue before adding it to the `issues` array.

> **Tip**
> The `issueNo` property is currently calculated according to the length of the `issues` array. A better approach would be to implement a generator mechanism for creating unique and random `issueNo` values.

3. Return to the `issue-report.component.ts` file, import `IssuesService`, and inject it to the constructor of the TypeScript class:

```
constructor(private builder: FormBuilder, private
issueService: IssuesService) { }
```

4. Add a new component method that will call the `createIssue` method of the injected service:

```
addIssue() {
    this.issueService.createIssue(this.issueForm?.value);
}
```

We pass the value of each form control using the `value` property of the `issueForm` object.

> **Important Note**
>
> The `value` property of a `FormGroup` object contains the model of the form. The keys of the model match the property names of the `Issue` interface, which is the type that the `createIssue` method accepts as a parameter. If those were different, we should convert the form model before passing it to the method.

5. Open the `issue-report.component.html` file and bind the `ngSubmit` event of the form to the `addIssue` component method:

```
<form clrForm *ngIf="issueForm" [formGroup]="issueForm"
(ngSubmit)="addIssue()">
```

The `ngSubmit` event will be triggered when we click on the `Create` button of the form.

We have now completed all the processes involved to add a new issue to the system. In the following section, we will learn how to display a newly created issue in the table of pending issues.

Displaying a new issue in the list

Displaying issues and creating new ones are two tasks delegated to different Angular components. When we create a new issue with `IssueReportComponent`, we need to notify `IssueListComponent` to reflect that change in the table. First, let's see how we can configure `IssueReportComponent` to communicate that change:

1. Open the `issue-report.component.ts` file and use the `@Output()` decorator to add an `EventEmitter` property:

```
@Output() formClose = new EventEmitter();
```

`Output` and `EventEmitter` symbols can be imported from the `@angular/core` npm package.

2. Call the `emit` method of the `formClose` output property inside the `addIssue` component method, right after creating the issue:

```
addIssue() {
    this.issueService.createIssue(this.issueForm?.value);
    this.formClose.emit();
}
```

3. Add a second HTML `button` element in the template of the component and call the `emit` method on its `click` event:

```
<button class="btn btn-primary" type="submit">Create
    </button>
<button class="btn" type="button"
    (click)="formClose.emit()">Cancel</button>
```

`IssueListComponent` can now bind to the `formClose` event of `IssueReportComponent` and be notified when any of the buttons are clicked. Let's find out how:

1. Open the `issue-list.component.ts` file and add the following property in the `IssueListComponent` class:

```
showReportIssue = false;
```

The `showReportIssue` property will toggle the appearance of the report issue form.

2. Add the following component method that will be called when the report issue form emits the `formClose` event:

```
onCloseReport() {
    this.showReportIssue = false;
    this.getIssues();
}
```

The `onCloseReport` method will set the `showReportIssue` property to `false` so that the report issue form is no longer visible, and the table of pending issues is displayed instead. It will also fetch issues again to refresh the data in the table.

3. Open the `issue-list.component.html` file and add an HTML `button` element at the top of the template. The button will display the report issue form when clicked:

```
<button class="btn btn-primary" (click)=
 "showReportIssue = true">Add new issue</button>
```

4. Group the button and the data grid inside an `ng-container` element. As indicated by the `*ngIf` Angular directive, contents of the `ng-container` element will be displayed when the report issue form is not visible:

```
<ng-container *ngIf="showReportIssue === false">
  <button class="btn btn-primary" (click)=
   "showReportIssue = true">Add new issue</button>
  <clr-datagrid>
   <clr-dg-column [clrDgField]="'issueNo'"
    [clrDgColType]="'number'">Issue No</clr-dg-column>
   <clr-dg-column [clrDgField]="'type'">Type</clr-dg-
     column>
   <clr-dg-column [clrDgField]="'title'">Title</clr-
     dg-column>
   <clr-dg-column [clrDgField]="'description'">
     Description</clr-dg-column>
   <clr-dg-column [clrDgField]="'priority'">Priority
     </clr-dg-column>

   <clr-dg-row *clrDgItems="let issue of issues">
    <clr-dg-cell>{{issue.issueNo}}</clr-dg-cell>
    <clr-dg-cell>{{issue.type}}</clr-dg-cell>
    <clr-dg-cell>{{issue.title}}</clr-dg-cell>
    <clr-dg-cell>{{issue.description}}</clr-dg-cell>
    <clr-dg-cell>
      <span class="label" [class.label-
        danger]="issue.priority === 'high'">
        {{issue.priority}}</span>
    </clr-dg-cell>
   </clr-dg-row>
```

```
    <clr-dg-footer>{{issues.length}} issues</clr-dg-
        footer>
    </clr-datagrid>
</ng-container>
```

The ng-container element is an Angular component that is not rendered on the screen, and it is used to group HTML elements.

5. Add the app-issue-report component at the end of the template and use the *ngIf directive to display it when the showReportIssue property is true. Bind also its formClose event to the onCloseReport component method:

```
<app-issue-report *ngIf="showReportIssue == true"
    (formClose)="onCloseReport()"></app-issue-report>
```

We have successfully connected all the dots and completed the interaction between the report issue form and the table that displays issues. Now it is time to put them in action:

1. Run the Angular application using ng serve.

2. Click on the **ADD NEW ISSUE** button and enter the details of a new issue:

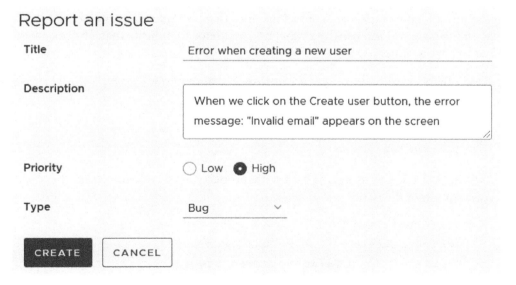

Figure 3.2 – Report issue form

3. Click on the **CREATE** button, and the new issue should appear in the table:

Figure 3.3 – Pending issues

4. Repeat *steps 2* and *3* without filling in any details, and you will notice that an empty issue is added to the table.

An empty issue can be created because we have not defined any required fields yet on our report issue form. In the following section, we will learn how to accomplish this task and add validations to our form to avoid unexpected behaviors.

Validating the details of an issue

When we create an issue with the report issue form, we can leave the value of a form control empty since we have not added any validation rules yet. To add validations in a form control, we use the `Validators` class from the `@angular/forms` npm package. A validator is added in each form control instance that we build using the `FormBuilder` service. In this case, we will use the `required` validator to indicate that a form control is required to have a value:

1. Open the `issue-report.component.ts` file and import `Validators` from the `@angular/forms` npm package:

```
import { FormBuilder, FormGroup, Validators } from
  '@angular/forms';
```

2. Set the `Validators.required` static property in all controls except the description of the issue:

```
ngOnInit(): void {
  this.issueForm = this.builder.group({
    title: ['', Validators.required],
    description: [''],
    priority: ['', Validators.required],
    type: ['', Validators.required]
  });
}
```

We can use various validators for a form control, such as `min`, `max`, and `email`. If we want to set multiple validators in a form control, we add them inside an array.

3. When we use validators in a form, we need to provide a visual indication to the user of the form. Open the `issue-report.component.html` file and add a `clr-control-error` component for each required form control:

```html
<clr-input-container>
  <label>Title</label>
  <input clrInput formControlName="title" />
  <clr-control-error>Title is required
    </clr-control-error>
</clr-input-container>
<clr-textarea-container>
  <label>Description</label>
  <textarea clrTextarea formControlName="description">
    </textarea>
</clr-textarea-container>
<clr-radio-container clrInline>
  <label>Priority</label>
  <clr-radio-wrapper>
    <input type="radio" value="low" clrRadio
      formControlName="priority" />
    <label>Low</label>
  </clr-radio-wrapper>
  <clr-radio-wrapper>
    <input type="radio" value="high" clrRadio
      formControlName="priority" />
    <label>High</label>
  </clr-radio-wrapper>
  <clr-control-error>Priority is required
    </clr-control-error>
</clr-radio-container>
<clr-select-container>
  <label>Type</label>
  <select clrSelect formControlName="type">
    <option value="Feature">Feature</option>
    <option value="Bug">Bug</option>
```

```
        <option value="Documentation">Documentation
            </option>
    </select>
    <clr-control-error>Type is required
        </clr-control-error>
</clr-select-container>
```

clr-control-error is a Clarity component that is used to provide validation messages in forms. It is displayed when we touch a control that is invalid. A control is invalid when at least one of its validation rules is violated.

4. The user may not always touch form controls to see the validation message. So, we need to take that into account upon form submission and act accordingly. To overcome this case, we will mark all form controls as touched when the form is submitted:

```
addIssue() {
    if (this.issueForm && this.issueForm.invalid) {
        this.issueForm.markAllAsTouched();
        return;
    }

    this.issueService.createIssue(this.issueForm?.value);
    this.formClose.emit();
}
```

In the preceding snippet, we use the markAllAsTouched method of the issueForm property to mark all controls as touched when the form is invalid. Marking controls as touched makes validation messages appear automatically. Additionally, we use a return statement to prevent the creation of the issue when the form is invalid.

5. Run ng serve to start the application. Click inside the **Title** input, and then move the focus out of the form control:

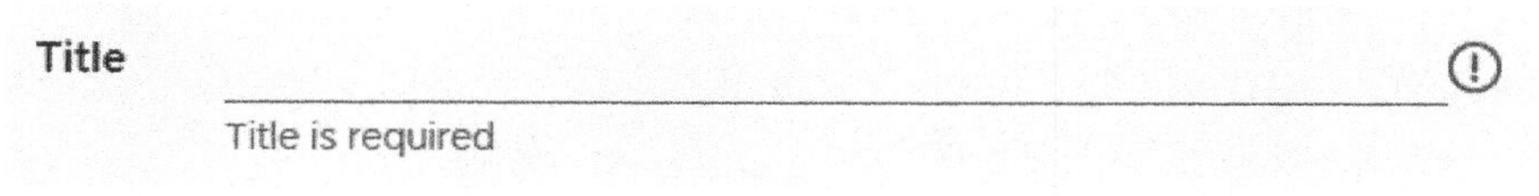

Title _____ !

Title is required

Figure 3.4 – Title validation message

A message should appear underneath the **Title** input stating that we have not entered any value yet. Validation messages in the Clarity library are indicated by text and an exclamation icon in red in the form control that is validated.

6. Now, click on the **CREATE** button:

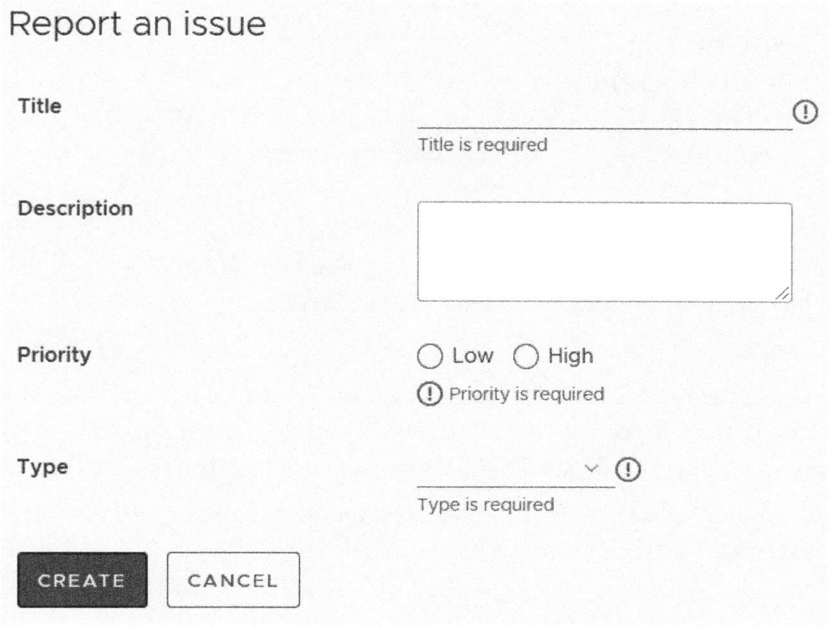

Figure 3.5 – Form validation messages

All validation messages will appear on the screen at once, and the form will not be submitted. Validations in reactive forms are an essential part of ensuring a smooth UX for our Angular applications. In the following section, we will learn how to create a modal dialog with Clarity and use it to resolve issues from our list.

Resolving an issue

The main idea behind having an issue tracking system is that an issue should be resolved at some point. We will create a user workflow in our application to accomplish such a task. We will be able to resolve an issue directly from the list of pending issues. The application will ask for confirmation from the user before resolving with the use of a modal dialog:

1. Create an Angular component to host the dialog:

```
ng generate component confirm-dialog
```

2. Open the `confirm-dialog.component.ts` file and create the following input and output properties in the `ConfirmDialogComponent` class:

```
import { Component, EventEmitter, Input, Output } from
    '@angular/core';

@Component({
  selector: 'app-confirm-dialog',
  templateUrl: './confirm-dialog.component.html',
  styleUrls: ['./confirm-dialog.component.css']
})
export class ConfirmDialogComponent {
  @Input() issueNo: number | null = null;
  @Output() confirm = new EventEmitter<boolean>();
}
```

We will use the `@Input()` decorator to get the issue number and display it on the template of the component. The `confirm` `EventEmitter` property will emit a `boolean` value to indicate whether the user confirmed to resolve the issue or not.

3. Create two methods that will call the `emit` method of the `confirm` output property, either with `true` or `false`:

```
agree() {
  this.confirm.emit(true);
  this.issueNo = null;
}

disagree() {
  this.confirm.emit(false);
  this.issueNo = null;
}
```

Both methods will set the `issueNo` property to `null` because that property will also control whether the modal dialog is opened or not. So, we want to close the dialog when the user agrees to resolve the issue or not.

We have set up the TypeScript class of our dialog component. Let's wire it up now with its template. Open the `confirm-dialog.component.html` file and replace its content with the following:

confirm-dialog.component.html

```html
<clr-modal [clrModalOpen]="issueNo !== null"
  [clrModalClosable]="false">
  <h3 class="modal-title">
    Resolve Issue #
    {{issueNo}}
  </h3>
  <div class="modal-body">
    <p>Are you sure you want to close the issue?</p>
  </div>
  <div class="modal-footer">
    <button type="button" class="btn btn-outline"
      (click)="disagree()">Cancel</button>
    <button type="button" class="btn btn-danger"
      (click)="agree()">Yes, continue</button>
  </div>
</clr-modal>
```

A Clarity modal dialog consists of a `clr-modal` component and a collection of HTML elements with specific classes:

- `modal-title`: The title of the dialog that displays the current issue number.

- `modal-body`: The main content of the dialog.

- `modal-footer`: The footer of the dialog that is commonly used to add actions for that dialog. We currently add two HTML `button` elements and bind their `click` events to the `agree` and `disagree` component methods, respectively.

Whether it is opened or closed, the current status of the dialog is indicated by the
clrModalOpen directive bound to the issueNo input property. When that property
is null, the dialog is closed. The clrModalClosable directive indicates that the
dialog cannot be closed by any means other than programmatically through the
issueNo property.

According to our specs, we want the user to resolve an issue directly from the list. Let's
find out how we can integrate the dialog that we created with the list of pending issues:

1. Open the issues.service.ts file and add a new method to set the completed
    property of an issue:

```
completeIssue(issue: Issue) {
  const selectedIssue: Issue = {
    ...issue,
    completed: new Date()
  };
  const index = this.issues.findIndex(i => i ===
    issue);
  this.issues[index] = selectedIssue;
}
```

The previous method first creates a clone of the issue that we want to resolve and
sets its completed property to the current date. It then finds the initial issue in the
issues array and replaces it with the cloned instance.

2. Open the issue-list.component.ts file and add a selectedIssue
    property and an onConfirm method:

```
export class IssueListComponent implements OnInit {

  issues: Issue[] = [];
  showReportIssue = false;
  selectedIssue: Issue | null = null;


  constructor(private issueService: IssuesService) { }

  ngOnInit(): void {
    this.getIssues();
```

```
    }


    onCloseReport() {
      this.showReportIssue = false;
      this.getIssues();
    }


    onConfirm(confirmed: boolean) {
      if (confirmed && this.selectedIssue) {
        this.issueService.completeIssue(this.
          selectedIssue);
        this.getIssues();
      }
      this.selectedIssue = null;
    }


    private getIssues() {
      this.issues =
        this.issueService.getPendingIssues();
    }
  }
```

The onConfirm method calls the completeIssue method of the issueService property only when the confirmed parameter is true. In this case, it also calls the getIssues method to refresh the table data. The selectedIssue property holds the issue object that we want to resolve, and it is reset whenever the onConfirm method is called.

3. Open the issue-list.component.html file and add an action overflow component inside the clr-dg-row component:

```
<clr-dg-row *clrDgItems="let issue of issues">
  <clr-dg-action-overflow>
    <button class="action-item" (click)="selectedIssue
      = issue">Resolve</button>
  </clr-dg-action-overflow>
  <clr-dg-cell>{{issue.issueNo}}</clr-dg-cell>
  <clr-dg-cell>{{issue.type}}</clr-dg-cell>
```

```
<clr-dg-cell>{{issue.title}}</clr-dg-cell>
<clr-dg-cell>{{issue.description}}</clr-dg-cell>
<clr-dg-cell>
  <span class="label" [class.label-danger]=
    "issue.priority === 'high'">{{issue.priority}}
      </span>
</clr-dg-cell>
</clr-dg-row>
```

The `clr-dg-action-overflow` component of Clarity adds a drop-down menu in each row of the table. The menu contains a single button that will set the `selectedIssue` property to the current `issue` when clicked.

4. Finally, add the `app-confirm-dialog` component at the end of the template:

```
<app-confirm-dialog *ngIf="selectedIssue"
  [issueNo]="selectedIssue.issueNo"
    (confirm)="onConfirm($event)"></app-confirm-dialog>
```

We pass the `issueNo` of the `selectedIssue` property to the input binding of the dialog component. We use the ? safe navigation operator to avoid errors in our application because initially there is no issue selected and the `issueNo` property is not available.

We also bind the `onConfirm` component method to the `confirm` event so that we can be notified when the user either agrees or not. The `$event` parameter is a reserved keyword in Angular and contains the event binding result, which is dependent on the type of the HTML element. In this case, it contains the Boolean result of the confirmation.

We have put all the pieces into place for resolving an issue. Let's give it a try:

1. Run `ng serve` and open the application at `http://localhost:4200`.

2. If you don't have any issues, use the **ADD NEW ISSUE** button to create one.

3. Click on the action menu of one row and select **Resolve**. The menu is the three vertical dots icon next to the **Issue No** column:

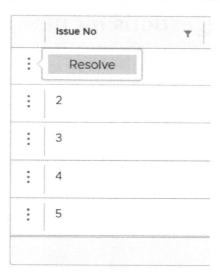

Figure 3.6 – Action menu

4. In the **Resolve Issue** dialog that appears, click on the **YES, CONTINUE** button:

Resolve Issue # 1

Are you sure you want to close the issue?

Figure 3.7 – Resolve Issue dialog

After clicking the button, the dialog will close, and the issue should not be visible on the list anymore.

We have provided a way for users of our application to resolve issues. Our issue tracking system is now complete and ready to put into action! Sometimes, users are in a hurry and may report an issue already reported. In the following section, we will learn how to leverage advanced reactive forms techniques to help them in this case.

Turning on suggestions for new issues

The reactive forms API contains a mechanism for getting notified when the value of a particular form control changes. We will use it in our application to find related issues when reporting a new one. More specifically, we will display a list of suggested issues when the user starts typing in the title form control:

1. Open the `issues.service.ts` file and add the following method:

    ```
    getSuggestions(title: string): Issue[] {
      if (title.length > 3) {
        return this.issues.filter(issue =>
          issue.title.indexOf(title) !== -1);
      }
      return [];
    }
    ```

    The `getSuggestions` method takes the title of an issue as a parameter and searches for any issues that contain the same title. The search mechanism is triggered when the `title` parameter is more than three characters long to limit results down to a reasonable amount.

2. Open the `issue-report.component.ts` file and add the following `import` statement:

    ```
    import { Issue } from '../issue';
    ```

3. Create a new component property to hold the suggested issues:

    ```
    suggestions: Issue[] = [];
    ```

4. The `controls` property of a `FormGroup` object contains all form controls as a key-value pair. The key is the name of the control, and the value is the actual form control object of the `AbstractControl` type. We can get notified about changes in the value of a form control by accessing its name, in this case the title, in the following way:

    ```
    ngOnInit(): void {
      this.issueForm = this.builder.group({
        title: ['', Validators.required],
        description: [''],
        priority: ['', Validators.required],
    ```

```
    type: ['', Validators.required]
  });
  this.issueForm.controls.title.valueChanges.subscribe((
  title: string) => {
    this.suggestions =
      this.issueService.getSuggestions(title);
  });
}
```

Each control exposes a valueChanges observable that we can subscribe to and get a continuous stream of values. The valueChanges observable emits new values as soon as the user starts typing in the title control of the form. We set the result of the getSuggestions method in the suggestions component property when that happens.

5. To display the suggested issues on the template of the component, open the issue-report.component.html file and add the following HTML code right after the clr-input-container element:

```html
<div class="clr-row" *ngIf="suggestions.length">
  <div class="clr-col-lg-2"></div>
  <div class="clr-col-lg-6">
    <clr-stack-view>
      <clr-stack-header>Similar issues
        </clr-stack-header>
      <clr-stack-block *ngFor="let issue of
        suggestions">
        <clr-stack-label>#{{issue.issueNo}}:
          {{issue.title}}</clr-stack-label>
        <clr-stack-content>{{issue.description}}
          </clr-stack-content>
      </clr-stack-block>
    </clr-stack-view>
  </div>
</div>
```

We use the `clr-stack-view` component from the Clarity library to display suggested issues in a key-value pair representation. The key is indicated by the `clr-stack-header` component and displays the title and the number of the issue. The value is indicated by the `clr-stack-content` component and displays the description of the issue.

> **Important Note**
> We display similar issues only when there are any available suggested ones.

Run `ng serve` and open the report issue form to create a new issue. When you start typing in the **Title** input, the application will suggest any related issues with the one that you are trying to create:

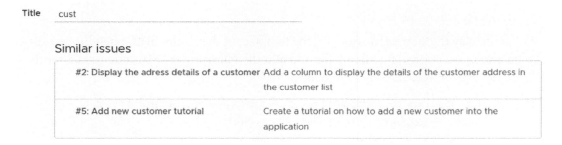

Figure 3.8 – Similar issues

The user will now see if there are any similar issues and avoid reporting a duplicate issue.

Summary

In this chapter, we built an Angular application for managing and tracking issues using reactive forms and Clarity Design System.

First, we installed Clarity to an Angular application and used a data grid component to display a list of pending issues. Then, we introduced reactive forms and used them to build a form for reporting a new issue. We added validations in the form to give our users a visual indication of the required fields and guard against unwanted behavior.

An issue tracking system is not efficient if our users are not able to resolve them. We built a modal dialog using Clarity to resolve a selected issue. Finally, we improved the UX of our application by suggesting related issues when reporting a new one.

In the next chapter, we will build a progressive web application for the weather using the Angular service worker.

Exercise

Create an Angular component to edit the details of an existing issue. The component should display the number of the issue and allow the user to change the title, description, and priority. The title and the description should be required fields.

The user should be able to access the previous component using the action menu in the list of pending issues. Add a new button in the action menu that will open the edit issue form.

After the user has completed updating an issue, the form should be closed, and the list of pending issues should be refreshed.

You can find the solution to the exercise in the `Chapter03` folder of the `exercise` branch at `https://github.com/PacktPublishing/Angular-Projects-Second-Edition/tree/exercise`.

Further reading

- Angular forms: `https://angular.io/guide/forms-overview`

- Reactive forms: `https://angular.io/guide/reactive-forms`

- Validating reactive forms: `https://angular.io/guide/form-validation#validating-input-in-reactive-forms`

- Passing data to a component: `https://angular.io/guide/component-interaction#pass-data-from-parent-to-child-with-input-binding`

- Getting data from a component: `https://angular.io/guide/component-interaction#parent-listens-for-child-event`

- Getting started with Clarity: `https://clarity.design/documentation/get-started`

4

Building a PWA Weather Application Using Angular Service Worker

We can access a web application using different types of devices, such as a desktop, mobile, tablet, and various network types, such as broadband, Wi-Fi, and cellular. A web application should work seamlessly and provide the same user experience independently of the device and the network of the user.

Progressive Web Apps (PWA) is a collection of web techniques for building web applications with previous considerations in mind. One popular technique is the **service worker**, which improves the loading time of a web application. In this chapter, we will use the service worker implementation of the Angular framework to build a PWA that displays the weather of a city using the **OpenWeather API**.

We will cover the following topics in detail:

- Setting up the OpenWeather API
- Displaying weather data
- Enabling offline mode with the service worker
- Staying up to date with in-app notifications
- Deploying our app with **Firebase** hosting

Essential background theory and context

Traditional web applications are usually hosted in a web server and are immediately available to any user at any given time. Native applications are installed on the device of the user, have access to its native resources, and can work seamlessly with any network. PWA applications stand between the two worlds of web and native applications and share characteristics from both. A PWA application is a web application that is based on the following pillars to convert into a native one:

- **Capable**: It can access locally saved data and interact with peripheral hardware that is connected to the device of the user.
- **Reliable**: It can have the same performance and experience in any network connection, even in areas with low connectivity and coverage.
- **Installable**: It can be installed on the device of the user, can be launched directly from the home screen, and interact with other installed native applications.

Converting a web application into a PWA involves several steps and techniques. The most essential one is configuring a service worker. The service worker is a mechanism that is run on the web browser and acts as a proxy between the application and an external HTTP endpoint or other in-app resources such as JavaScript and CSS files. The main job of the service worker is to intercept requests to those resources and act on them by providing a cached or live response.

> **Important note**
> The service worker is persisted after the tab of the browser is closed.

The Angular framework provides an implementation for the service worker that we can use to convert our Angular applications into PWA.

It also contains a built-in HTTP client that we can use to communicate with a server over HTTP. The Angular HTTP client exposes an observable-based API with all standard HTTP methods such as POST and GET. Observables are based on the **observer pattern**, which is the core of reactive functional programming. In the observer pattern, multiple objects called **observers** can subscribe to an observable and get notified about any changes to its state. An observable dispatches changes to observers by emitting event streams asynchronously. The Angular framework uses a library called **RxJS** that contains various artifacts for working with observables. One of these artifacts is a set of functions called **operators** that can apply various actions on observables such as transformations and filtering. Next, let's get an overview of our project.

Project overview

In this project, we will build a PWA application to display the weather conditions of a city. Initially, we will learn how to configure the OpenWeather API, which we will use to get weather data. We will then learn how to use the API to display weather information in an Angular component. We will see how to convert our Angular application into PWA using a service worker. We will also implement a notification mechanism for our application updates. Finally, we will deploy our PWA application into the Firebase hosting provider.

Build time: 90 minutes

Getting started

The following software tools are required to complete this project:

- Angular CLI: A command-line interface for Angular that you can find at `https://angular.io/cli`.

- GitHub material: The related code for this chapter can be found in the `Chapter04` folder at `https://github.com/PacktPublishing/Angular-Projects-Second-Edition`.

Setting up the OpenWeather API

The OpenWeather API has been created by the OpenWeather team and contains current and historical weather information from over 200,000 cities worldwide. It also supports forecast weather data for more detailed information. In this project, we will focus on the current weather data.

We need to get an API key first to start using the OpenWeather API:

1. Navigate to the OpenWeather API website: `https://openweathermap.org/api`.

    You will see a list of all available APIs from the OpenWeather team.

2. Find the section entitled **Current Weather Data** and click on the **Subscribe** button.

    You will be redirected to the page with the available pricing schemes of the service. Each scheme supports a different combination of API calls per minute and month. For this project, we are going to use the **Free** tier.

3. Click on the **Get API key** button.

    You will be redirected to the sign-up page of the service.

4. Fill in all the required details and click on the **Create Account** button.

    A confirmation message will be sent to the email address that you used to create your account.

5. Find the confirmation email and click on the **Verify your email** button to complete your registration.

    You will shortly receive another email from OpenWeather with details about your current subscription, including your API key and the HTTP endpoint that we will use for communicating with the API.

> **Important note**
> The API key may take some time to be activated, usually a couple of hours, before you can use it.

As soon as the API key has been activated, we can start using it within an Angular application. We will learn how to do this in the following section.

Displaying weather data

In this section, we will create an Angular application to display weather information for a city. The user will enter the name of the city in an input field, and the application will use the OpenWeather API to get weather data for the specified city. We will cover the following topics in more detail:

- Setting up the Angular application
- Communicating with the OpenWeather API
- Displaying weather information for a city

Let's start by creating the Angular application first in the following section.

Setting up the Angular application

We will use the ng new command of the Angular CLI to create a new Angular application from scratch:

```
ng new weather-app --style=scss --routing=false
```

The preceding command will create a new Angular CLI application with the following properties:

- weather-app: The name of the Angular application
- --style=scss: Indicates that our Angular application will use the SCSS stylesheet format
- --routing=false: Disables Angular routing in the application

The user should be able to enter the name of the city in an input field, and the weather information of the city should be visualized in a card layout. The **Angular Material** library provides a set of Angular UI components, including an input and a card, to use for our needs.

Angular Material components adhere to the Material Design principles and are maintained by the Components team of Angular. We can install the Angular Material using the following command of the Angular CLI:

```
ng add @angular/material --theme=indigo-pink --typography=true
--animations=true
```

The preceding code uses the `ng add` command of the Angular CLI, passing additional configuration options:

- `@angular/material`: The npm package name of the Angular Material library. It will also install the `@angular/cdk` package, a set of behaviors and interactions used to build Angular Material. Both packages will be added to the `dependencies` section of the `package.json` file of the application.

- `--theme=indigo-pink`: The name of the Angular Material theme that we want to use. Adding a theme involves modifying several files of the Angular CLI workspace. It adds entries of the CSS theme file to the `angular.json` configuration file:

  ```
  ./node_modules/@angular/material/prebuilt-themes/indigo-
  pink.css
  ```

  It also includes the Material Design icons in the `index.html` file:

  ```
  <link href="https://fonts.googleapis.com/
  icon?family=Material+Icons" rel="stylesheet">
  ```

  Angular Material comes with a set of predefined themes that we can use. Alternatively, we can build a custom one that fits our specific needs.

- `--typography=true`: Enables Angular Material typography globally in our application. Typography defines how text content is displayed and uses the **Roboto** Google font by default, which is included in the `index.html` file:

  ```
  <link href="https://fonts.googleapis.com/
  css2?family=Roboto:wght@300;400;500&display=swap"
  rel="stylesheet">
  ```

  It adds the following class to the `body` of the HTML file:

  ```
  <body class="mat-typography">
      <app-root></app-root>
  </body>
  ```

  It also adds some CSS styles to the global `styles.scss` file of our application:

  ```
  html, body { height: 100%; }
  body { margin: 0; font-family: Roboto, "Helvetica Neue",
  sans-serif; }
  ```

- `--animations=true`: Enables browser animations in our application by importing `BrowserAnimationsModule` into the main application module, `app.module.ts`:

```typescript
import { NgModule } from '@angular/core';
import { BrowserModule } from '@angular/platform-browser';

import { AppComponent } from './app.component';
import { BrowserAnimationsModule } from '@angular/platform-browser/animations';

@NgModule({
  declarations: [
    AppComponent
  ],
  imports: [
    BrowserModule,
    BrowserAnimationsModule
  ],
  providers: [],
  bootstrap: [AppComponent]
})
export class AppModule { }
```

We have nearly completed the setup and configuration of our Angular application. The last step is to add the API key that we created in the *Setting up the OpenWeather API* section.

The Angular CLI workspace contains the `src\environments` folder that we can use for defining application settings such as API keys and endpoints. It contains one TypeScript file for each environment that we want to support in our application. The Angular CLI creates two files by default:

- `environment.ts`: The TypeScript file for the development environment. It is used when we start an Angular application using `ng serve`.

- `environment.prod.ts`: The TypeScript file for the production environment. It is used when we build the application using `ng build`.

Each environment file exports an `environment` object. Add the following properties to the object in both development and production files:

```
apiUrl: 'https://api.openweathermap.org/data/2.5/',
apiKey: '<Your API key>'
```

In the preceding snippet, the `apiUrl` property is the URL of the endpoint that we will use to make calls to the OpenWeather API, and `apiKey` is our API key. Replace the `<Your API key>` value with the API key that you have.

We now have all the moving parts in place to build our Angular application. In the following section, we will create a mechanism for interacting with the OpenWeather API.

Communicating with the OpenWeather API

The application should interact with the OpenWeather API over HTTP to get weather data. Let's see how we can set up this type of communication in our application:

1. First, we need to create an interface for describing the type of data we will get from the API. Use the following `generate` command of the Angular CLI to create one:

    ```
    ng generate interface weather
    ```

    The preceding command will create the `weather.ts` file in the `src\app` folder of our Angular CLI project.

2. Open the `weather.ts` file and modify it as follows:

    ```
    export interface Weather {
      weather: WeatherInfo[],
      main: {
        temp: number;
        pressure: number;
        humidity: number;
      };
      wind: {
        speed: number;
      };
      sys: {
        country: string
      };
    ```

```
  name: string;
}

interface WeatherInfo {
  main: string;
  icon: string;
}
```

Each property corresponds to a weather field in the OpenWeather API response. You can find a description for each one at `https://openweathermap.org/current#parameter`.

Then, we need to set up the built-in HTTP client provided by the Angular framework.

3. Open the `app.module.ts` file and add `HttpClientModule` to the `imports` array of the `@NgModule` decorator:

```typescript
import { HttpClientModule } from '@angular/common/http';
import { NgModule } from '@angular/core';
import { BrowserModule } from '@angular/platform-browser';

import { AppComponent } from './app.component';
import { BrowserAnimationsModule } from '@angular/platform-browser/animations';

@NgModule({
  declarations: [
    AppComponent
  ],
  imports: [
    BrowserModule,
    BrowserAnimationsModule,
    HttpClientModule
  ],
  providers: [],
  bootstrap: [AppComponent]
})
export class AppModule { }
```

4. Use the `generate` command of the Angular CLI to create a new Angular service:

```
ng generate service weather
```

The preceding command will create the `weather.service.ts` file in the `src\app` folder of our Angular CLI project.

5. Open the `weather.service.ts` file and inject the `HttpClient` service into its constructor:

```
import { HttpClient } from '@angular/common/http';
import { Injectable } from '@angular/core';


@Injectable({
  providedIn: 'root'
})
export class WeatherService {
  constructor(private http: HttpClient) { }

}
```

6. Add a method in the service that accepts the name of the city as a single parameter and queries the OpenWeather API for that city:

```
getWeather(city: string): Observable<Weather> {
  const options = new HttpParams()
    .set('units', 'metric')
    .set('q', city)
    .set('appId', environment.apiKey);


  return this.http.get<Weather>(environment.apiUrl +
    'weather', { params: options });
}
```

The `getWeather` method uses the `get` method of the `HttpClient` service that accepts two parameters. The first one is the URL endpoint of the OpenWeather API, which is available from the `apiUrl` property of the `environment` object.

> **Important note**
>
> The `environment` object is imported from the default `environment.ts` file. The Angular CLI is responsible for replacing it with the `environment.prod.ts` file when we build our application.

The second parameter is an `options` object used to pass additional configuration to the request, such as URL query parameters with the `params` property. We use the constructor of the `HttpParams` object and call its `set` method for each query parameter that we want to add to the URL. In our case, we pass the `q` parameter for the city name, the `appId` for the API key that we get from the `environment` object, and the type of `units` we want to use. You can learn more about supported units at `https://openweathermap.org/current#data`.

> **Tip**
>
> We used the `set` method to create query parameters because the `HttpParams` object is immutable. Calling the constructor for each parameter that you want to pass will throw an error.

We also set the type of response data as `Weather` in the `get` method. Notice that the `getWeather` method does not return `Weather` data, but instead an `Observable` of this type.

7. Add the following `import` statements at the top of the file:

```
import { HttpClient, HttpParams } from '@angular/common/
http';
import { Injectable } from '@angular/core';
import { Observable } from 'rxjs';
import { environment } from '../environments/
environment';
import { Weather } from './weather';
```

The Angular service that we created contains all the necessary artifacts for interacting with the OpenWeather API. In the following section, we will create an Angular component for initiating requests and displaying data from it.

Displaying weather information for a city

The user should be able to use the UI of our application and enter the name of a city that wants to view weather details. The application will use that information to query the OpenWeather API, and the result of the request will be displayed on the UI using a card layout. Let's start building an Angular component for creating all these types of interactions:

1. Use the `generate` command of the Angular CLI to create an Angular component:

```
ng generate component weather
```

2. Open the template of the main component, `app.component.html`, and replace its content with the selector of the new component, `app-weather`:

```
<app-weather></app-weather>
```

3. Open the `app.module.ts` file and add the following modules from the Angular Material library to the `imports` array of the `@NgModule` decorator:

```
@NgModule({
  declarations: [
    AppComponent,
    WeatherComponent
  ],
  imports: [
    BrowserModule,
    BrowserAnimationsModule,
    HttpClientModule,
    MatIconModule,
    MatInputModule,
    MatCardModule
  ],
  providers: [],
  bootstrap: [AppComponent]
})
```

Also, add the necessary `import` statements at the top of the file:

```
import { MatCardModule } from '@angular/material/card';
import { MatIconModule } from '@angular/material/icon';
import { MatInputModule } from '@angular/material/input';
```

4. Open the weather.component.ts file, create a weather property of the Weather type, and inject WeatherService into the constructor of the WeatherComponent class:

```typescript
import { Component, OnInit } from '@angular/core';

import { Weather } from '../weather';
import { WeatherService } from '../weather.service';

@Component({
  selector: 'app-weather',
  templateUrl: './weather.component.html',
  styleUrls: ['./weather.component.scss']
})
export class WeatherComponent implements OnInit {

  weather: Weather | undefined;

  constructor(private weatherService: WeatherService)
    { }

  ngOnInit(): void {
  }
}
```

5. Create a component method that subscribes to the getWeather method of WeatherService and assigns the result to the weather component property:

```typescript
search(city: string) {
  this.weatherService.getWeather(city).subscribe(weather
    => this.weather = weather);
}
```

We have already finished working with the TypeScript class file of our component. Let's wire it up with its template. Open the `weather.component.html` file and replace its content with the following HTML code:

weather.component.html

```
<mat-form-field>
  <input matInput placeholder="Enter city" #cityCtrl
    (keydown.enter)="search(cityCtrl.value)">
  <mat-icon matSuffix
    (click)="search(cityCtrl.value)">search</mat-icon>
</mat-form-field>
<mat-card *ngIf="weather">
  <mat-card-header>
    <mat-card-title>{{weather.name}},
      {{weather.sys.country}}</mat-card-title>
    <mat-card-subtitle>{{weather.weather[0].main}}
      </mat-card-subtitle>
  </mat-card-header>
  <img mat-card-image
    src="https://openweathermap.org/img/wn/
      {{weather.weather[0].icon}}@2x.png"
      [alt]="weather.weather[0].main">
  <mat-card-content>
    <h1>{{weather.main.temp | number:'1.0-0'}} &#8451;</h1>
    <p>Pressure: {{weather.main.pressure}} hPa</p>
    <p>Humidity: {{weather.main.humidity}} %</p>
    <p>Wind: {{weather.wind.speed}} m/s</p>
  </mat-card-content>
</mat-card>
```

The preceding template consists of several components from the Angular Material library, including a `mat-form-field` component that contains the following child elements:

- An `input` HTML element for entering the name of the city. When the user has finished editing and presses the *Enter* key, it calls the `search` component method passing the `value` property of the `cityCtrl` variable as a parameter. The `cityCtrl` variable is a **template reference variable** and indicates the actual object of the native HTML `input` element.

- A `mat-icon` component displays a *magnifier* icon and is located at the end of the input element, as indicated by the `matSuffix` directive. It also calls the `search` component method when clicked.

> **Important note**
>
> The `cityCtrl` template reference variable is indicated by a # and is accessible everywhere inside the template of the component.

A `mat-card` component presents information in a card layout and is displayed only when the `weather` component property has a value. It consists of the following child elements:

- `mat-card-header`: The header of the card. It consists of a `mat-card-title` component that displays the name of the city and the country code and a `mat-card-subtitle` component that displays the current weather conditions.

- `mat-card-image`: The image of the card that displays the icon of the weather conditions, along with a description as an alternate text.

- `mat-card-content`: The main content of the card. It displays the temperature, pressure, humidity, and wind speed of the current weather. The temperature is displayed without any decimal points, as indicated by the `number` pipe.

Let's now spice things up a bit by adding some styles to our component:

weather.component.scss

```scss
:host {
  display: flex;
  align-items: center;
  justify-content: center;
  flex-direction: column;
  padding-top: 25px;
}

mat-form-field {
  width: 20%;
}

mat-icon {
  cursor: pointer;
}

mat-card {
  margin-top: 30px;
  width: 250px;
}

h1 {
  text-align: center;
  font-size: 2.5em;
}
```

The :host selector is an Angular unique CSS selector that targets the HTML element hosting our component, which in our case, is the app-weather HTML element.

If we run our application using `ng serve`, navigate to `http://localhost:4200` and search for weather information in **Athens**, we should get the following output on the screen:

Enter city

Athens   Q

Athens, GR

Clouds

16 °C

Pressure: 1015 hPa

Humidity: 51 %

Wind: 3.1 m/s

Figure 4.1 – Application output

Congratulations! At this point, you have a fully working Angular application that displays weather information for a specific city. The application consists of a single Angular component that communicates with the OpenWeather API using an Angular service through HTTP. We learned how to style our component using Angular Material and give our users a pleasant experience with our app. But what happens when we are offline? Does the application work as expected? Does the user's experience remain the same? Let's find out in the following section.

Enabling offline mode with the service worker

Users from anywhere can now access our Angular application to get weather information for any city they are interested in. When we say *anywhere*, we mean any network type such as broadband, cellular (3G/4G/5G), and Wi-Fi. Consider the case where a user is in a place with low coverage or frequent network outages. How is our application going to behave? Let's find out by conducting an experiment:

1. Run the Angular application using the `serve` command of the Angular CLI:

    ```
    ng serve
    ```

2. Open your favorite browser and navigate to `http://localhost:4200`, which is the default address and port number for an Angular CLI project. You should see the input field for entering the name of the city:

    Enter city   🔍

    Figure 4.2 – Entering the name of a city

3. Open the developer tools of your browser and navigate to the **Network** tab. Set the value of the **Throttling** dropdown to **Offline**:

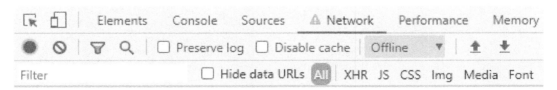

Figure 4.3 – Offline network mode

4. Try to refresh your browser. You will see an indication that you are disconnected from the internet, as shown in the following screenshot:

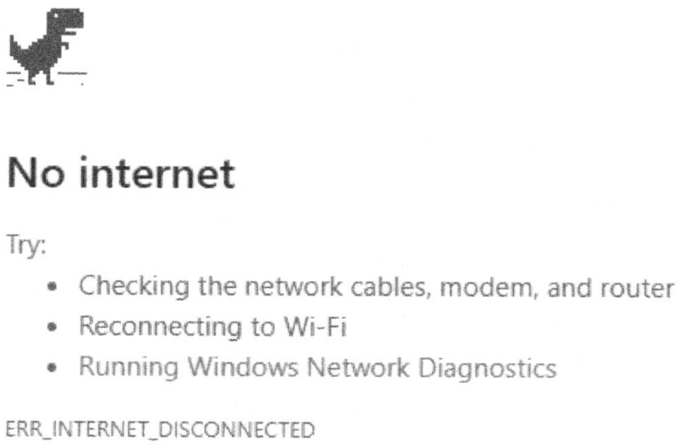

No internet

Try:

- Checking the network cables, modem, and router
- Reconnecting to Wi-Fi
- Running Windows Network Diagnostics

ERR_INTERNET_DISCONNECTED

Figure 4.4 – No internet connection (Google Chrome)

The previous case is pretty standard in areas with low-quality internet connections. So, what can we do for our users in such areas? Luckily, the Angular framework contains an implementation of a service worker that can significantly enhance the UX of our application when running in offline mode. It can cache certain parts of the application and deliver them accordingly instead of making real requests.

> **Tip**
> The Angular service worker can also be used in environments with large network latency connections. Consider using a service worker in this type of network to also improve the experience of your users.

Run the following command of the Angular CLI to enable the service worker in our Angular application:

```
ng add @angular/pwa
```

The preceding command will transform the Angular CLI workspace accordingly for PWA support:

- It adds the `@angular/service-worker` npm package to the `dependencies` section of the `package.json` file of the application.

- It creates the `manifest.webmanifest` file in the `src` folder of the application. The manifest file contains information about the application needed to install and run the application as a native one. It also adds it to the `assets` array of the `build` options in the `angular.json` file.

- It creates the `ngsw-config.json` file at the root of the project, which is the service worker configuration file. We use it to define configuration-specific artifacts, such as which resources are cached and how they are cached. You can find more details about the configuration of the service worker at the following link: `https://angular.io/guide/service-worker-config#service-worker-configuration`.

  The configuration file is also set in the `ngswConfigPath` property of the `build` configuration in the `angular.json` file.

- It sets the `serviceWorker` property to `true` in the `build` configuration of the `angular.json` file.

- It registers the service worker in the `app.module.ts` file:

```
import { ServiceWorkerModule } from '@angular/service-worker';
import { environment } from '../environments/environment';


@NgModule({
  declarations: [
    AppComponent,
    WeatherComponent
  ],
  imports: [
    BrowserModule,
    BrowserAnimationsModule,
    HttpClientModule,
    MatIconModule,
    MatInputModule,
```

```
    MatCardModule,
    ServiceWorkerModule.register('ngsw-worker.js', {
    enabled: environment.production,
    // Register the ServiceWorker as soon as the app is
    // stable
    // or after 30 seconds (whichever comes first).
    registrationStrategy: 'registerWhenStable:30000'
})
    ],
    providers: [],
    bootstrap: [AppComponent]
})
```

The ngsw-worker.js file is the JavaScript file that contains the actual implementation of the service worker. It is created automatically for us when we build our application in production mode. Angular uses the register method of the ServiceWorkerModule class to register it within our application.

- It creates several icons to be used when the application is installed as a native one in the device of the user.

- It includes the manifest file and a meta tag for theme-color in the head of the index.html file:

```
<link rel="manifest" href="manifest.webmanifest">
<meta name="theme-color" content="#1976d2">
```

Now that we have completed the installation of the service worker, it is time to test it! Before moving on, we should install an external web server because the built-in function of the Angular CLI does not work with service workers. A good alternative is http-server:

1. Run the install command of the npm client to install http-server:

```
npm install -D http-server
```

The preceding command will install http-server as a development dependency of our Angular CLI project.

2. Build the Angular application using the build command of the Angular CLI:

```
ng build
```

3. Open the `package.json` file of the Angular CLI workspace and add the following entry to the `scripts` property:

```
"scripts": {
  "ng": "ng",
  "start": "ng serve",
  "build": "ng build",
  "watch": "ng build --watch -configuration
    development",
  "test": "ng test",
  "server": "http-server -p 8080 -c-1
    dist/weather-app"
}
```

4. Start the HTTP web server using the following command:

```
npm run server
```

The preceding command will start `http-server` at port `8080` and will have caching disabled.

5. Open your browser and navigate to `http://localhost:8080`.

> **Tip**
> Prefer opening the page in private or incognito mode to avoid unexpected behavior from the service worker.

6. Repeat the process that we followed at the beginning of the section for switching to offline mode.

7. If you refresh the page now, you will notice that the application is working as expected.

The service worker did all the work for us, and the process was so transparent that we could not tell whether we are online or offline. You can verify that by inspecting the **Network** tab:

Figure 4.5 – Service worker (offline mode)

The (**ServiceWorker**) value in the **Size** column indicates that the service worker served a cached version of our application.

We have now successfully installed the service worker and went one step closer to converting our application into a PWA. In the following section, we will learn how to notify users of the application about potential updates.

Staying up to date with in-app notifications

When we want to apply a change in a web application, we make the change and build a new version of our application. The application is then deployed to a web server, and every user has access to the new version immediately. But this is not the case with PWA applications.

When we deploy a new version of our PWA application, the service worker must act accordingly and apply a specific update strategy. It should either notify the user of the new version or install it immediately. Whichever update strategy we follow depends on our needs. In this project, we want to show a prompt to the user and decide whether they want to update. Let's see how to implement this feature in our application:

1. Open the `app.module.ts` file and add `MatSnackBarModule` to the `imports` array of the `@NgModule` decorator:

```
import { MatSnackBarModule } from '@angular/material/
snack-bar';


@NgModule({
  declarations: [
    AppComponent,
    WeatherComponent
  ],
  imports: [
    BrowserModule,
    BrowserAnimationsModule,
    HttpClientModule,
    MatIconModule,
    MatInputModule,
    MatCardModule,
    MatSnackBarModule,
    ServiceWorkerModule.register('ngsw-worker.js', {
      enabled: environment.production,
```

```
        // Register the ServiceWorker as soon as the app
        // is stable
        // or after 30 seconds (whichever comes first).
        registrationStrategy: 'registerWhenStable:30000'
      })
    ],
    providers: [],
    bootstrap: [AppComponent]
})
```

MatSnackBarModule is an Angular Material module that allows us to interact with snack bars. A snack bar is a pop-up window that usually appears on the bottom of the page and is used for notification purposes.

2. Open the app.component.ts file and add the OnInit interface to the implemented interfaces of the AppComponent class:

```
import { Component, OnInit } from '@angular/core';

@Component({
  selector: 'app-root',
  templateUrl: './app.component.html',
  styleUrls: ['./app.component.scss']
})
export class AppComponent implements OnInit {
  title = 'weather-app';
}
```

3. Inject the MatSnackBar and SwUpdate services in the constructor of the AppComponent class:

```
import { Component, OnInit } from '@angular/core';
import { MatSnackBar } from '@angular/material/snack-bar';
import { SwUpdate } from '@angular/service-worker';

@Component({
  selector: 'app-root',
```

```
    templateUrl: './app.component.html',
    styleUrls: ['./app.component.scss']
})
export class AppComponent implements OnInit {
    title = 'weather-app';


    constructor(private updates: SwUpdate, private
        snackbar: MatSnackBar) {}
}
```

The MatSnackBar service is an Angular service exposed from
MatSnackBarModule. The SwUpdate service is part of the service worker
and contains observables that we can use to notify regarding the update process
on our application.

4. Create the following ngOnInit method:

```
ngOnInit() {
    this.updates.available.pipe(
        switchMap(() => this.snackbar.open('A new version
            is available!', 'Update now').afterDismissed()),
        filter(result => result.dismissedByAction),
        map(() => this.updates.activateUpdate().then(() =>
            location.reload()))
    ).subscribe();
}
```

The ngOnInit method is an implementation method of the OnInit interface
and is called upon initialization of the component. The SwUpdate service contains
an available observable property that we can use to get notified when a new
version of our application is available. Typically, we tend to subscribe to observables,
but in this case, we don't. Instead, we subscribe to the pipe method, an RxJS
operator for composing multiple operators.

5. Add the following import statements at the top of the app.component.ts file:

```
import { filter, map, switchMap } from 'rxjs/operators';
```

A lot is going on inside the `pipe` method that we defined previously, so let's break it down into pieces to understand it further. The `pipe` operator combines three RxJS operators:

- `switchMap`: This is called when a new version of our application is available. It uses the `open` method of the `snackbar` property to show a snack bar with an action button and subscribes to its `afterDismissed` observable. The `afterDismissed` observable emits when the snack bar is closed either by clicking on the action button or programmatically using its API methods.

- `filter`: This is called when the snack bar is dismissed using the action button.

- `map`: This calls the `activateUpdate` method of the `updates` property to apply the new version of the application. Once the application has been updated, it reloads the window of the browser for the changes to take effect.

Let's see the whole process of updating to a new version in action:

1. Run the `build` command of the Angular CLI to build the Angular application:

    ```
    ng build
    ```

2. Start the HTTP server to serve the application:

    ```
    npm run server
    ```

3. Open a private or incognito window of your browser and navigate to `http://localhost:8080`.

4. Without closing the browser window, let's introduce a change in our application and add a header. Run the `generate` command of the Angular CLI to create a component:

    ```
    ng generate component header
    ```

5. Open the `app.module.ts` file and import a couple of Angular Material modules:

    ```
    import { MatButtonModule } from '@angular/material/
    button';
    import { MatToolbarModule } from '@angular/material/
    toolbar';

    @NgModule({
      declarations: [
        AppComponent,
        WeatherComponent,
    ```

```
        HeaderComponent
    ],
    imports: [
      BrowserModule,
      BrowserAnimationsModule,
      HttpClientModule,
      MatIconModule,
      MatInputModule,
      MatCardModule,
      MatSnackBarModule,
      MatButtonModule,
      MatToolbarModule,
      ServiceWorkerModule.register('ngsw-worker.js', {
      enabled: environment.production,
      // Register the ServiceWorker as soon as the app is
      // stable
      // or after 30 seconds (whichever comes first).
      registrationStrategy: 'registerWhenStable:30000'
    })
    ],
    providers: [],
    bootstrap: [AppComponent]
})
```

6. Open the `header.component.html` file and create a `mat-toolbar` component with two HTML `button` elements, each one containing a `mat-icon` component:

```html
<mat-toolbar color="primary">
  <span>Weather App</span>
  <span class="spacer"></span>
  <button mat-icon-button>
    <mat-icon>refresh</mat-icon>
  </button>
  <button mat-icon-button>
    <mat-icon>share</mat-icon>
  </button>
</mat-toolbar>
```

7. Add the following CSS style to the `header.component.scss` file to position buttons at the far right end of the header:

```
.spacer {
  flex: 1 1 auto;
}
```

8. Open the `app.component.html` file and add the `app-header` component on the top:

```
<app-header></app-header>
<app-weather></app-weather>
```

9. Repeat steps *1* and *2* to build and start the application. Open a new tab in the browser window that you have already opened and you will see the following notification at the bottom of the page after a few seconds:

Figure 4.6 – New version notification

10. Click on the **Update now** button, wait for the browser window to reload, and you should see your change:

Figure 4.7 – Application output

Our Angular application has begun to transform into a PWA one. Additional to the caching mechanism that the Angular service worker provides, we have added a mechanism for installing new versions of our application. In the following section, we will learn how to deploy our application and install it natively on our device.

Deploying our app with Firebase hosting

Firebase is a hosting solution provided by Google that we can use to deploy our Angular applications. The Firebase team has put a lot of effort into creating an Angular CLI schematic for deploying an Angular application using one single command. Before diving deeper, let's learn how to set up Firebase hosting:

1. Use a Google account to log in to Firebase at `https://console.firebase. google.com`.

2. Click on the **Add project** button to create a new Firebase project.

3. Enter the name of the project, `weather-app`, and click the **Continue** button.

> **Important note**
>
> Firebase generates a unique identifier for your project, such as **weather-app-b11a2**, underneath the name of the project. The identifier will be used in the hosting URL of your project later on.

4. Disable the use of **Google Analytics** for your project and click the **Create project** button.

5. Once the project has been created, the following will appear on the screen:

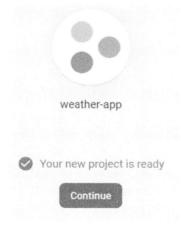

Figure 4.8 – Firebase project creation

6. Click on the **Continue** button, and you will be redirected to the dashboard of your new Firebase project.

We have now completed the configuration of the Firebase hosting. It is now time to integrate it with our Angular application. Run the following command of the Angular CLI to install the `@angular/fire` npm package in your Angular CLI project:

```
ng add @angular/fire
```

The preceding command will also authenticate you with Firebase and prompt you to select a Firebase project for deployment. Use the arrow keys to select the **weather-app** project that we created earlier and press *Enter*. The process will modify the Angular CLI workspace accordingly to accommodate its deployment to Firebase:

- It will add several npm packages to the `dependencies` and `devDependencies` sections of the `package.json` file of the project.

- It will create a `.firebaserc` file at the root folder that contains details of the selected Firebase project.

- It will create a `firebase.json` file at the root folder, which is the Firebase configuration file:

```
{
  "hosting": [
    {
      "target": "weather-app",
      "public": "dist/weather-app",
      "ignore": [
        "**/.*"
      ],
      "headers": [
        {
          "source": "*.[0-9a-f][0-9a-f][0-9a-f]
          [0-9a-f][0-9a-f][0-9a-f][0-9a-f][0-9a-f]
          [0-9a-f][0-9a-f][0-9a-f][0-9a-f][0-9a-f]
          [0-9a-f][0-9a-f][0-9a-f][0-9a-f][0-9a-f]
          [0-9a-f][0-9a-f].+(css|js)",
          "headers": [
            {
              "key": "Cache-Control",
              "value": "public,
```

```
                              max-age=31536000,immutable"
                }
            ]
          }
      ],
      "rewrites": [
          {
              "source": "**",
              "destination": "/index.html"
          }
        ]
      }
    ]
  }
```

The configuration file specifies settings such as the folder that will be deployed to Firebase as stated from the `public` property and any rewrite rules with the `rewrites` property.

> **Important note**
> The folder that will be deployed by default is the `dist` output folder created by the Angular CLI when we run the `ng build` command.

- It will add a `deploy` entry to the `architect` section of the `angular.json` configuration file:

```
"deploy": {
  "builder": "@angular/fire:deploy",
  "options": {}
}
```

To deploy the application, we only need to run a single Angular CLI command, and the Angular CLI will take care of the rest:

```
ng deploy
```

The preceding command will build the application and start deploying it to the selected Firebase project. Once deployment is complete, the Angular CLI will report back the following information:

- **Project Console**: The dashboard of the Firebase project.

- **Hosting URL**: The URL of the deployed version of the application. It consists of the unique identifier of the Firebase project and the .web.app suffix that is added automatically from Firebase.

> **Important note**
>
> The service worker requires an application to be served with HTTPS to work properly as a PWA, except in the **localhost** that is used for development. Firebase hosts web applications with HTTPS by default.

Now that we have deployed our application, let's see how we can install it as a PWA on our device:

1. Navigate to the hosting URL and click on the **plus** button next to the address bar of the browser:

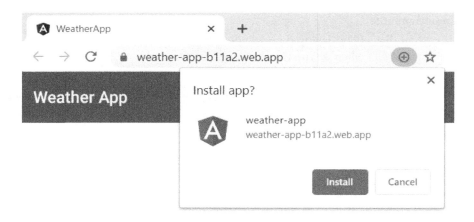

Figure 4.9 – Installing the application (Google Chrome)

> **Important note**
> The **Install** button may be found in different locations in other browsers.

The browser will prompt us to install the **weather-app** application.

2. Click the **Install** button, and the application will open as a native window on our device:

Figure 4.10 – PWA application

It will also install a shortcut for launching the application directly from our device. Congratulations! We now have a full PWA application that displays weather information for a city.

Summary

In this chapter, we built a PWA application that displays weather information for a given city.

Initially, we set up the OpenWeather API to get weather data and created an Angular application from scratch to integrate it. We learned how to use the built-in HTTP client of the Angular framework to communicate with the OpenWeather API. We also installed the Angular Material library and used some of the ready-made UI components for our application.

After creating the Angular application, we introduced the Angular service worker and enabled it to work offline. We learned how to interact with the service worker and provide notifications for updates in our application. Finally, we deployed a production version of our application into the Firebase hosting and installed it locally on our device.

In the next chapter, we will learn how to create an Angular desktop application with Electron, the big rival of PWA applications.

Practice questions

Let's take a look at a few practice questions:

1. What is the purpose of environment files in Angular?

2. How do we pass query parameters in an HTTP request?

3. How do we get results back from an HTTP `get` method?

4. Why do we use a service worker?

5. Which Angular Material component is used for notifications?

6. How are we notified regarding updates from the service worker?

7. What is the primary use of the `pipe` RxJS operator?

8. How can we change the theme color of a PWA application?

9. Which npm package do we use for deploying to Firebase?

10. How can we change the folder that is deployed in Firebase?

Further reading

Add this before the bullet points:

- PWA: `https://web.dev/progressive-web-apps/`

- OpenWeather API: `https://openweathermap.org/api`

- Angular Material: `https://material.angular.io/`

- Angular HTTP client: `https://angular.io/guide/http`

- Angular service worker: `https://angular.io/guide/service-worker-getting-started`

- Communicating with the Angular service worker: `https://angular.io/guide/service-worker-communications`

- HTTP server: `https://www.npmjs.com/package/http-server`

- Firebase hosting: `https://firebase.google.com/docs/hosting`

- Deployment in Angular: `https://angular.io/guide/deployment#automatic-deployment-with-the-cli`

5

Building a WYSIWYG Editor for the Desktop using Electron

Web applications are traditionally built with HTML, CSS, and JavaScript. Their use has also been widely spread to server development using **Node.js**. Various tools and frameworks have emerged in recent years that use HTML, CSS, and JavaScript to create applications for desktop and mobile. In this chapter, we are going to investigate how to create desktop applications using Angular and **Electron**.

Electron is a JavaScript framework that is used to build native desktop applications with web technologies. If we combine it with the Angular framework, we can create fast and highly performant web applications. In this chapter, we will build a desktop **WYSIWYG** editor and cover the following topics:

- Adding a WYSIWYG editor library for Angular
- Integrating Electron in the workspace

- Communicating between Angular and Electron
- Packaging a desktop application

Essential background theory and context

Electron is a cross-platform framework that is used to build desktop applications for Windows, Linux, and Mac. Many popular applications are built with Electron, such as **Visual Studio Code**, **Skype**, and **Slack**. The Electron framework is built on top of Node.js and **Chromium**. Web developers can leverage their existing HTML, CSS, and JavaScript skills to create desktop applications without learning a new language such as C++ or C#.

> Tip
>
> Electron applications have many similarities with PWA applications. Consider building an Electron application for scenarios such as advanced filesystem manipulation or when you need a more native look and feel for your application. Another use case is when you are building a complementary tool for your primary desktop product and you want to ship them together.

An Electron application consists of two processes:

- **Main**: This interacts with the native local resources using the Node.js API.
- **Renderer**: This is responsible for managing the user interface of the application.

An Electron application can have only one main process that can communicate with one or more renderer processes. Each renderer process operates in complete isolation from the others.

The Electron framework provides the `ipcMain` and `ipcRenderer` interfaces, which we can use to interact with these processes. The interaction is accomplished using **Inter-Process Communication (IPC)**, a mechanism that exchanges messages securely and asynchronously over a common channel via a Promise-based API.

Project overview

In this project, we will build a desktop WYSIWYG editor that keeps its content local to the filesystem. Initially, we will build it as an Angular application using **ngx-wig**, a popular WYSIWYG Angular library. We will then convert it to a desktop application using Electron and learn how to sync content between Angular and Electron. We will also see how to persist the content of the editor into the filesystem. Finally, we will package our application as a single executable file that can be run in a desktop environment.

Build time: 1 hour.

Getting started

The following software tools are required to complete this project:

- Angular CLI: A command-line interface for Angular that you can find at `https://angular.io/cli`.

- Visual Studio Code: A code editor that you can download from `https://code.visualstudio.com/Download`.

- GitHub material: The code for this chapter can be found in the `Chapter05` folder at `https://github.com/PacktPublishing/Angular-Projects-Second-Edition`.

Adding a WYSIWYG editor library for Angular

We will kick off our project by creating a WYSIWYG editor as a standalone Angular application first. Use the Angular CLI to create a new Angular application from scratch:

```
ng new my-editor --defaults
```

We pass the following options to the `ng new` command:

- `my-editor`: Defines the name of the application

- `--defaults`: Defines CSS as the preferred stylesheet format of the application and disables routing because our application will consist of a single component that will host the editor

A WYSIWYG editor is a rich text editor, such as Microsoft Word. We could create one from scratch using the Angular framework, but it would be a time-consuming process, and we would only re-invent the wheel. The Angular ecosystem contains a wide variety of libraries to use for this purpose. One of them is the ngx-wig library, which has no external dependencies, just Angular! Let's add the library to our application and learn how to use it:

1. Use the npm client to install ngx-wig from the npm package registry:

    ```
    npm install ngx-wig
    ```

2. Open the app.module.ts file and add NgxWigModule into the imports array of the @NgModule decorator:

    ```
    import { NgModule } from '@angular/core';
    import { BrowserModule } from '@angular/platform-browser';
    import { NgxWigModule } from 'ngx-wig';

    import { AppComponent } from './app.component';

    @NgModule({
      declarations: [
        AppComponent
      ],
      imports: [
        BrowserModule,
        NgxWigModule
      ],
      providers: [],
      bootstrap: [AppComponent]
    })
    export class AppModule { }
    ```

    NgxWigModule is the main module of the ngx-wig library.

3. Create a new Angular component that will host our WYSIWYG editor:

    ```
    ng generate component editor
    ```

4. Open the template file of the newly generated component, `editor.component.html`, and replace its content with the following HTML snippet:

```
<ngx-wig placeholder="Enter your content"></ngx-wig>
```

`NgxWigModule` exposes a set of Angular services and components that we can use in our application. The main component of the module is the `ngx-wig` component, which displays the actual WYSIWYG editor. It exposes a collection of input properties that we can set, such as the placeholder of the editor. You can find more options at `https://github.com/stevermeister/ngx-wig`.

5. Open the `app.component.html` file and replace its content with the `app-editor` selector:

```
<app-editor></app-editor>
```

6. Open the `styles.css` file, which contains global styles for the Angular application, and add the following styles to make the editor dockable and take up the full page:

```
html, body {
    margin: 0;
    width: 100%;
    height: 100%;
}

.ng-wig, .nw-editor-container, .nw-editor {
    display: flex !important;
    flex-direction: column;
    height: 100% !important;
    overflow: hidden;
}
```

7. Open the main HTML file of the Angular application, `index.html`, and remove the `base` tag from the `head` element. The `base` tag is used from the browser to reference scripts and CSS files with a relative URL. Leaving the `base` tag will make our desktop application fail because it will load all necessary assets directly from the local filesystem. We will learn more in the *Integrating Angular with Electron* section.

Let's see what we have achieved so far. Run `ng serve` and navigate to `http://localhost:4200` to preview the application:

Figure 5.1 – Application output

Our application consists of the following:

- A toolbar with buttons that allows us to apply different styles to the content of the editor

- A text area that is used as the main container for adding content to the editor

We now have created a web application using Angular that features a fully operational WYSIWYG editor. In the following section, we will learn how to convert it into a desktop one using Electron.

Integrating Electron in the workspace

The Electron framework is an npm package that we can install using the following command:

```
npm install -D electron
```

The previous command will install the latest version of the `electron` npm package into the Angular CLI workspace. It will also add a respective entry into the `devDependencies` section of the `package.json` file of our project.

> **Important Note**
>
> Electron is added to the `devDependencies` section of the `package.json` file because it is a development dependency of our application. It is used only to prepare and build our application as a desktop one and not during runtime.

Electron applications run on the Node.js runtime and use the Chromium browser for rendering purposes. A Node.js application has at least a JavaScript file, usually called `index.js` or `main.js`, which is the main entry point of the application. Since we are using Angular and TypeScript as our development stack, we will start by creating a respective TypeScript file that will be finally compiled to JavaScript:

1. Create a folder named `electron` inside the `src` folder of the Angular CLI workspace. The `electron` folder will contain any source code that is related to Electron.

> **Tip**
>
> We can think of our application as two different platforms. The web platform is the Angular application, which resides in the `src\app` folder. The desktop platform is the Electron application, which resides in the `src\electron` folder. This approach has many benefits, including that it enforces the separation of concerns in our application and allows each one to develop independently from the other. From now on, we will refer to them as the Angular application and the Electron application.

2. Create a `main.ts` file inside the `electron` folder with the following content:

```typescript
import { app, BrowserWindow } from 'electron';

function createWindow () {
  const mainWindow = new BrowserWindow({
    width: 800,
    height: 600
  });

  mainWindow.loadFile('index.html');
}

app.whenReady().then(() => {
  createWindow();
});
```

We first import the `BrowserWindow` and `app` artifacts from the `electron` npm package. The `BrowserWindow` class is used to create a desktop window for our application. We define the window dimensions, passing an options object in its constructor that sets the `width` and `height` values of the window. We then call the `loadFile` method, passing as a parameter the HTML file that we want to load inside the window.

> **Important Note**
>
> The `index.html` file that we pass in the `loadFile` method is the main HTML file of the Angular application. It will be loaded using the `file://` protocol, which is why we removed the `base` tag in the *Adding a WYSIWYG Angular library* section.

The `app` object is the global object of our desktop application, just like the `window` object on a web page. It exposes a `whenReady` promise that, when resolved, means we can run any initialization logic for our application, including the creation of the window.

3. Create a `tsconfig.json` file inside the `electron` folder and add the following contents:

```
{
    "extends": "../../tsconfig.json",
    "compilerOptions": {
      "importHelpers": false
    },
    "include": [
      "**/*.ts"
    ]
}
```

The `main.ts` file needs to be compiled to JavaScript because browsers currently do not understand TypeScript. The compilation process is called **transpilation** and requires a TypeScript configuration file. The configuration file contains options that drive the TypeScript **transpiler**, which is responsible for the transpilation process.

The preceding TypeScript configuration file defines the path of the Electron source code files using the `include` property and sets the `importHelpers` property to `false`.

> **Important Note**
> If we enable the `importHelpers` flag, it will include helpers from the **tslib** library into our application, resulting in a larger bundle size.

4. Run the following command to install the **webpack CLI**:

```
npm install -D webpack-cli
```

The webpack CLI is used to invoke **webpack**, a popular module bundler, from the command line. We will use webpack to build and bundle our Electron application.

5. Install the `ts-loader` npm package using the following npm command:

```
npm install -D ts-loader
```

The `ts-loader` library is a webpack plugin that can load TypeScript files.

We have now created all the individual pieces needed to convert our Angular application into a desktop one using Electron. We only need to put them together so that we can build and run our desktop application. The main piece that orchestrates the Electron application is the webpack configuration file that we need to create in the root folder of our Angular CLI workspace:

webpack.config.js

```js
const path = require('path');
const src = path.join(process.cwd(), 'src', 'electron');

module.exports = {
  mode: 'development',
  devtool: 'source-map',
  entry: path.join(src, 'main.ts'),
  output: {
    path: path.join(process.cwd(), 'dist', 'my-editor'),
    filename: 'shell.js'
  },
  module: {
    rules: [
      {
        test: /\.ts$/,
        loader: 'ts-loader',
```

```
      options: {
        configFile: path.join(src, 'tsconfig.json')
      }
    }
  ]
},
target: 'electron-main'
};
```

The preceding file configures webpack in our application using the following options:

- `mode`: Indicates that we are currently running in a development environment.

- `devtool`: Enables source map file generation for debugging purposes.

- `entry`: Indicates the main entry point of the Electron application, which is the `main.ts` file.

- `output`: Defines the path and the filename of the Electron bundle that will be generated from webpack. The `path` property points to the same folder that is used from the Angular CLI to generate the bundle of the Angular application. The `filename` property is set to `shell.js` because the default one generated from webpack is `main.js`, and it will cause a conflict with the `main.js` file generated from the Angular application.

- `module`: Instructs webpack to load the `ts-loader` plugin for handling TypeScript files.

- `target`: Indicates that we are currently running in the main process of Electron.

webpack now contains all information needed to build and bundle the Electron application. On the other hand, the Angular CLI takes care of building the Angular application. Let's see how we can combine them and run our desktop application:

1. Run the following npm command to install the `concurrently` npm package:

```
npm install -D concurrently
```

The `concurrently` library enables us to execute multiple processes concurrently. In our case, it will enable us to run the Angular and Electron applications in parallel.

2. Open the `package.json` file and add a new entry in the `scripts` property:

```
"scripts": {
  "ng": "ng",
  "start": "ng serve",
  "build": "ng build",
  "watch": "ng build --watch --configuration
    development",
  "test": "ng test",
  "start:desktop": "concurrently \"ng build --delete-
    output-path=false --watch\" \"webpack --watch\""
}
```

The `start:desktop` script builds the Angular application using the `ng build` command of the Angular CLI and the Electron application using the `webpack` command. Both applications run in watch mode using the `--watch` option, so that every time we make a change in the code, the application will rebuild to reflect the change. Whenever we modify the Angular application, the Angular CLI will delete the `dist` folder by default. We can prevent this behavior using the `--delete-output-path=false` option because the Electron application is also built in the same folder.

> **Important Note**
> We did not pass the webpack configuration file to the `webpack` command because it assumes the `webpack.config.js` filename by default.

3. Click on the **Run** menu that exists in the sidebar of Visual Studio Code:

Figure 5.2 – Run menu

4. In the **RUN** pane that appears, click on the **create a launch.json file** link:

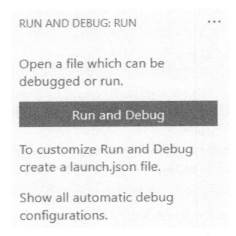

Figure 5.3 – RUN pane

5. Visual Studio Code will open a drop-down menu that allows us to select the environment to run our application. An Electron application uses Node.js, so select any of the available Node.js options.

6. Visual Studio Code will create a .vscode folder in our Angular CLI workspace with a launch.json file inside it. In the launch.json file that has been opened, set the value of the program property to ${workspaceRoot}/dist/ my-editor/shell.js. The program property indicates the absolute path of the Electron bundle file.

7. Add the following entry below the program property in the launch.json file:

```
"runtimeExecutable": "${workspaceRoot}/node_modules/.bin/
electron"
```

The runtimeExecutable property defines the absolute path of the Electron executable.

We are now ready to run our desktop application and preview it. Run the following npm command to build the application:

```
npm run start:desktop
```

The previous command will build first the Electron application and then the Angular one. Wait for the Angular build to finish and then press *F5* to preview the application:

Figure 5.4 – Application window

In the preceding screenshot, we can see that our Angular application with the WYSIWYG editor is hosted inside a native desktop window. It contains the following characteristics that we usually find in desktop applications:

- The header with an icon
- The main menu
- Minimize, maximize, and close buttons

The Angular application is rendered inside the Chromium browser. To verify that, click on the **View** menu item and select the **Toggle Developer Tools** option.

Well done! You have successfully managed to create your own desktop WYSIWYG editor. In the following section, we will learn how to interact between Angular and Electron.

Communicating between Angular and Electron

According to the specifications of the project, the content of the WYSIWYG editor needs to be persisted in the local filesystem. Additionally, the content will be loaded from the filesystem upon application startup.

The Angular application handles any interaction between the WYSIWYG editor and its data using the renderer process, whereas the Electron application manages the filesystem with the main process. Thus, we need to establish an IPC mechanism to communicate between the two Electron processes as follows:

- Configuring the Angular CLI workspace
- Interacting with the editor
- Interacting with the filesystem

Let's start with the first one, to set up the Angular CLI project for supporting the desired communication mechanism.

Configuring the Angular CLI workspace

We need to modify several files to configure the workspace of our application:

1. Open the `main.ts` file that exists in the `src\electron` folder and set the `nodeIntegration` property to `true` in the `BrowserWindow` constructor:

```
function createWindow () {
  const mainWindow = new BrowserWindow({
    width: 800,
    height: 600,
    webPreferences: {
      nodeIntegration: true,
      contextIsolation: false
    }
  });

  mainWindow.loadFile('index.html');
}
```

    The preceding flag will enable Node.js in the renderer process and expose the `ipcRenderer` interface, which we will need for communicating with the main process.

2. Open the `tsconfig.app.json` file that exists in the root folder of the Angular CLI workspace and add the `electron` entry inside the `types` property:

```
{
  "extends": "./tsconfig.json",
  "compilerOptions": {
    "outDir": "./out-tsc/app",
    "types": [
      "electron"
    ]
  },
  "files": [
    "src/main.ts",
    "src/polyfills.ts"
  ],
```

```
"include": [
    "src/**/*.d.ts"
  ]
}
```

The Electron framework includes types that we can use in our Angular application.

3. Create a new file named `window.ts` inside the `src\app` folder and enter the following code:

```
import { InjectionToken } from '@angular/core';

export const WINDOW = new
  InjectionToken<Window>('Global window object', {
  factory: () => window
});

export interface ElectronWindow extends Window {
  require(module: string): any;
}
```

The Electron framework is a JavaScript module that can be loaded from the global `window` object of the browser. We use the `InjectionToken` interface to make the `window` object injectable so that we can use it in our Angular components and services. Additionally, we use a `factory` method to return it so that it is easy to replace it in platforms with no access to the `window` object, such as the server.

Electron is loaded using the `require` method of the `window` object, which is available only in the Node.js environment. To use it in an Angular application, we create the `ElectronWindow` interface that extends the `Window` interface by defining that method.

The Angular and Electron applications are now ready to interact with each other using the IPC mechanism. Let's start implementing the necessary logic in the Angular application first.

Interacting with the editor

The Angular application is responsible for managing the WYSIWYG editor. The content of the editor is kept in sync with the filesystem using the renderer process of Electron. Let's find out how to use the renderer process:

1. Create a new Angular service using the `generate` command of the Angular CLI:

```
ng generate service editor
```

2. Open the `editor.service.ts` file and inject the `WINDOW` token in the constructor of the `EditorService` class:

```
import { Inject } from '@angular/core';
import { Injectable } from '@angular/core';
import { ElectronWindow, WINDOW } from './window';

@Injectable({
  providedIn: 'root'
})
export class EditorService {

  constructor(@Inject(WINDOW) private window:
    ElectronWindow) {}

}
```

3. Create a getter property that returns the `ipcRenderer` object from the `electron` module:

```
private get ipcRenderer(): Electron.IpcRenderer {
  return this.window.require('electron').ipcRenderer;
}
```

The `electron` module is the main module of the Electron framework that gives access to various properties, including the main and the renderer process. We also set the type of the `ipcRenderer` property to `Electron.IpcRenderer`, which is part of the built-in types of Electron.

4. Create a method that will be called to get the content of the editor from the filesystem:

```
getContent(): Promise<string> {
  return this.ipcRenderer.invoke('getContent');
}
```

We use the `invoke` method of the `ipcRenderer` property, passing the name of the communication channel as a parameter. The result of the `getContent` method is a `Promise` object of the `string` type since the content of the editor is raw text data. The `invoke` method initiates a connection with the main process through the `getContent` channel. In the *Interacting with the filesystem* section, we will see how to set up the main process for responding to the `invoke` method call in that channel.

5. Create a method that will be called to save the content of the editor to the filesystem:

```
setContent(content: string) {
  this.ipcRenderer.invoke('setContent', content);
}
```

The `setContent` method calls the `invoke` method of the `ipcRenderer` object again but with a different channel name. It also uses the second parameter of the `invoke` method to pass data to the main process. In this case, the `content` parameter will contain the content of the editor. We will see how to configure the main process for handling data in the *Interacting with the filesystem* section.

6. Open the `editor.component.ts` file and create a `myContent` property to hold editor data. Also, inject `EditorService` in the constructor of the `EditorComponent` class:

```
import { Component, OnInit } from '@angular/core';
import { EditorService } from '../editor.service';

@Component({
  selector: 'app-editor',
  templateUrl: './editor.component.html',
  styleUrls: ['./editor.component.css']
})
export class EditorComponent implements OnInit {
```

```
    myContent = '';

    constructor(private editorService: EditorService) {}

    ngOnInit(): void {
    }

}
```

7. Create a method that calls the getContent method of the editorService variable and execute it inside the ngOnInit method:

```
ngOnInit(): void {
    this.getContent();
}

private async getContent() {
    this.myContent = await
        this.editorService.getContent();
}
```

We use the async/await syntax, which allows the synchronous execution of our code in promise-based method calls.

8. Create a method that calls the setContent method of the editorService variable:

```
saveContent(content: string) {
    this.editorService.setContent(content);
}
```

9. Let's wire up those methods that we have created with the template of the component. Open the editor.component.html file and add the following bindings:

```
<ngx-wig placeholder="Enter your content"
 [ngModel]="myContent"
    (contentChange)="saveContent($event)"></ngx-wig>
```

We use the ngModel directive to bind the model of the editor to the myContent component property, which will be used to display the content initially. We also use the contentChange event binding to save the content of the editor whenever it changes, that is, while the user types.

10. The ngModel directive is part of the @angular/forms npm package. Import FormsModule in the app.module.ts file to use it:

```
import { NgModule } from '@angular/core';
import { BrowserModule } from '@angular/platform-
browser';
import { NgxWigModule } from 'ngx-wig';

import { AppComponent } from './app.component';
import { EditorComponent } from './editor/editor.
component';
import { FormsModule } from '@angular/forms';

@NgModule({
  declarations: [
    AppComponent,
    EditorComponent
  ],
  imports: [
    BrowserModule,
    FormsModule,
    NgxWigModule
  ],
  providers: [],
  bootstrap: [AppComponent]
})
export class AppModule { }
```

We have now implemented all the logic for our Angular application to communicate with the main process. It is now time to implement the other end of the communication mechanism, the Electron application, and its main process.

Interacting with the filesystem

The main process interacts with the filesystem using the `fs` Node.js library, which is built into the Electron framework. Let's see how we can use it:

1. Open the `main.ts` file that exists in the `src\electron` folder and import the following artifacts:

```
import { app, BrowserWindow, ipcMain } from 'electron';
import * as fs from 'fs';
import * as path from 'path';
```

The `fs` library is responsible for interacting with the filesystem. The `path` library provides utilities for working with file and folder paths. The `ipcMain` object allows us to work with the main process of Electron.

2. Create a variable that holds the path of the file containing the content of the editor:

```
const contentFile = path.join(app.getPath('userData'),
'content.html');
```

The file that keeps the content of the editor is the `content.html` file that exists inside the reserved `userData` folder. The `userData` folder is an alias for a special purpose system folder, different for each OS, and it is used to store application-specific files such as configuration. You can find more details about the `userData` folder as well as other system folders at `https://www.electronjs.org/docs/api/app#appgetpathname`.

> **Important Note**
>
> The `getPath` method of the `app` object works cross-platform and is used to get the path of special folders such as the home directory of a user or the application data.

3. Call the `handle` method of the `ipcMain` object to start listening for requests in the `getContent` channel:

```
ipcMain.handle('getContent', () => {
  if (fs.existsSync(contentFile)) {
    const result = fs.readFileSync(contentFile);
    return result.toString();
  }
  return '';
});
```

When the main process receives a request in this channel, it uses the `existsSync` method of the `fs` library to check whether the file with the content of the editor exists already. If it exists, it reads it using the `readFileSync` method and returns its content to the renderer process.

4. Call the `handle` method again, but this time for the `setContent` channel:

```
ipcMain.handle('setContent', ({}, content: string) => {
    fs.writeFileSync(contentFile, content);
});
```

In the preceding snippet, we use the `writeFileSync` method of the `fs` library to write the value of the `content` property in the file.

5. Open the `package.json` file and change the version of the `@types/node` npm package:

```
"@types/node": "^15.6.0"
```

Now that we have connected the Angular and the Electron application, it is time to preview our WYSIWYG desktop application:

1. Execute the `start:desktop` npm script and press *F5* to run the application.

2. Use the editor and its toolbar to enter some content such as the following:

Figure 5.5 – Editor content

3. Close the application window and re-run the application. If everything worked correctly, you should see the content that you had entered inside the editor.

Congratulations! You have enriched your WYSIWYG editor by adding persistence capabilities to it. In the following section, we will take the last step toward creating our desktop application, and we will learn how to package it and distribute it.

Packaging a desktop application

Web applications are usually bundled and deployed to a web server that hosts them. On the other hand, desktop applications are bundled and packaged as a single executable file that can be easily distributed. Packaging our WYSIWYG application requires the following steps:

- Configuring webpack for production mode

- Using an Electron bundler

We will look at both of them in more detail in the following sections.

Configuring webpack for production

We have already created a webpack configuration file for the development environment. We now need to create a new one for production. Both configuration files will share some functionality, so let's start by creating a common one:

1. Create a `webpack.dev.config.js` file in the root folder of the Angular CLI workspace with the following content:

    ```
    const path = require('path');
    const baseConfig = require('./webpack.config');

    module.exports = {
      ...baseConfig,
      mode: 'development',
      devtool: 'source-map',
      output: {
        path: path.join(process.cwd(), 'dist', 'my-
          editor'),
        filename: 'shell.js'
      }
    };
    ```

2. Remove the `mode`, `devtool`, and `output` properties from the `webpack.config.js` file.

3. Open the `package.json` file and pass the new webpack development configuration file at the `start:desktop` script:

```
"start:desktop": "concurrently \"ng build --delete-
output-path=false --watch\" \"webpack --config webpack.
dev.config.js --watch\""
```

4. Create a `webpack.prod.config.js` file in the root folder of the Angular CLI workspace with the following content:

```
const path = require('path');
const baseConfig = require('./webpack.config');

module.exports = {
  ...baseConfig,
  output: {
    path: path.join(process.cwd(), 'dist', 'my-
      editor'),
    filename: 'main.js'
  }
};
```

The main difference with the webpack configuration file for the development environment is that we changed the filename of the output bundle to `main.js`. The Angular CLI adds a hashed number in the `main.js` file of the Angular application in production, so there will be no conflicts. Other things to notice are that `mode` is set to `production` by default when we omit it, and the `devtool` property is missing because we do not want to enable source maps in production mode.

5. Add a new entry in the `scripts` property of the `package.json` file for building our application in production mode:

```
"scripts": {
  "ng": "ng",
  "start": "ng serve",
  "build": "ng build",
  "watch": "ng build --watch --configuration
development",
  "test": "ng test",
  "start:desktop": "concurrently \"ng build --delete-
```

```
      output-path=false --watch\" \"webpack --config
        webpack.dev.config.js --watch\"",
    "build:electron": "ng build && webpack --config
      webpack.prod.config.js"
}
```

The `build:electron` script builds the Angular and Electron application in production mode simultaneously.

We have completed all the configurations needed for packaging our desktop application. In the following section, we will learn how to convert it into a single bundle specific to each operating system.

Using an Electron bundler

The Electron framework has a wide variety of tools that are created and maintained by the open source community.

You can see a list of available projects in the **Tools** section at the following link:

`https://www.electronjs.org/community`

One of these tools is the **electron-packager** library, which we can use to package our desktop application as a single executable file for each OS (Windows, Linux, and macOS). Let's see how we can integrate it into our development workflow:

1. Run the following npm command to install `electron-packager` as a development dependency to our project:

    ```
    npm install -D electron-packager
    ```

2. Add a new entry in the `scripts` property of the `package.json` file for packaging our application:

    ```
    "scripts": {
        "ng": "ng",
        "start": "ng serve",
        "build": "ng build",
        "watch": "ng build --watch --configuration
          development",
        "test": "ng test",
        "start:desktop": "concurrently \"ng build --
    ```

```
        delete-output-path=false --watch\" \"webpack --
            config webpack.dev.config.js --watch\"",
    "build:electron": "ng build && webpack --config
        webpack.prod.config.js",
    "package": "electron-packager dist/my-editor --
        out=dist --asar"
    }
```

In the preceding script, `electron-packager` will read all files in the `dist/my-editor` folder, package them, and output the final bundle in the `dist` folder. The `--asar` option instructs the packager to archive all files in the **ASAR** format, similar to a **ZIP** or **TAR** file.

3. Create a `package.json` file in the `src\electron` folder and add the following content:

```
{
    "name": "my-editor",
    "main": "main.js"
}
```

The `electron-packager` library requires a `package.json` file to be present in the output folder and points to the main entry file of the Electron application.

4. Open the `webpack.prod.config.js` file and add the `CopyWebpackPlugin` in the `plugins` property:

```
const path = require('path');
const baseConfig = require('./webpack.config');
const CopyWebpackPlugin = require('copy-webpack-
    plugin');

module.exports = {
    ...baseConfig,
    output: {
        path: path.join(process.cwd(), 'dist', 'my-
            editor'),
        filename: 'main.js'
    },
```

```
plugins: [
  new CopyWebpackPlugin({
    patterns: [
      {
        context: path.join(process.cwd(), 'src',
          'electron'),
        from: 'package.json'
      }
    ]
  })
]
};
```

We use the `CopyWebpackPlugin` to copy the `package.json` file from the `src\electron` folder into the `dist\my-editor` folder while building the application in production mode.

5. Run the following command to build the application in production mode:

```
npm run build:electron
```

6. Now run the following npm command to package it:

```
npm run package
```

The preceding command will package the application for the OS that you are currently running on, which is the default behavior of the `electron-packager` library. You can alter this behavior by passing additional options, which you will find in the GitHub repository of the library listed in the *Further reading* section.

7. Navigate to the `dist` folder of the Angular CLI workspace. You will find a folder called `my-editor-{OS}`, where `{OS}` is your current OS and its architecture. For example, in Windows, it will be `my-editor-win32-x64`. Open the folder, and you will get the following files:

Figure 5.6 – Application package (Windows)

In the preceding screenshot, the `my-editor.exe` file is the executable file of our desktop application. Our application code is not included in this file but rather in the `app.asar` file, which exists in the `resources` folder.

Run the executable file, and the desktop application should open normally. You can take the whole folder and upload it to a server or distribute it by any other means. Your WYSIWYG editor can now reach many more users, such as those that are offline most of the time. Awesome!

Summary

In this chapter, we built a WYSIWYG editor for the desktop using Angular and Electron. Initially, we created an Angular application and added `ngx-wig`, a popular Angular WYSIWYG library. Then, we learned how to build an Electron application and implemented a communication mechanism for exchanging data between the Angular application and the Electron application. Finally, we learned how to bundle our application for packaging and getting it ready for distribution.

In the next chapter, we will learn how to build a mobile photo geotagging application with Angular and Ionic.

Practice questions

Let's take a look at a few practice questions:

1. Which class is responsible for creating a desktop window in Electron?

2. How do we communicate between the main and renderer processes in Electron?

3. Which flag enables the use of Node.js in the renderer process?

4. How do we convert a global JavaScript object into an Angular injectable one?

5. How do we load Electron in an Angular application?

6. Which interface do we use for interacting with Electron in an Angular application?

7. How do we pass data to the main Electron process from an Angular application?

8. Which package do we use for filesystem manipulation in Electron?

9. Which library do we use for packaging an Electron application?

Further reading

Here are some links to build upon what we learned in the chapter:

*   Electron: `https://www.electronjs.org/`

*   Electron quick start: `https://www.electronjs.org/docs/tutorial/quick-start`

*   ngx-wig: `https://github.com/stevermeister/ngx-wig`

*   webpack configuration: `https://webpack.js.org/configuration/`

*   ts-loader: `https://webpack.js.org/guides/typescript/`

*   Injecting an object in Angular: `https://angular.io/guide/dependency-injection-providers#injecting-an-object`

*   Filesystem Node.js API: `https://nodejs.org/api/fs.html`

*   electron-packager: `https://github.com/electron/electron-packager`

*   concurrently: `https://github.com/kimmobrunfeldt/concurrently`

6

Building a Mobile Photo Geotagging Application Using Capacitor and 3D Maps

Angular is a cross-platform JavaScript framework that can be used to build applications for different platforms such as web, desktop, and mobile. Moreover, it allows developers to use the same code base and apply the same web techniques to each platform, enjoying the same experience and performance. In this chapter, we will investigate how we can build mobile applications using Angular.

Ionic is a popular UI toolkit that allows us to build mobile applications using web technologies such as Angular. The **Capacitor** library greatly enhances Ionic applications by enabling them to run natively on Android and iOS devices. In this chapter, we will use both technologies to build a mobile application that can take geotagged photos and display them on a 3D map.

We will cover the following topics in detail:

- Creating a mobile application with **Ionic**
- Taking photos with **Capacitor**
- Storing data in **Firebase**
- Previewing photos with **CesiumJS**

Essential background theory and context

Capacitor is a native mobile runtime that enables us to build native **Android** and **iOS** applications with web technologies, including Angular. It provides an abstraction API layer for web applications to interact with the native resources of a mobile OS. It does not include a UI layer or any other way of interacting with the user interface.

Ionic is a mobile framework that contains a collection of UI components that we can use in an application built with Capacitor. The main advantage of Ionic is that we maintain a single code base across all native mobile platforms. That is, we write the code once, and it works everywhere. Ionic supports all popular JavaScript frameworks, including Angular.

> **Important note**
> When we create a new Ionic application from scratch, we also get Capacitor installed and configured out of the box.

Firebase is a **Backend-as-a-Service (BaaS)** platform provided by Google that contains a set of tools and services for building applications. **Cloud Firestore** is a database solution provided by Firebase that features a flexible and scalable NoSQL document-oriented database that can be used in web and mobile applications. **Storage** is a Firebase service that allows us to interact with a storage mechanism and upload or download files.

CesiumJS is a JavaScript library for creating interactive 3D maps in the browser. It is an open source, cross-platform library that uses **WebGL** and allows us to share geospatial data on multiple platforms. It is empowered by **Cesium**, a platform for building high-quality and performant 3D geospatial applications.

Project overview

In this project, we will build a mobile application that can take photos according to the current location and preview them on a map. Initially, we will learn how to create a mobile application using Angular and Ionic. We will then use Capacitor to take photos using the camera of the mobile device and tag them with the current location via the GPS. We will upload those photos in Firebase along with their location data. Finally, we will use CesiumJS to load location data on a 3D globe along with a preview of the photo.

> **Important note**
>
> In this chapter, you will learn how to build a mobile application with Angular and Ionic. To follow up with the project and preview your application, you will need to follow the getting started guide for your development environment (Android or iOS), which you can find in the *Further reading* section.

Build time: 2 hours

Getting started

You will need the following software and tools to complete the project:

- For Android: **Android Studio** with a minimum of Android SDK 21 or higher and **Android WebView** with Chrome 50 or later.
- For iOS: **Xcode** 11 or above and **Xcode Command Line Tools.**
- A physical mobile device.
- GitHub material: The related code for this chapter can be found in the Chapter06 folder at https://github.com/PacktPublishing/Angular-Projects-Second-Edition.

Creating a mobile application with Ionic

The first step toward building our application is creating a new mobile application using the Ionic toolkit. We will start building our application with the following tasks:

- Scaffolding the application
- Building the main menu

Ionic has a pretty straightforward process for creating a new mobile application from scratch, which can be done from the Ionic website without entering a single line of code.

Scaffolding the application

To create a new Ionic application, we need to head over to `https://www.ionicframework.com` and complete the following steps:

1. Click on the **Get Started** button that is displayed on the header of the landing page:

Figure 6.1 – Start an Ionic application

You will be redirected to the **Create your Ionic App** page to fill in all the necessary details to create your Ionic application.

2. Enter the name of your application in the **App name** field:

Welcome to Ionic

Let's start your first app

Figure 6.2 – Enter the application name

3. Use the **Pick an icon** field to define the icon of your application. Hover with your mouse over the default icon, and either pick one from the emoji gallery or upload one of your choice.

4. Select the brand color of your application in the **Pick a theme color** field. The brand color is used in various places of an application, such as the background, toolbars, and text. You can select either a predefined color or create a custom one using an RGB combination.

5. Choose the layout of your application using the **Pick a layout template** field. You can select among three different templates. In this project, we will use the **MENU** template:

Pick a layout template (i)

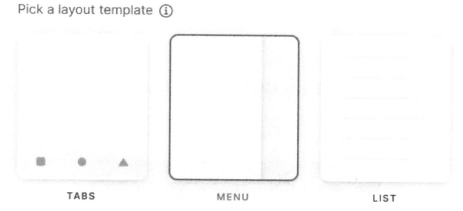

Figure 6.3 – Layout template selection

6. Finally, select the JavaScript framework that you want to work with in your mobile application. Currently, Ionic supports the three most popular ones: React, Angular, and Vue. Select **Angular** and click the **Continue** button:

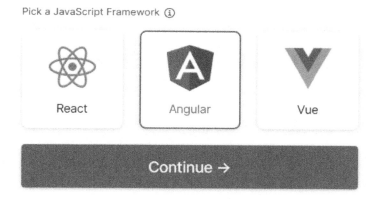

Figure 6.4 – JavaScript framework selection

7. You will be redirected to the signup page, where you will need to create an Ionic account. You can either create a new one from scratch or select to use one of the free Git services:

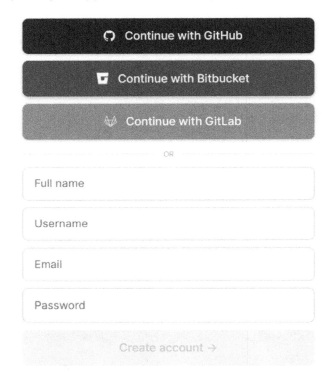

Figure 6.5 – Create an Ionic account

> **Tip**
> Ionic will create a repository for your application automatically and connect it with your Ionic dashboard if you select the latter.

For this project, it is recommended to select one of the free Git services available. When you choose to do so, you will be asked to be authorized with the selected Git service.

8. Click the **Connect** button on the Git host of your choice to connect your new Ionic account with the Git service:

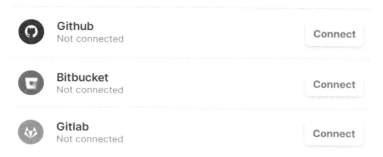

Choose a git host

We will automatically create a repo for your app
and connect it to your Ionic dashboard.

Github Not connected		Connect
Bitbucket Not connected		Connect
Gitlab Not connected		Connect

Figure 6.6 – Connect to a Git host

9. Click the **Choose** button to select your Git account, and Ionic will start building your application:

Compiling your app

Hang tight for just a moment.

Provisioning resources...

Figure 6.7 – Building the Ionic application

After the build has finished, you will be redirected to the Ionic dashboard of your application. From there, you can accomplish specific tasks for your application, such as setting up a **Continuous Integration/Development (CI/CD)** pipeline, building, and previewing your application.

Ionic has created a sample application for us with some ready-made data. To modify it according to our needs, we need to get a copy of the application locally. Let's see how we can accomplish that in the following section.

Building the main menu

Ionic provides a command-line tool called the **Ionic CLI** that is used to build and run an Ionic mobile application. Let's see how we can install it and start building the main menu of our application:

1. Install the Ionic CLI using the following npm command:

```
npm install -g @ionic/cli cordova-res
```

The cordova-res library is used to generate the icons and splash screens of our application for native mobile devices.

2. Ionic has already created a Git repository for our Ionic application in our Git host. Clone the repository locally into your system and run the following command to install all the dependencies of the application:

```
npm install
```

3. Open the main HTML file of the application, index.html, and add the name of your application in the title tag:

```
<title>Phototag App</title>
```

4. Open the template file of the main component, app.component.html, and remove the second ion-list element. An ion-list element displays a collection of items in a list view.

5. Add the name of your application in the ion-list-header element and change the text of the ion-note element:

```
<ion-list-header>Phototag</ion-list-header>
<ion-note>Capture geotagged photos</ion-note>
```

An `ion-list-header` element is the header of a list. An `ion-note` element is a text element that is used to provide additional information, such as the subtitle of a list.

6. Open the TypeScript file of the main component, `app.component.ts`, and modify it as follows:

```typescript
import { Component } from '@angular/core';
@Component({
  selector: 'app-root',
  templateUrl: 'app.component.html',
  styleUrls: ['app.component.scss'],
})
export class AppComponent {
  public appPages = [
    {
      title: 'Take a photo',
      url: '/capture',
      icon: 'camera'
    },
    {
      title: 'View gallery',
      url: '/view',
      icon: 'globe'
    }
  ];
}
```

The `appPages` property contains all the pages of our application. Each page has a `title`, the URL from which it is accessible, and an `icon`. Our application will consist of two pages, one that will be used for taking photos using the camera and another for displaying them on a map.

7. Run the `serve` command of the Ionic CLI to start the application:

```
ionic serve
```

The preceding command will build your application and open your default browser at `http://localhost:8100`.

Click on the **Menu** button, and you should see the following output:

Figure 6.8 – Main menu

> **Tip**
> Try to adjust your browser window size to achieve a more realistic view for
> a mobile device, or use the **Device toolbar** in the **Google Chrome** developer
> tools. You can find more details about the Device toolbar at `https://`
> `developers.google.com/web/tools/chrome-devtools/`
> `device-mode#viewport`.

We have learned how to create a new Ionic application using the getting started page of
the Ionic website. We also saw how to get the application locally on our machine and
make modifications according to our needs.

If we now try to click on a menu item, we will notice that nothing happens since we have
not created the necessary pages that will be activated in each case. In the following section,
we will learn how to complete this task by building the functionality of the first page.

Taking photos with Capacitor

The first page of our application will allow the user to take photos using the camera.
We will use the Capacitor runtime to get access to the native resource of the camera. To
implement the page, we need to take the following actions:

- Create the user interface.
- Interact with Capacitor.

Let's start building the user interface of the page.

Creating the user interface

Each page in our application is a different Angular module. To create an Angular module in Ionic, we can use the `generate` command of the Ionic CLI:

```
ionic generate page capture
```

The previous command will perform the following actions:

- Create an Angular module named `capture`.
- Create a related routing module.
- Create the main component of the module.
- Register the new module in the `app-routing.module.ts` file.

Let's start building the logic of our new page now:

1. First, let's make our page the default one when the user opens the application. Open the `app-routing.module.ts` file and change the first entry of the `routes` property:

    ```
    {
        path: '',
        redirectTo: 'capture',
        pathMatch: 'full'
    }
    ```

    The empty path is called the **default** routing path, and it is activated when our application starts up. The `redirectTo` property tells Angular to redirect to the `capture` path, which will load the page we created.

    > **Tip**
    > You can also remove the `folder/:id` path as it is no longer needed, and the whole `folder` module from the application, which is part of the template layout.

2. Open the `capture.page.html` file and replace the contents of the `ion-toolbar` element as follows:

    ```
    <ion-header>
      <ion-toolbar>
        <ion-buttons slot="start">
    ```

```
    <ion-menu-button color="primary">
      </ion-menu-button>
    </ion-buttons>
    <ion-title>Take a photo</ion-title>
  </ion-toolbar>
</ion-header>
```

The `ion-toolbar` element is part of the `ion-header` element, which is the top navigation bar of the page. It contains an `ion-menu-button` element for toggling the main menu of the application and an `ion-title` element that depicts the title of the page.

3. Add a second `ion-header` element inside the `ion-content` element with the following HTML code:

```
<ion-content>
  <ion-header collapse="condense">
    <ion-toolbar>
      <ion-title size="large">Take a photo</ion-title>
    </ion-toolbar>
  </ion-header>
</ion-content>
```

The header will be displayed when the page is expanded and the main menu is displayed on the screen. The `size` attribute of the `ion-title` element is set to `large` for supporting collapsible large tiles on iOS devices.

4. Add the following HTML code immediately after the second header:

```
<div id="container">
  <strong class="capitalize">Take a nice photo with
    your camera</strong>
  <ion-fab vertical="center" horizontal="center"
    slot="fixed">
    <ion-fab-button>
      <ion-icon name="camera"></ion-icon>
    </ion-fab-button>
  </ion-fab>
</div>
```

It contains an `ion-fab-button` element, which, when clicked, will open the camera of the device to take a photo.

5. Finally, let's add some cool styles to our page. Open the `capture.page.scss` file and enter the following CSS styles:

```scss
#container {
    text-align: center;
    position: absolute;
    left: 0;
    right: 0;
    top: 50%;
    transform: translateY(-50%);
}

#container strong {
    font-size: 20px;
    line-height: 26px;
}

#container ion-fab {
    margin-top: 60px;
}
```

Let's run the application using `ionic serve` to get a quick preview of what we have built so far:

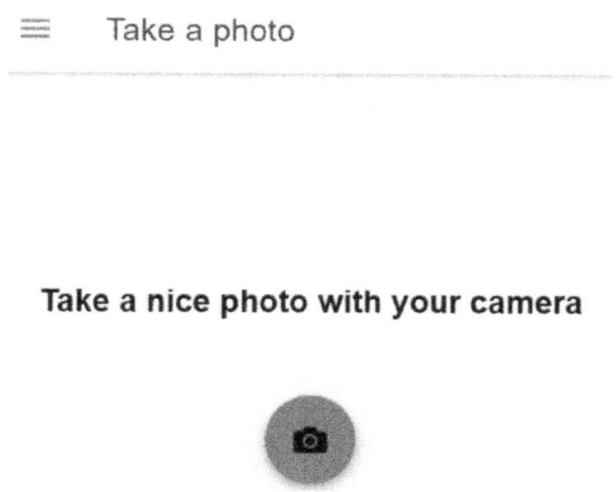

≡   Take a photo

Take a nice photo with your camera

Figure 6.9 – Capture page

The camera button on the page needs to open the camera to take a photo. In the following section, we will learn how to use Capacitor to interact with the camera.

Interacting with Capacitor

Taking photos in our application involves using two APIs from the Capacitor library. The **Camera** API will open the camera to take a photo, and the **Geolocation** API will read the current location from the GPS. Let's see how we can use both in our application:

1. Execute the following npm command to install both APIs:

    ```
    npm install @capacitor/camera @capacitor/geolocation
    ```

2. Create an Angular service using the following Ionic CLI command:

    ```
    ionic generate service photo
    ```

3. Open the photo.service.ts file and add the following import statements:

    ```
    import { Camera, CameraResultType, CameraSource } from '@
    capacitor/camera';
    import { Geolocation } from '@capacitor/geolocation';
    ```

4. Create a method in the PhotoService class to read the current position from the GPS device:

    ```
    private async getLocation() {
      const location = await
        Geolocation.getCurrentPosition();
      return location.coords;
    }
    ```

    The getCurrentPosition method of the Geolocation object contains a coords property with various location-based data such as the latitude and the longitude.

5. Create another method that calls the getLocation method and opens the camera of the device to take a photo:

    ```
    async takePhoto() {
      await this.getLocation();

      await Camera.getPhoto({
    ```

```
      resultType: CameraResultType.DataUrl,
      source: CameraSource.Camera,
      quality: 100
    });
  }
```

We use the getPhoto method of the Camera object and pass a configuration object to define the properties for each photo. The resultType property indicates that the photo will be in a **data URL** format to easily save it later to the cloud. The source property indicates that we will use the camera device to get the photo, and the quality property defines the quality of the actual photo.

6. Open the capture.page.ts file and inject PhotoService in the constructor of the CapturePage class:

```
import { Component, OnInit } from '@angular/core';
import { PhotoService } from '../photo.service';

@Component({
  selector: 'app-capture',
  templateUrl: './capture.page.html',
  styleUrls: ['./capture.page.scss'],
})
export class CapturePage implements OnInit {

  constructor(private photoService: PhotoService) { }

  ngOnInit() {
  }

}
```

7. Create a component method that will call the takePhoto method of the photoService variable:

```
openCamera() {
  this.photoService.takePhoto();
}
```

8. Open the `capture.page.html` file and bind the `click` event of the `ion-fab-button` element to the `openCamera` component method:

```
<ion-fab vertical="center" horizontal="center"
slot="fixed">
  <ion-fab-button (click)="openCamera()">
    <ion-icon name="camera"></ion-icon>
  </ion-fab-button>
</ion-fab>
```

We have now added all the necessary pieces to take a photo using the camera of the device. Let's try to run the application on a real device to test the interaction with the camera:

1. First, we need to build our application using the following Ionic CLI command:

```
ionic build
```

The preceding command will create a www folder in the root folder of your project that contains your application bundle.

2. Install the appropriate platform on which you want to run the application using the following command:

```
npm install @capacitor/<os>
```

In the previous command, the `<os>` parameter can be either `android` or `ios`. If your application is targeted at both platforms, you must execute the command twice.

3. Then, add the installed platform in the capacitor using the following command:

```
ionic cap add <os>
```

The `cap` command is the executable file of the Capacitor library.

The command will create one folder for each platform and will also add the required npm package in the `dependencies` section of the `package.json` file.

> **Important note**
> You must add the specific platform folder to your source control for it to be available to the rest of the project.

4. Finally, run the following command to open the application:

```
ionic cap open <os>
```

In the previous command, `<os>` can be either `android` or `ios`. Upon execution, it will open the native mobile project in the respective IDE, Android Studio or Xcode, depending on the platform that you are targeting. The IDE must then be used to run the native application.

> **Important note**
>
> Every time you re-build the application, you need to run the `npx cap copy` command to copy the application bundle from the www folder into the native mobile project.

5. Click on the camera button, and the application will ask for your permission to use the GPS and the camera, respectively.

> **Important note**
>
> You may need to add additional permissions in the native mobile project of your development environment. Check the respective documentation of the APIs on the Capacitor website.

The first page of our application now has a sleek interface that allows the user to interact with the camera. We have also created an Angular service that ensures a seamless interaction with Capacitor to get location-based data and take photos. In the following section, we will see how to save them in the cloud using Firebase.

Storing data in Firebase

The application will be able to store photos and their location in Firebase. We will use the Storage service to upload our photos and the Cloud Firestore database to keep their location. We will further expand our application in the following tasks:

- Creating a Firebase project
- Integrating the **AngularFire** library

First, we need to set up a new Firebase project for our application.

Creating a Firebase project

We can set up and configure a Firebase project using the Firebase console at `https://console.firebase.google.com`:

1. Click on the **Add project** button to create a new Firebase project:

Figure 6.10 – Create a new Firebase project

2. Enter a name for your project and click the **Continue** button:

Figure 6.11 – Enter the project name

> **Important note**
>
> Firebase generates a unique identifier for your project, which is located underneath the project name and is used in various Firebase services.

3. Disable **Google Analytics** for this project and click on the **Create project** button:

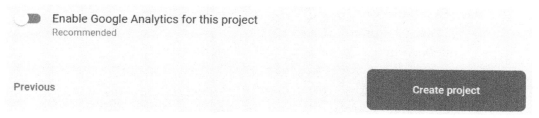

Figure 6.12 – Disable Google Analytics

4. Wait for the new project to be created and click on the **Continue** button. You will be redirected to the dashboard of your new project, which contains a list of options:

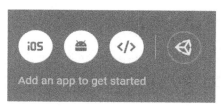

Figure 6.13 – Select the type of your application

Click on the third option with the *code* icon to add Firebase to a web application.

5. Enter a name for your application in the **App nickname** field and click on the **Register app** button:

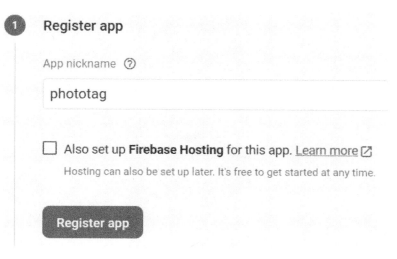

Figure 6.14 – Application registration

6. Firebase will generate a configuration that we will use later in the mobile application:

```
var firebaseConfig = {
  apiKey: "<Your API key>",
  authDomain: "<Your project auth domain>",
  projectId: "<Your project ID>",
  storageBucket: "<Your storage bucket>",
  messagingSenderId: "<Your messaging sender ID>",
  appId: "<Your application ID>"
};
```

Take a note of the `firebaseConfig` object and click the **Continue to console** button.

> **Tip**
>
> The Firebase configuration can also be accessed later at `https://console.firebase.google.com/project/<project-id>/settings/general` where `project-id` is the ID of your Firebase project.

7. Back in the dashboard console, select the **Cloud Firestore** option to enable Cloud Firestore in your application:

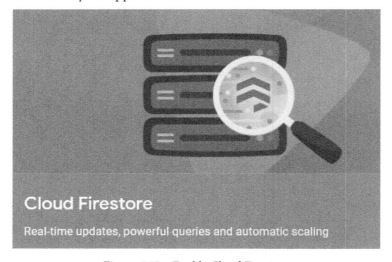

Figure 6.15 – Enable Cloud Firestore

8. Click on the **Create database** button to create a new Cloud Firestore database:

Cloud Firestore
Real-time updates, powerful queries and automatic scaling
Create database

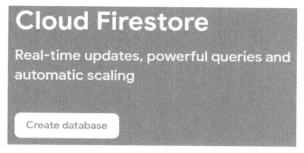

Figure 6.16 – Create a database

9. Select the operation mode of your database. Choose **Start in test mode** for development purposes and click the **Next** button:

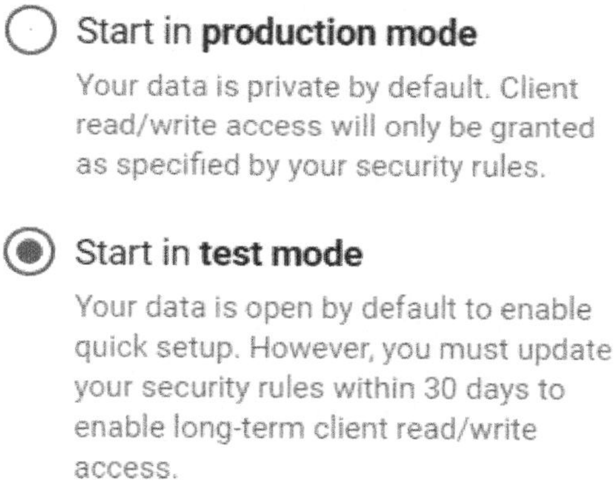

Start in production mode
Your data is private by default. Client read/write access will only be granted as specified by your security rules.
Start in test mode
Your data is open by default to enable quick setup. However, you must update your security rules within 30 days to enable long-term client read/write access.

Figure 6.17 – Select operation mode

Choosing a mode is nothing less than setting rules for your database. Test mode allows faster setup and keeps your data public for 30 days. When you are ready to move your application into production, you can modify the rules of your database accordingly to make your data private.

10. Choose a location for your database according to your regional settings and click the **Enable** button:

Figure 6.18 – Select the database location

Congratulations! You have created a new Cloud Firestore database. In the next section, we will learn how to put the new database into saving data with our mobile application.

Integrating the AngularFire library

The AngularFire library is an Angular library that we can use in an Angular application to interact with Firebase family products such as Cloud Firestore and the Storage service. To install it in our application, run the following command of the Angular CLI:

```
ng add @angular/fire
```

The preceding command will ask you to select the Firebase project that we created in the previous section and will modify the structure of the application accordingly to use AngularFire. Let's see now how we can use the AngularFire library in our application:

1. Open the src\environments\environment.ts file and copy the contents of your Firebase configuration into the environment object as follows:

```
export const environment = {
  production: false,
  firebaseConfig: {
    apiKey: '<Your API key>',
    authDomain: '<Your project auth domain>',
    projectId: '<Your project ID>',
    storageBucket: '<Your storage bucket>',
    messagingSenderId: '<Your messaging sender ID>',
    appId: '<Your application ID>'
  }
};
```

The `environment.ts` file is used when we are running our application in development mode.

2. We need the same Firebase configuration when we run the application in production mode. Copy the Firebase configuration contents into the `src\environments\environment.prod.ts` file that is used in production mode.

3. Open the `app.module.ts` file and add the following `import` statements:

```
import { AngularFireModule } from '@angular/fire';
import { AngularFirestoreModule } from '@angular/fire/firestore';
import { AngularFireStorageModule } from '@angular/fire/storage';
import { environment } from '../environments/environment';
```

`AngularFireModule` is the main module of the AngularFire library. `AngularFirestoreModule` is a specific module of AngularFire that we need when working with Cloud Firestore databases. `AngularFireStorageModule` is a module that we can use to interact with the Storage service.

In the preceding code, we also import the `environment` object that contains the Firebase configuration.

> **Important note**
>
> We import the `environment` object from the development environment file and not the production one. The Angular framework is smart enough to understand which environment we are currently running our application in and use the appropriate file during runtime.

4. Add the AngularFire modules also to the `imports` array of the `@NgModule` decorator:

```
imports: [BrowserModule, IonicModule.forRoot(),
  AppRoutingModule,
  AngularFireModule.initializeApp
    (environment.firebaseConfig),
  AngularFirestoreModule,
  AngularFireStorageModule
]
```

In the preceding code, we use the `initializeApp` method of the `AngularFireModule` class to register our application with our Firebase project.

5. Before moving on, we need to create a model for the data that will be saved in the Cloud Firestore database. Execute the following command of the Ionic CLI to create one:

```
ionic generate interface photo
```

6. Open the `photo.ts` file and add the following properties in the `Photo` interface:

```
export interface Photo {
    url: string;
    lat: number;
    lng: number;
}
```

The `url` property will be the URL of the actual photo, and the `lat`/`lng` properties represent the latitude and longitude of the current location.

7. Open the `photo.service.ts` file and add the following `import` statements:

```
import { AngularFirestore } from '@angular/fire/
firestore';
import { AngularFireStorage } from '@angular/fire/
storage';
import { Photo } from './photo';
```

The `AngularFirestore` service contains all the necessary methods that we will need to interact with our Cloud Firestore database. The `AngularFireStorage` service contains methods for uploading files to the Storage service.

8. Inject both services into the constructor of the `PhotoService` class:

```
constructor(private firestore: AngularFirestore, private
storage: AngularFireStorage) {}
```

9. Create the following method to save a photo in Firebase:

```
private async savePhoto(dataUrl: string, latitude:
number, longitude: number) {
  const name = new
    Date().getUTCMilliseconds().toString();
  const upload = await
```

```
    this.storage.ref(name).putString(dataUrl,
      'data_url');
  const photoUrl = await upload.ref.getDownloadURL();

  await
    this.firestore.collection<Photo>('photos').add({
    url: photoUrl,
    lat: latitude,
    lng: longitude
  });
}
```

First, we create a random `name` for our photo and use the `putString` method of the `storage` variable to upload it to Firebase storage. As soon as uploading has been completed, we get a downloadable URL using the `getDownloadURL` method, which can be used to access that photo. Finally, we use the `add` method to add a new `Photo` object in the `collection` property of the `firestore` variable. We use the `collection` property because we want to work with a list of photos in our application.

> **Tip**
> The `firestore` variable also contains a `doc` property that can be used when we want to work with single objects. The `collection` property internally keeps a list of `doc` objects.

10. Modify the `takePhoto` method to call the `savePhoto` method that we created in *step 9*:

```
async takePhoto() {
  const {latitude, longitude} = await
    this.getLocation();

  const cameraPhoto = await Camera.getPhoto({
    resultType: CameraResultType.DataUrl,
    source: CameraSource.Camera,
    quality: 100
  });
```

```
await this.savePhoto(cameraPhoto.dataUrl, latitude,
    longitude);
}
```

We are now ready to check the full functionality of the photo-shooting process:

1. Build the application using the following Ionic CLI command:

    ```
    ionic build
    ```

2. Run the following command of Capacitor to copy the application bundle to the native mobile projects:

    ```
    ionic cap copy
    ```

3. Open the native mobile project using the open command of Capacitor and run the project using the respective IDE.

4. Open the Firebase console of your application and select the **Storage** option in the **Build** section. Select the **Rules** tab, remove the authentication check at line 5 and click the **Publish** button. The resulting rules should be the following:

    ```
    rules_version = '2';
    service firebase.storage {
      match /b/{bucket}/o {
        match /{allPaths=**} {
          allow read, write;
        }
      }
    }
    ```

5. Use the application to take a nice photo. To verify that your photo has been successfully uploaded to Firebase, select the **Files** tab. You should see an entry like the following:

	Name	Size	Type	Last modified
☐	🖼 669	2.9 MB	image/jpeg	6 Feb 2021

Figure 6.19 – Firebase storage

In the preceding screenshot, the file named **669** is the physical file of the photo that you have taken.

6. Similarly, select the **Firestore Database** option in the **Build** section, and you should see something like the following:

Figure 6.20 – Cloud Firestore

In the preceding screenshot, the **1oFxxWgQseIwqWUrYBkN** entry is the logical object of the photo that contains the URL of the actual file and its location data.

The first page of our application is now feature-complete. We have gone through the full process of taking a photo and uploading it to the cloud along with its location data. We started by setting up and configuring a Firebase project and finished by learning how to use the AngularFire library to interact with that project. In the next section, we will reach our final destination by implementing the second page of our application.

Previewing photos with CesiumJS

The next feature of our application will be to display all the photos that we have taken with the camera on a 3D map. The CesiumJS library provides a viewer with a 3D globe that we can use to visualize various things, such as images in specific locations. This new feature of our application will consist of the following:

- Configuring CesiumJS
- Displaying photos on viewer

We will begin by learning how to set up the CesiumJS library.

Configuring CesiumJS

The CesiumJS library is an npm package that we can install to start working with 3D maps and visualizations:

1. Run the following npm command to install CesiumJS:

```
npm install cesium
```

2. Open the `angular.json` configuration file and add the following entry in the `assets` array of the `build` architect option:

```
"assets": [
  {
    "glob": "**/*",
    "input": "src/assets",
    "output": "assets"
  },
  {
    "glob": "**/*.svg",
    "input":
      "node_modules/ionicons/dist/ionicons/svg",
    "output": "./svg"
  },
  {
    "glob": "**/*",
    "input": "node_modules/cesium/Build/Cesium",
    "output": "/assets/cesium"
  }
]
```

The preceding entry will copy runtime all CesiumJS source files into a `cesium` folder inside the `assets` folder of our application.

3. Also add the CesiumJS widgets style sheet file into the `styles` array of the `build` section:

```
"styles": [
  "node_modules/cesium/Build/Cesium/Widgets/
    widgets.css",
  "src/theme/variables.scss",
  "src/global.scss"
]
```

The viewer of CesiumJS contains a toolbar with widgets, including a search bar and a dropdown for selecting a specific type of map, such as **Bing Maps** or **Mapbox**.

4. Open the main entry point file of our application, `main.ts`, and add the following line:

```
// eslint-disable-next-line @typescript-eslint/dot-
// notation
window['CESIUM_BASE_URL'] = '/assets/cesium/';
```

The `CESIUM_BASE_URL` global variable indicates the location of the CesiumJS source files.

5. Install a custom webpack builder using the following npm command:

```
npm install -D @angular-builders/custom-webpack
```

A **builder** is an Angular library that extends the default functionality of the Angular CLI. The `@angular-builders/custom-webpack` builder allows us to provide an additional webpack configuration file while building our application. It is beneficial in cases where we want to include additional webpack plugins or override existing functionality.

6. Create a new webpack configuration file named `extra-webpack.config.js` in the root folder of the project and add the following content:

```
module.exports = {
  resolve: {
    fallback: {
      fs: "empty",
      Buffer: false,
      http: "empty",
      https: "empty",
      zlib: "empty"
    }
  },
  module: {
    unknownContextCritical: false
  }
};
```

The configuration file will ensure that webpack will not try to load CesiumJS code that cannot understand. CesiumJS uses modules in a format that cannot be statically analyzed from webpack.

7. Open the `angular.json` file and change the `builder` property of the `build` architect section to use the custom webpack builder:

```
"builder": "@angular-builders/custom-webpack:browser"
```

8. Define the path of the custom webpack configuration file in the `options` property of the `build` section:

```
"customWebpackConfig": {
    "path": "./extra-webpack.config.js"
}
```

9. Configure the `serve` architect section to use the custom webpack builder:

```
"serve": {
    "builder": "@angular-builders/custom-webpack:
      dev-server",
    "options": {
      "browserTarget": "app:build"
    },
    "configurations": {
      "production": {
        "browserTarget": "app:build:production"
      },
      "ci": {
        "progress": false
      }
    }
}
```

10. Open the `tsconfig.app.json` file and add the `cesium` types in the `compilerOptions` property:

```
"compilerOptions": {
    "outDir": "./out-tsc/app",
    "types": ["cesium"]
}
```

Now that we have completed the configuration of the CesiumJS library, we can start creating the page for our feature:

1. Run the following command of the Ionic CLI to create a new page:

```
ionic generate page view
```

2. Open the `view.page.html` file and modify the `ion-header` element so that it includes a menu toggle button:

```
<ion-header>
  <ion-toolbar>
    <ion-buttons slot="start">
      <ion-menu-button color="primary">
      </ion-menu-button>
    </ion-buttons>
    <ion-title>View gallery</ion-title>
  </ion-toolbar>
</ion-header>
```

3. Add a `div` element inside the `ion-content` element that will be the container for our viewer:

```
<ion-content>
  <div #mapContainer></div>
</ion-content>
```

`#mapContainer` is a **template reference variable** and we use it to declare an alias for an element in our template.

4. Open the `view.page.scss` file and set the size of the map container element:

```
div {
  height: 100%;
  width: 100%;
}
```

5. Let's create our viewer now. Open the `view.page.ts` file and modify it as follows:

```
import { AfterViewInit, Component, OnInit, ElementRef,
ViewChild } from '@angular/core';
import { Viewer } from 'cesium';

@Component({
  selector: 'app-view',
  templateUrl: './view.page.html',
  styleUrls: ['./view.page.scss'],
})
export class ViewPage implements OnInit, AfterViewInit {

  @ViewChild('mapContainer') content: ElementRef;

  constructor() { }

  ngOnInit() {
  }

  ngAfterViewInit() {
    const viewer = new
      Viewer(this.content.nativeElement);
  }

}
```

We create a new `Viewer` object inside the `ngAfterViewInit` method of the component. The `ngAfterViewInit` method is called when the view of the component has finished loading, and it is defined in the `AfterViewInit` interface. The constructor of the `Viewer` class accepts as a parameter the native HTML element on which we want to create the viewer. In our case, we want to attach it to the map container element that we created earlier. Thus, we use the `@ViewChild` decorator to reference that element by passing the template reference variable name as a parameter.

6. Run the application using `ionic serve` and click on the **View gallery** option from the main menu. You should see the following output:

Figure 6.21 – View gallery page

> **Tip**
> If the map on the viewer is not displayed correctly, try to select a different provider from the map button on the viewer toolbar, next to the question button.

We have now successfully configured the CesiumJS library in our application. In the next section, we will see how to benefit from it and display our photos on the 3D globe of the CesiumJS viewer.

Displaying photos on viewer

The next thing that we need to do for our application to be ready is to display our photos on the map. We will get all the photos from Firebase and add them to the viewer in the specified locations. Let's see how we can accomplish that:

1. Create a new Angular service using the following command of the Ionic CLI:

```
ionic generate service cesium
```

2. Open the `cesium.service.ts` file and add the following `import` statements:

```
import { AngularFirestore } from '@angular/fire/
firestore';
import { Cartesian3, Color, PinBuilder, Viewer } from
'cesium';
import { Observable } from 'rxjs';
import { map } from 'rxjs/operators';
import { Photo } from './photo';
```

3. Inject the `AngularFirestore` service in the constructor of the `CesiumService` class and create a `viewer` property, which we will use to store our `Viewer` object:

```
export class CesiumService {

  private viewer: Viewer;

  constructor(private firestore: AngularFirestore) { }
}
```

4. Create a `register` method to set the `viewer` property:

```
register(viewer: Viewer) {
  this.viewer = viewer;
}
```

5. Create a method to get the `photos` collection from Cloud Firestore:

```
private getPhotos(): Observable<Photo[]> {
  return this.firestore.collection<Photo>('photos').
    snapshotChanges().pipe(
    map(actions => actions.map(a => a.payload.doc.data()
      as Photo))
```

```
    );
  }
```

In the preceding method, we call the snapshotChanges method to get the data of the photos collection. We have already learned that a collection consists of doc objects. Thus, we can reach the actual photo object using the data method on the doc property for each action object.

6. Create the following method for adding all the photos to the viewer:

```
addPhotos() {
  const pinBuilder = new PinBuilder();

  this.getPhotos().subscribe(photos => {
    photos.forEach(photo => {
      const entity = {
        position: Cartesian3.fromDegrees(photo.lng,
          photo.lat),
        billboard: {
          image: pinBuilder.fromColor
            (Color.fromCssColorString('#de6b45'),
              48).toDataURL()
        },
        description: `<img width="100%"
          style="margin:auto; display: block;"
            src="${photo.url}" />`
      };
      this.viewer.entities.add(entity);
    });
  });
}
```

The location of each photo on the viewer will be displayed as a pin. Thus, we need to initialize a PinBuilder object first. The preceding method subscribes to the getPhotos method to get all photos from Cloud Firestore. For each photo, it creates an entity object that contains the position, which is the location of the photo in degrees, and a billboard property that displays a pin of 48 pixels in size. It also defines a description property that will display the actual image of the photo when we click on the pin.

Each `entity` object is added to the `entities` collection of `viewer` using its `add` method.

7. The description of each entity is displayed inside an info box. Open the `global.scss` file that contains the global styles of the application and add the following CSS styles for the info box:

```
.cesium-infoBox, .cesium-infoBox-iframe {
  height: 100% !important;
  width: 100%;
}
```

8. Now, let's use `CesiumService` from our page. Open the `view.page.ts` file and inject the `CesiumService` class into the constructor of the `ViewPage` class:

```
import { AfterViewInit, Component, OnInit, ElementRef,
ViewChild } from '@angular/core';
import { Viewer } from 'cesium';
import { CesiumService } from '../cesium.service';


@Component({
  selector: 'app-view',
  templateUrl: './view.page.html',
  styleUrls: ['./view.page.scss'],
})
export class ViewPage implements OnInit, AfterViewInit {

    @ViewChild('mapContainer') content: ElementRef;


    constructor(private cesiumService: CesiumService) {}


    ngOnInit() {
    }


    ngAfterViewInit() {
      const viewer = new
        Viewer(this.content.nativeElement);
    }


}
```

9. Modify the `ngAfterViewInit` method to register the viewer and add the photos:

```
ngAfterViewInit() {
  this.cesiumService.register(new
    Viewer(this.content.nativeElement));
  this.cesiumService.addPhotos();
}
```

We are now set to view our photos on the map:

1. Run the application using the `ionic serve` command.

2. Use the application to take some nice photos, preferably in different locations.

3. Select the **View gallery** option from the main menu, and you should get an output like the following:

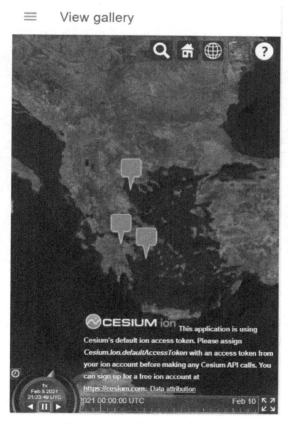

Figure 6.22 – Photos on the map

4. Click on one of the pins on the map and you should see your photo:

Figure 6.23 – Photo display

We now have a complete mobile application for taking geotagged photos and displaying them on a map. We saw how to set up the CesiumJS library and get our photos from Cloud Firestore. The API of the CesiumJS viewer provided us with an easy way to visualize our photos on the map and interact with them.

Summary

In this chapter, we built a mobile application for taking photos, tagging them with the current location, and displaying them on a 3D map. Initially, we learned how to create a new mobile application using the Ionic framework. We built the application locally, and then we integrated Capacitor to interact with the camera and the GPS device. The camera was used to take photos and the GPS to mark them with the location.

Later on, we used Firebase services to store our photo files and data in the cloud. Finally, we learned how to retrieve the stored photos from Firebase and displayed them on a 3D globe using the CesiumJS library.

In the next chapter, we will investigate another way to prerender content in Angular. We will use server-side rendering techniques to create a GitHub portfolio website.

Practice questions

1. Which toolkit can we use to create a UI in a Capacitor application?
2. Which method do we use to take photos with the camera in a Capacitor application?
3. How do we read the current location in a Capacitor application?
4. How do we add a menu toggle button with Ionic?
5. Which Capacitor command do we use to sync the application bundle with native mobile projects?
6. What is the difference between test and production mode in Cloud Firestore?
7. Which method do we use to initialize an application with the AngularFire library?
8. Which method do we use to fetch data from a Cloud Firestore collection?
9. How do we create a pin using the CesiumJS library?
10. How do we convert latitude and longitude to degrees using CesiumJS?

Further reading

- Getting started with Capacitor: `https://capacitorjs.com/docs/getting-started`
- Android getting started guide for Capacitor: `https://capacitorjs.com/docs/android#getting-started`
- iOS getting started guide for Capacitor: `https://capacitorjs.com/docs/ios#getting-started`

- Angular development with Ionic: `https://ionicframework.com/docs/angular/overview`

- AngularFire library documentation: `https://firebaseopensource.com/projects/angular/angularfire2/`

- CesiumJS quick start guide: `https://cesium.com/docs/tutorials/quick-start/`

- CesiumJS and Angular article: `https://cesium.com/blog/2018/03/12/cesium-and-angular/`

7

Building an SSR Application for a GitHub Portfolio Using Angular

A typical Angular application follows the **Single-Page Application** (**SPA**) approach, where each page is created in the DOM of the browser while the user interacts with the application. A web server hosts the application and is responsible for serving only the main page, usually called `index.html`, at application startup.

Server-Side Rendering (**SSR**) is a technique that follows an entirely different approach for application rendering than SPA. It uses the server to prerender pages while they are requested at runtime from the user. Rendering content on the server dramatically enhances the performance of a web application and improves its **Search Engine Optimization** (**SEO**) capabilities. To perform SSR in an Angular application, we use a library called **Angular Universal**.

In this chapter, we will learn how to benefit from Angular Universal by building a portfolio application using the **GitHub API**. We will cover the following topics:

- Building an Angular application with the GitHub API

- Integrating Angular Universal

- Prerendering content during build

- Enhancing SEO capabilities

- Replaying events with preboot

Essential background theory and context

An Angular application consists of several pages that are created dynamically in the DOM of the browser by the Angular framework while we use the application. Angular Universal enables the Angular framework to create these pages on the server statically during application runtime. In other words, it can create a fully static version of an Angular application that can run even without needing to have JavaScript enabled. Prerendering an application on the server has the following advantages:

- It allows web crawlers to index the application and make it discoverable and linkable on social media websites.

- It makes the application usable to mobile and other low-performant devices that cannot afford to execute JavaScript on their side.

- It improves the user experience by loading the first page quickly and, at the same time, loading the actual client page in the background (**First Contentful Paint** (**FCP**)).

> **Important note**
> The application does not respond to user events during the FCP other than navigation events initiated from the `routerLink` directive of the Angular router. However, we can use a special-purpose library called **preboot** to replay those events after the entire application has been loaded.

The GitHub API is an HTTP REST API for interacting with GitHub data. It can be used either publicly or in private using an authentication mechanism provided out of the box.

> **Important note**
>
> Unauthorized requests to the GitHub API are limited to *60* requests per hour. For an overview of available authentication methods, you can find more details at `https://docs.github.com/en/rest/overview/other-authentication-methods`.

To communicate over HTTP in Angular, we use the built-in HTTP client that is available in the `@angular/common/http` npm package. Interacting with HTTP in SSR applications may result in duplicated HTTP requests due to the page prerendering at the FCP. However, Angular Universal can overcome this type of duplication using a mechanism called **TransferState**.

Project overview

In this project, we will build a portfolio application for our GitHub user profile. We will initially use the Angular CLI to scaffold an Angular application that interacts with the GitHub API. We will learn how to use the GitHub API and fetch user-specific data. We will also use the **Bootstrap CSS** library to style our application and create a beautiful user interface.

After creating our Angular application, we will turn it into a server-side rendered application using Angular Universal. We will see how to install and configure Angular Universal, and we will learn how to prerender it during build time. Then, we will configure our application to be correctly rendered using SEO in the most popular social platforms. Finally, we will find out how to use the preboot library to play back browser events that are not fully supported in SSR applications.

Build time: 2 hours

Getting started

The following prerequisites and software tools are required for completing this project:

- **GitHub account**: A valid GitHub user account.

- **Angular CLI**: A CLI for Angular that you can find at `https://angular.io/cli`.

- **GitHub material**: The related code for this chapter can be found in the `Chapter07` folder at `https://github.com/PacktPublishing/Angular-Projects-Second-Edition`.

Building an Angular application with the GitHub API

GitHub contains an API that we can use to fetch various information about the profile of a GitHub user. The Angular application that we are building will communicate with the GitHub API and display a brief portfolio for our GitHub profile. Our application will consist of the following features:

- **Dashboard**: This will be the landing page of the application, and it will display a summary of our GitHub profile.

- **Info**: This will display personal information about us.

- **Repositories**: This will display a list of our *public* repositories.

- **Organizations**: This will display a list of GitHub organizations of which we are members.

> **Important note**
>
> The resulting output of each feature that is displayed in the screenshots of this chapter will be different according to your GitHub profile.

The dashboard will be the main page of the application, and it will contain all the other features. We will learn how to build the dashboard page in the following section.

Building the dashboard

Before we can start creating the main features of our application, we need to scaffold and configure an Angular application first by running the following command:

```
ng new gh-portfolio --routing=false --style=scss
```

The preceding command will use the ng new command of the Angular CLI, passing the following options:

- gh-portfolio: The name of the Angular application that we want to create

- --routing=false: Disables routing because our application will consist of a single page

- --style=scss: Configures the Angular application to use the SCSS stylesheet format when working with CSS styles

We will use the Bootstrap CSS library for styling our portfolio application. Let's see how to install and configure it in the Angular CLI application that we have just created:

1. Execute the following npm command to install the Bootstrap CSS library:

```
npm i bootstrap
```

2. Open the `src\styles.scss` file and import the Bootstrap SCSS stylesheet:

```
@import "~bootstrap/scss/bootstrap";
```

The `styles.scss` file contains CSS styles that are applied globally to the application. The `@import` CSS rule accepts the absolute path of a stylesheet file that we want to load.

> **Important note**
>
> When we import a stylesheet format using the `@import` rule, we omit the extension of the file.

The ~ character denotes the `node_modules` folder in the root folder of our Angular CLI application.

3. Execute the following command to install **Bootstrap Icons**, a free and open source icon library:

```
npm install bootstrap-icons
```

Bootstrap Icons can be used in various formats, such as SVG or font. In this project, we are going to use the latter.

4. Import the font icons format of the Bootstrap Icons library into the `styles.scss` file:

```
@import "~bootstrap/scss/bootstrap";
@import "~bootstrap-icons/font/bootstrap-icons";
```

We have already created the Angular application and added the necessary artifacts for styling it. We are now ready to start creating the main page of our Angular application:

1. Download an Angular logo of your choice from the **press kit** of the official Angular documentation at `https://angular.io/presskit`.

2. Copy the downloaded logo file into the `src\assets` folder of the Angular CLI workspace. The `assets` folder is used for static files such as images, fonts, and JSON files.

3. Open the `environment.ts` file in the `src\environments` folder and add a new property to the `environment` object:

```
export const environment = {
  production: false,
  username: '<Your GitHub login>'
};
```

Replace the value of the `username` property with your GitHub login. The `environment` object is used to define application-wide properties such as configuration settings or the URL of a backend API.

4. Open the `environment.prod.ts` file that exists in the same folder and add the same property as in *step 3*. The `environment.prod.ts` file is used when we run an Angular CLI application in production mode. The `environment.ts` file is the default one, and it is used in development mode.

> **Important note**
> The `environment` object must have the same structure and properties in all environment files.

5. Open the `app.component.ts` file and create a property in the `AppComponent` class to get the `username` property from the `environment` object:

```
import { Component } from '@angular/core';
import { environment } from
  '../environments/environment';

@Component({
  selector: 'app-root',
  templateUrl: './app.component.html',
  styleUrls: ['./app.component.scss']
})
export class AppComponent {
  username = environment.username;
}
```

> **Important note**
>
> We import the `environment` object from the default environment file. The Angular CLI replaces it with the respective environment file according to the mode that we are currently running, either development or production.

6. Open the `app.component.html` file and replace its content with the following HTML template:

```html
<div class="toolbar d-flex align-items-center">
  <img width="40" alt="Angular Logo"
    src="assets/angular.png" />
  <span>Welcome to my GitHub portfolio</span>
  <a class="ms-auto p-2" target="_blank"
  rel="noopener" href="https://github.com/{{username}}
  " title="GitHub">
    <i class="bi-github"></i>
  </a>
</div>
```

In the preceding template, we define the header of our application. It contains an anchor element that links to our GitHub profile. We have also added the GitHub icon using the `bi-github` class from the Bootstrap Icon set.

7. Insert the following HTML snippet after the header of the application:

```html
<div class="content d-flex flex-column">
  <div class="row">
    <div class="col-sm-3"></div>
    <div class="col-sm-9">
      <div class="row">
        <div class="col-12 col-sm-12"></div>
      </div>
      <div class="row">
        <div class="col-12 col-sm-12"></div>
      </div>
    </div>
  </div>
</div>
```

In the preceding snippet, we create the container element for the basic features of our application. The element with the `col-sm-3` class selector will display the personal information feature. The element with the `col-sm-9` class selector will be split into two rows, each one for the repositories and organizations feature. The resulting layout of the content will look like the following:

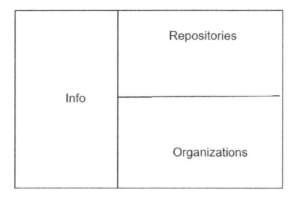

Figure 7.1 – Main content

8. Open the `app.component.scss` file and add the following CSS styles for the header and the content of our application:

```scss
.toolbar {
  height: 60px;
  background-color: #1976d2;
  color: white;
  font-weight: 600;
}

.toolbar img {
  margin: 0 16px;
}

.toolbar i {
  font-size: 1.5rem;
  color: white;
  margin: 0 16px;
}
```

```
.toolbar a {
  margin-bottom: 5px;
}


.toolbar i:hover {
  opacity: 0.8;
}


.content {
  margin: 52px auto 32px;
  padding: 0 16px;
}
```

9. Run `ng serve` to start the application and navigate to `http://localhost:4200`. The header of the application should look like the following:

Figure 7.2 – Application header

The main page of our portfolio application is now ready. It contains a header and an empty container element for adding the main features. In the following section, we will start building the personal information feature of our application.

Displaying personal information

The first feature of our application will be to display personal information from our GitHub profile, such as the full name, the profile photo, and some social media links. Before creating the feature, we first need to configure our application so that it can communicate with the GitHub API:

1. Open the main module of the application, the `app.module.ts` file, and add the `HttpClientModule` class to the `imports` array of the `@NgModule` decorator:

```
import { NgModule } from '@angular/core';
import { BrowserModule } from '@angular/platform-
  browser';
import { HttpClientModule } from
```

```
    '@angular/common/http';

import { AppComponent } from './app.component';

@NgModule({
  declarations: [
    AppComponent
  ],
  imports: [
    BrowserModule,
    HttpClientModule
  ],
  providers: [],
  bootstrap: [AppComponent]
})
export class AppModule { }
```

The `HttpClientModule` class is the main Angular module of the built-in HTTP library that exports all necessary services for interacting with an HTTP resource.

2. Create a new Angular service using the following Angular CLI command:

```
ng generate service github
```

3. Open the `github.service.ts` file and inject the `HttpClient` service into the constructor of the `GithubService` class:

```
import { HttpClient } from '@angular/common/http';
import { Injectable } from '@angular/core';

@Injectable({
  providedIn: 'root'
})
export class GithubService {

  constructor(private http: HttpClient) { }

}
```

The `HttpClient` class is an Angular service of the built-in HTTP client that provides all the primary methods for interacting with an HTTP, such as **GET**, **POST**, and **PUT**.

4. Open the `environment.ts` file and add a new property for the URL of the GitHub API:

```
export const environment = {
  production: false,
  username: '<Your GitHub login>',
  apiUrl: 'https://api.github.com'
};
```

Make sure that you add the same property to the environment file for production.

All interaction between our application and the GitHub API will be delegated to `GithubService`. Now, let's focus on building our feature:

1. Execute the following command of the Angular CLI to create a new Angular component for our feature:

```
ng generate component personal-info
```

2. Create a `user` interface to define the data model of our component using the following Angular CLI command:

```
ng generate interface user
```

3. Open the `user.ts` file and add the following properties to the `User` interface:

```
export interface User {
  avatar_url: string;
  name: string;
  blog: string;
  location: string;
  bio: string;
  twitter_username: string;
  followers: number;
}
```

4. Open the `github.service.ts` file and add the following `import` statements:

```
import { Observable } from 'rxjs';
import { environment } from
  '../environments/environment';
import { User } from './user';
```

5. Create a new method for getting the details of our profile from the GitHub API:

```
getUser(): Observable<User> {
  return this.http.get<User>(`${environment.apiUrl}/
    users/${environment.username}`);
}
```

6. Open the `personal-info.component.ts` file and add the following `import` statements:

```
import { Observable } from 'rxjs';
import { GithubService } from '../github.service';
import { User } from '../user';
```

7. Inject `GithubService` into the constructor of the `PersonalInfoComponent` class and create a component property to get the result of the `getUser` method:

```
export class PersonalInfoComponent implements OnInit {

  user$: Observable<User> | undefined;

  constructor(private githubService: GithubService) { }

  ngOnInit(): void {
    this.user$ = this.githubService.getUser();
  }

}
```

8. Open the `personal-info.component.html` file and replace its content with the following HTML template:

```html
<div class="card" *ngIf="user$ | async as user">
  <img [src]="user.avatar_url" class="card-img-top"
    alt="{{user.name}} photo">
  <div class="card-body">
    <h5 class="card-title">{{user.name}}</h5>
    <p class="card-text">{{user.bio}}</p>
  </div>
  <ul class="list-group list-group-flush">
    <li class="list-group-item" title="Location">
      <i class="bi-geo me-2"></i>{{user.location}}
    </li>
    <li class="list-group-item" title="Followers">
      <i class="bi-people me-2"></i>{{user.followers}}
    </li>
  </ul>
  <div class="card-body">
    <a href="https://www.twitter.com/{{user.twitter_
      username}}" class="card-link">Twitter</a>
    <a [href]="user.blog" class="card-link">
      Personal blog</a>
  </div>
</div>
```

In the preceding template, we use the `async` pipe because the `user$` property is an observable, and we need to subscribe to it so that we can get its values. The main advantage of the `async` pipe is that it unsubscribes from the observable automatically when a component is destroyed, avoiding potential memory leaks.

We also create the `user` alias for the observable to reference it easily in various locations around the template of the component.

9. Open the `app.component.html` file and add the selector of `PersonalInfoComponent` to the element with the `col-sm-3` class selector:

```html
<div class="col-sm-3">
  <app-personal-info></app-personal-info>
</div>
```

If we run `ng serve` to preview the application, we should see the personal information panel on the left side of the page:

Figure 7.3 – Personal information

The first feature of our portfolio application is now complete. It displays the personal information of our GitHub profile along with a short bio and some social network links. In the next section, we will build the repositories feature of our application.

Listing user repositories

The GitHub user profile contains a list of repositories that the user owns, called **sources**, or contributes, called **forks**. The repositories feature of our application will only display the sources repositories.

The repositories and organizations features will have a similar user interface. Thus, we need to create a component for use in both features:

1. Execute the following command of the Angular CLI to create a new component:

```
ng generate component panel
```

2. Open the `panel.component.ts` file and define two input properties using the @ Input decorator:

```
import { Component, Input, OnInit } from '@angular/core';

@Component({
  selector: 'app-panel',
  templateUrl: './panel.component.html',
  styleUrls: ['./panel.component.scss']
})
export class PanelComponent implements OnInit {

  @Input() caption: string = '';
  @Input() icon: string = '';

  constructor() { }

  ngOnInit(): void {
  }

}
```

3. Open the `panel.component.html` file and replace its content with the following HTML template:

```
<div class="card mb-4">
  <div class="card-header">
    <i class="bi bi-{{icon}} me-1"></i>
```

```
    {{caption}}
  </div>
  <div class="card-body">
    <ng-content></ng-content>
  </div>
</div>
```

The panel component is a Bootstrap `card` element that consists of a header and a body. The header uses the `caption` and `icon` input properties to display text with an icon. The body uses the `ng-content` Angular component to define a placeholder where the content from our features will be displayed.

We can now start using the panel component to create our feature:

1. Create an interface for representing the data model of a GitHub repository:

    ```
    ng generate interface repository
    ```

2. Open the `repository.ts` file and add the following properties:

    ```
    export interface Repository {
      name: string;
      html_url: string;
      description: string;
      fork: boolean;
      stargazers_count: number;
      language: string;
      forks_count: number;
    }
    ```

3. Open the `github.service.ts` file and import the `Repository` interface:

    ```
    import { Repository } from './repository';
    ```

4. Now it is time for some refactoring in our service. The URL that we will use for getting repositories has some similarities with that of the `getUser` method. Extract the URL of that method in a property of the `GithubService` class:

    ```
    export class GithubService {

      private userUrl: string = '';
    ```

```
constructor(private http: HttpClient) {
  this.userUrl = `${environment.apiUrl}/users/${
    environment.username}`;
}

getUser(): Observable<User> {
  return this.http.get<User>(this.userUrl);
}
}
```

5. Create a new method to fetch repositories of the current GitHub user:

```
getRepos(): Observable<Repository[]> {
  return this.http.get<Repository[]>(this.userUrl +
    '/repos');
}
```

Now that we have created the prerequisites for fetching the user repositories from the GitHub API, we can start building the component that will display those repositories:

1. Execute the following command to create a new Angular component using the Angular CLI:

```
ng generate component repositories
```

2. Open the repositories.component.ts file and add the following import statements:

```
import { Observable } from 'rxjs';
import { map } from 'rxjs/operators';
import { GithubService } from '../github.service';
import { Repository } from '../repository';
```

3. Inject GithubService into the constructor of the RepositoriesComponent class and create a component property to get the result of the getRepos method:

```
export class RepositoriesComponent implements OnInit {

  repos$: Observable<Repository[]> | undefined;

  constructor(private githubService: GithubService) { }
```

```
ngOnInit(): void {
    this.repos$ = this.githubService.getRepos().pipe(
      map(repos => repos.filter(repo => !repo.fork))
    );
  }

}
```

We use the `pipe` RxJS operator to combine the observable returned from the `getRepos` method with the `map` operator to filter out fork repositories and get only sources. Filtering is accomplished using the standard `filter` method for arrays.

4. Open the `repositories.component.html` file and replace its content with the following HTML template:

```html
<app-panel caption="Repositories" icon="archive">
  <div class="row row-cols-1 row-cols-md-3 g-4">
    <div class="col p-2" *ngFor="let repo of repos$ |
      async">
      <div class="card h-100">
        <div class="card-body">
          <h5 class="card-title">
            <a [href]="repo.html_url">{{repo.name}}
            </a>
          </h5>
          <p class="card-text">{{repo.description}}
          </p>
        </div>
      </div>
    </div>
  </div>
</app-panel>
```

In the preceding template, we wrap the main content of the component inside the `app-panel` component and we set the `caption` and `icon` properties for the header.

Our component iterates over the `repos$` observable and displays the name and the description of each repository. The name is an anchor element that points to the actual GitHub URL of the repository.

5. Add the following list immediately after the element with the `card-body` class selector:

```
<ul class="list-group list-group-flush list-group-
    horizontal">
  <li class="list-group-item border-0">
    <i class="bi-code me-2"></i>{{repo.language}}
  </li>
  <li class="list-group-item border-0">
    <i class="bi-star me-2">
    </i>{{repo.stargazers_count}}
  </li>
  <li class="list-group-item border-0">
    <i class="bi-diagram-2 me-2">
    </i>{{repo.forks_count}}
  </li>
</ul>
```

In the preceding snippet, we display the language of each repository, how many have starred it, and how many have forked it.

6. Open the `app.component.html` file and add the selector of `RepositoriesComponent` in the first HTML element with the `col-12 col-sm-12` class selector:

```
<div class="col-sm-9">
  <div class="row">
    <div class="col-12 col-sm-12">
      <app-repositories></app-repositories>
    </div>
  </div>
  <div class="row">
    <div class="col-12 col-sm-12"></div>
  </div>
</div>
```

7. Run `ng serve` to preview the application, and you should see the new panel next to the personal information feature:

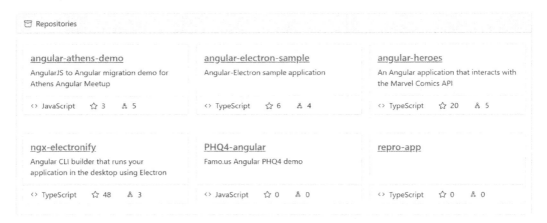

Figure 7.4 – Repositories

The second feature of our application has been completed. It displays a list of public repositories that exist in our GitHub profile. Our application now also features a panel component that we can use to build the organizations feature of our application in the following section.

Visualizing the organization membership

A GitHub user can be a member of a GitHub organization. Our application will display a list of user organizations along with some additional information about each one. Let's start building our organization list:

1. Create an interface to define the properties of an organization:

```
ng generate interface organization
```

2. Open the `organization.ts` file and add the following properties:

```
export interface Organization {
    login: string;
    description: string;
    avatar_url: string;
}
```

3. Open the `github.service.ts` file and import the `Organization` interface:

```
import { Organization } from './organization';
```

4. Create a new method to get organizations of the current GitHub user:

```
getOrganizations(): Observable<Organization[]> {
  return this.http.get<Organization[]>(this.userUrl +
    '/orgs');
}
```

5. Execute the following command to create an Angular component for our feature:

```
ng generate component organizations
```

6. Open the `organizations.component.ts` file and add the following `import` statements:

```
import { Observable } from 'rxjs';
import { GithubService } from '../github.service';
import { Organization } from '../organization';
```

7. Inject `GithubService` into the constructor of the `OrganizationsComponent` class and set the result of its `getOrganizations` method to an observable component property:

```
export class OrganizationsComponent implements OnInit {

  orgs$: Observable<Organization[]> | undefined;

  constructor(private githubService: GithubService) { }

  ngOnInit(): void {
    this.orgs$ =
      this.githubService.getOrganizations();
  }

}
```

8. Open the `organizations.component.html` file and replace its content with the following HTML template:

```html
<app-panel caption="Organizations" icon="diagram-3">
  <div class="list-group">
    <a href="https://www.github.com/{{org.login}}"
      class="list-group-item list-group-item-action"
      *ngFor="let org of orgs$ | async">
      <div class="row">
        <img [src]="org.avatar_url">
        <div class="col-sm-9">
          <div class="d-flex w-100 justify-content-
            between">
            <h5 class="mb-1">{{org.login}}</h5>
          </div>
          <p class="mb-1">{{org.description}}</p>
        </div>
      </div>
    </a>
  </div>
</app-panel>
```

In the preceding HTML template, we place the main content of our component inside the app-panel component, passing an appropriate caption and icon. We display the name and description of each organization. Each organization is wrapped to an anchor element that points to the GitHub page of the organization.

9. Open the `organizations.component.scss` file and add the following CSS styles for the organization logos:

```css
img {
  width: 60px;
  height: 40px;
}
```

10. Open the `app.component.html` file and add the selector of `OrganizationsComponent` in the second element with the `col-12 col-sm-12` class selector:

```html
<div class="col-sm-9">
  <div class="row">
    <div class="col-12 col-sm-12">
      <app-repositories></app-repositories>
    </div>
  </div>
  <div class="row">
    <div class="col-12 col-sm-12">
      <app-organizations></app-organizations>
    </div>
  </div>
</div>
```

11. Run `ng serve` to start the application, and you should see the organization list under the repositories feature:

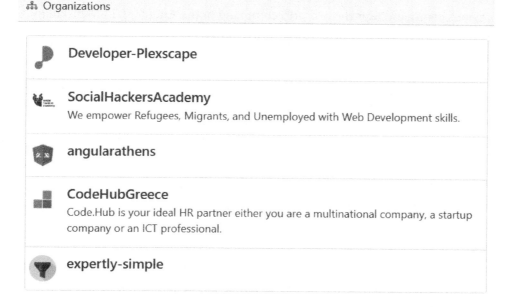

Figure 7.5 – Organizations

Our application now features a complete portfolio for the profile of a GitHub user. It displays the following:

- Personal information, a short biography, and social media links

- A list of public user repositories that contains links to each one for more information

- A list of organizations where the user is a member with links to each one for further details

In the next section, we will learn how to integrate Angular Universal and render our application in the server.

Integrating Angular Universal

Angular Universal is an Angular library that enables an Angular CLI application to be rendered on the server. An SSR application increases the loading speed of an Angular application and improves the loading of the first page.

To install Angular Universal in an existing Angular CLI application, we will use the following command of the Angular CLI:

```
ng add @nguniversal/express-engine
```

The previous command uses the ng add command of the Angular CLI to install the @nguniversal/express-engine npm package. The @nguniversal/express-engine package is the heart of the Angular Universal library and consists of a **Node.js Express** web server at its core.

When we execute the preceding command to install Angular Universal, we are not only installing the library but also modifying our Angular CLI workspace with the following files:

- angular.json: This creates new entries in the architect section to build and enable our Angular Universal application. One of these entries is the server property, which is responsible for building our application with SSR. It outputs the generated bundle into a separate server folder, inside the standard output folder of the Angular CLI application:

```
"options": {
  "outputPath": "dist/gh-portfolio/server",
  "main": "server.ts",
  "tsConfig": "tsconfig.server.json",
  "inlineStyleLanguage": "scss"
}
```

The original application bundle is now generated into a `browser` folder, inside the standard output folder:

```json
"options": {
  "outputPath": "dist/gh-portfolio/browser",
  "index": "src/index.html",
  "main": "src/main.ts",
  "polyfills": "src/polyfills.ts",
  "tsConfig": "tsconfig.app.json",
  "inlineStyleLanguage": "scss",
  "assets": [
    "src/favicon.ico",
    "src/assets"
  ],
  "styles": [
    "src/styles.scss"
  ],
  "scripts": []
}
```

Thus, an Angular Universal application generates two versions of the same Angular application, one version for the server and another one for the browser.

- `package.json`: This adds all the necessary npm dependencies and creates a handful set of npm scripts to start building with Angular Universal:

```json
"scripts": {
  "ng": "ng",
  "start": "ng serve",
  "build": "ng build",
  "watch": "ng build --watch --configuration
    development",
  "test": "ng test",
  "dev:ssr": "ng run gh-portfolio:serve-ssr",
  "serve:ssr": "node dist/gh-portfolio/server/
    main.js",
  "build:ssr": "ng build && ng run gh-
    portfolio:server",
  "prerender": "ng run gh-portfolio:prerender"
}
```

Scripts that contain the `:ssr` suffix are related to building and serving the Angular Universal application. The `prerender` script will create a prerendered version of an Angular application during build time. We will learn about the `prerender` script in the *Prerendering content during build* section.

- `server.ts`: This contains the Node.js Express application that will host the server-side rendered version of our portfolio application.

- `main.server.ts`: This is the main entry point of our Angular Universal application.

- `app.server.module.ts`: This is the main application module of the server-side rendered application.

- `tsconfig.server.json`: This is the TypeScript configuration for our Angular Universal application.

- `main.ts`: The main entry point of our Angular application loads the main application module only after the DOM has been loaded completely:

```
document.addEventListener('DOMContentLoaded', () => {
  platformBrowserDynamic().bootstrapModule(AppModule)
  .catch(err => console.error(err));
});
```

- `app.module.ts`: This calls the `withServerTransition` method of `BrowserModule` to load our application as a server-side rendered one:

```
@NgModule({
  declarations: [
    AppComponent,
    PersonalInfoComponent,
    PanelComponent
    RepositoriesComponent,
    OrganizationsComponent
  ],
  imports: [
    BrowserModule.withServerTransition({ appId:
      'serverApp' }),
    HttpClientModule
  ],
  providers: [],
```

```
    bootstrap: [AppComponent]
})
export class AppModule { }
```

> **Important note**
>
> Global JavaScript objects such as `window` and `document` are not available when rendering an Angular application in the server because there is no browser. Angular provides abstraction APIs for some of these objects, such as the DOCUMENT injection token. If you need to enable them conditionally, you can inject the PLATFORM_ID token and use the `isPlatformServer` or `isPlatformBrowser` methods from the `@angular/common` npm package to check on which platform your application is currently running:

```
import { Inject, PLATFORM_ID } from '@angular/core';
import { isPlatformBrowser } from '@angular/common';

export class CheckPlatformComponent {
  isBrowser: boolean;

  constructor( @Inject(PLATFORM_ID) platformId: any) {
    this.isBrowser = isPlatformBrowser(platformId);
  }
}
```

We can now run our GitHub portfolio application on the server using the following npm command:

```
npm run dev:ssr
```

To preview your GitHub portfolio application on the server, open your browser at `http://localhost:4200`.

You should typically see the application as it was before. So, what have we gained here? Angular Universal applications do not reveal their full potential when running in a development machine with a powerful processor and a lot of memory. Instead, we need to run and preview them in real-world cases, such as a slow network. We can use **Google Chrome Developer Tools** to emulate a slow network in a development environment:

1. Open the Google Chrome browser.
2. Toggle the developer tools and select the **Network** tab.

3. Select the **Slow 3G** option from the **Throttling** dropdown.

4. Enter `http://localhost:4200` in the address bar of your browser.

If you click on any link while the page is loading, you will notice that nothing happens. Why is that? The server first loads a static version of your application to display to the user until waiting for the actual Angular application to load in the background. During this FCP, all links except `routerLink` directives are not responding. Angular Universal will switch to the complete application when it has been fully loaded in the background.

Later, in the *Replaying events with preboot* section, we will see how to handle these events. In the meantime, we will investigate how to improve the loading speed of our application even more using prerendering in the following section.

Prerendering content during build

The `package.json` file of our Angular CLI workspace contains the `prerender` npm script that we can use to improve the first loading of our application. The script runs the `prerender` command from the `architect` section of the `angular.json` configuration file and prerenders the content of our application during build time. Let's see the effect that prerendering will have on our GitHub portfolio application:

1. Execute the following npm command to generate a prerendered version of the application:

```
npm run prerender
```

> **Important note**
> The `username` and `apiUrl` properties in the environment production file should be set correctly. Otherwise, the command will output errors in the terminal window of VSCode.

The preceding command will output a production bundle of the application into the `dist\gh-portfolio\browser` folder.

2. Navigate to the `dist\gh-portfolio\browser` folder and you should see two HTML files, `index.html` and the `index.original.html` file.

3. Open the `index.original.html` file and find the `app-root` HTML element. This is the main component of our Angular application where Angular will render the content of our application in the browser.

4. Open the `index.html` file and have a look again at the `app-root` element.

    The main component is not empty this time. Angular Universal has made all HTTP requests to the GitHub API and prefetched the content of our application during runtime. All component templates and styles have been prerendered in the main HTML file, which essentially means that we can view our application on a browser even without JavaScript enabled!

5. Execute the following command to start the prerendered version of our GitHub portfolio application:

```
npm run serve:ssr
```

    The preceding command will start the application at `http://localhost:4000`.

6. Disable JavaScript from the settings of your browser and navigate to `http://localhost:4000`.

The GitHub portfolio application that we created remains fully operational without having JavaScript enabled. The main page of the application is also rendered instantly without having the user wait for the application to load.

The previous scenario is a perfect fit for users who cannot afford to have JavaScript enabled on their devices. But what happens when the same prerendered version of the application is used by a user with JavaScript enabled? Let's learn more about that:

1. Enable JavaScript in your browser and toggle the developer tools.

2. Navigate to `http://localhost:4000`. Nothing different seems to happen at first sight. Nevertheless, the application loads instantly due to the prerendered content.

3. Inspect the **Network** tab and you will notice the following:

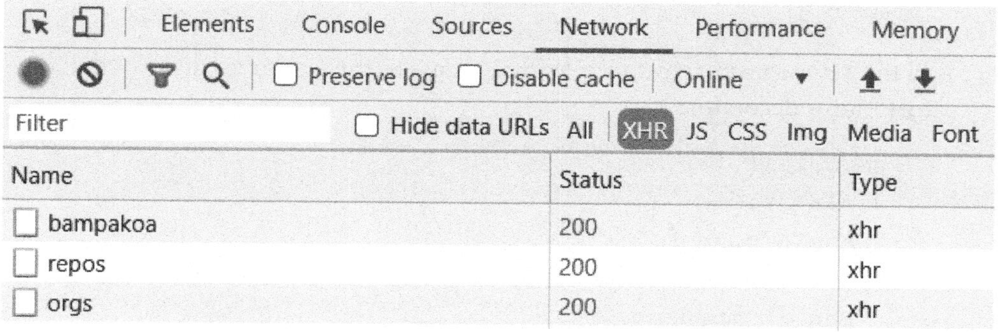

Figure 7.6 – Network tab (Google Chrome)

Our application initiates all HTTP requests to the GitHub API as if it was rendered from a browser. It essentially duplicates all HTTP requests needed from the application even if data has already been prerendered on the HTML page. Why is that?

The application makes one HTTP request for the browser rendered version and another for the SSR application because both versions have a different state. We can prevent the previous behavior by sharing the state between the server and the browser. More specifically, we can transfer the state of the server to the browser using a special-purpose Angular module of the Angular Universal library called `TransferHttpCacheModule`.

If we use `TransferHttpCacheModule`, the server will cache responses from the GitHub API and the browser will use the cache instead of initiating a new request. `TransferHttpCacheModule` solves the problem by installing an **HTTP interceptor** in the Angular application that ignores HTTP requests that have been handled by the server initially.

> **Important note**
>
> An HTTP interceptor is an Angular service that intercepts HTTP requests and responses that originate from the built-in HTTP client of the Angular framework.

To install `TransferHttpCacheModule` in our GitHub portfolio application, follow these steps:

1. Open the main module file of the Angular application, `app.module.ts`, and import `TransferHttpCacheModule` from the `@nguniversal/common` npm package:

```
import { TransferHttpCacheModule } from '@nguniversal/
common';
```

2. Add the `TransferHttpCacheModule` class to the `imports` array of the `@NgModule` decorator:

```
@NgModule({
  declarations: [
    AppComponent,
    PersonalInfoComponent,
    PanelComponent,
    RepositoriesComponent,
    OrganizationsComponent
```

```
    ],
    imports: [
      BrowserModule.withServerTransition({ appId:
      'serverApp' }),
      HttpClientModule,
      TransferHttpCacheModule
    ],
    providers: [],
    bootstrap: [AppComponent]
})
```

3. Open the main module file of the SSR application, app.server.module.ts, and import ServerTransferStateModule from the @angular/platform-server npm package:

```
import { ServerModule, ServerTransferStateModule }
  from '@angular/platform-server';
```

4. Add the ServerTransferStateModule class to the imports array of the @NgModule decorator:

```
@NgModule({
  imports: [
    AppModule,
    ServerModule,
    ServerTransferStateModule
  ],
  bootstrap: [AppComponent],
})
```

5. Execute the following command to prerender your application:

```
npm run prerender
```

6. Run the following command to start your prerendered application:

```
npm run serve:ssr
```

If you preview the portfolio application and inspect the **Network** tab of your browser, you will notice that it does not make additional HTTP requests. `TransferHttpCacheModule` intercepted all HTTP requests and stored them in the `TransferState` store of our application. TransferState is a key-value store that can be transferred from the server to the browser. The browser version of the application later can read the HTTP responses directly from the store without making an extra call.

We now have a fully prerendered version of our GitHub portfolio. But how can we optimize it further so that we can share it on a social media platform? We will learn more about SEO optimization techniques in the following section.

Enhancing SEO capabilities

SEO is the process of optimizing a website to be correctly indexed from a web crawler. A web crawler is a special-purpose software that is present on most search engines and can identify and index websites so that they are easily discoverable and linkable through their platforms.

Angular Universal does a great job of SEO by prerendering content during build time. Some web crawlers cannot execute JavaScript and build the dynamic content of an Angular application. Prerendering with Angular Universal eliminates the need for JavaScript, thus allowing web crawlers to do their best to identify the web application.

We can also help SEO by defining several tags in the `head` element of the main `index.html` file of an Angular application, such as `title`, `viewport`, and `charset`:

index.html

```html
<!doctype html>
<html lang="en">
<head>
  <meta charset="utf-8">
  <title>GhPortfolio</title>
  <base href="/">
  <meta name="viewport" content="width=device-width,
    initial-scale=1">
  <link rel="icon" type="image/x-icon" href="favicon.ico">
</head>
<body>
```

```
    <app-root></app-root>
</body>
</html>
```

You can find a list of available tags at `https://developer.mozilla.org/en-US/docs/Web/HTML/Element/meta/name`.

However, setting a tag in the `index.html` file is not adequate, especially when an Angular application has routing enabled and contains several routes. The Angular framework provides a couple of handy services that we can use to set tags programmatically. First, let's see how to set the title tag in our application:

1. Open the `app.component.ts` file and import the `Title` and `OnInit` Angular artifacts:

    ```
    import { Component, OnInit } from '@angular/core';
    import { environment } from
      '../environments/environment';
    import { Title } from '@angular/platform-browser';
    ```

2. Inject the `Title` service into the constructor of the `AppComponent` class:

    ```
    export class AppComponent {
        username = environment.username;

        constructor(private title: Title) {}
    }
    ```

3. Add the `OnInit` interface to the implemented interface list of the component and call the `setTitle` method of the `title` variable in the `ngOnInit` method:

    ```
    export class AppComponent implements OnInit {
        username = environment.username;

        constructor(private title: Title) {}

        ngOnInit() {
          this.title.setTitle('GitHub portfolio app');
        }
    }
    ```

4. Run `npm run dev:ssr` to preview the application, and you should see the title in the browser tab:

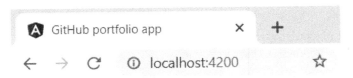

Figure 7.7 – Browser tab title

Similar to the `Title` service, we can use the `Meta` service to set meta tags for our application:

1. Open the `app.component.ts` file and import `Meta` from the `@angular/platform-browser` npm package:

```
import { Meta } from '@angular/platform-browser';
```

2. Inject the `Meta` service into the constructor of the `AppComponent` class:

```
constructor(private title: Title, private meta: Meta) {}
```

3. Use the `addTags` method of the `meta` variable to add some meta tags to the `ngOnInit` method:

```
ngOnInit(): void {
    this.title.setTitle('GitHub portfolio app');
    this.meta.addTags([
        {
            name: 'description',
            content: `${this.username}'s GitHub portfolio`
        },
        {
            name: 'author',
            content: this.username
        }
    ]);
}
```

In the preceding code, we add two meta tags. The first one sets the description that contains the username of the current GitHub profile. The second one sets the `author` tag to be the same as the username of the GitHub profile.

4. Run `npm run dev:ssr` to start the application and navigate to
    `http://localhost:4200`.

5. Use your browser to inspect the page, and you should see the following meta tags in
    the `head` element of the page:

```html
▼<head>
    <meta charset="utf-8">
    <title>GitHub portfolio app</title>
    <base href="/">
    <meta name="viewport" content="width=device-width, initial-scale=1">
    <link rel="icon" type="image/x-icon" href="favicon.ico">
    <link rel="stylesheet" href="styles.css">
  ▶<style>…</style>
  ▶<style>…</style>
  ▶<style>…</style>
  ▶<style>…</style>
  ▶<style>…</style>
    <meta name="description" content="<Your GitHub login>'s GitHub portfolio">
    <meta name="author" content="<Your GitHub login>">
```

Figure 7.8 – Application head element

Each of the popular social platforms, such as **Twitter**, **Facebook**, and **LinkedIn**, requires
its own meta tags so that the URL of an SSR application can be correctly displayed on
their platforms. If you do not want to add them manually using the `Meta` service of the
Angular framework, you can use the **ngx-seo** library, which provides built-in methods for
each platform. You can get the library from the npm registry at `https://www.npmjs.com/package/ngx-seo`.

In the following section, we will conclude our project by learning how to replay events not
supported by an SSR application.

Replaying events with preboot

In the *Integrating Angular Universal* section, we saw that an SSR application does not
respond to user events other than navigations with the `routerLink` directive until it is
entirely bootstrapped. We will now learn how to queue those events and replay them when
the application has been fully loaded using the preboot library. Let's see how to use it:

1. Execute the following npm command to install the library:

```
npm install preboot
```

2. Open the `app.module.ts` file and import `PrebootModule` from the `preboot` npm package:

```
import { PrebootModule } from 'preboot';
```

3. Add the `PrebootModule` class to the `imports` array of the `@NgModule` decorator:

```
@NgModule({
  declarations: [
    AppComponent,
    PersonalInfoComponent,
    PanelComponent,
    RepositoriesComponent,
    OrganizationsComponent
  ],
  imports: [
    BrowserModule.withServerTransition({ appId:
      'serverApp' }),
    HttpClientModule,
    TransferHttpCacheModule,
    PrebootModule.withConfig({ appRoot: 'app-root' })
  ],
  providers: [],
  bootstrap: [AppComponent]
})
```

We use the `withConfig` method of `PrebootModule` to define the main component of our Angular application. It accepts an options object of the `PrebootOptions` type that contains various properties, which you can find at `https://github.com/angular/preboot#PrebootOptions`. One of the options is the `appRoot` property, which defines the selector of the main component.

The purpose of the preboot library is to maintain a consistent user experience while the state of the application is transferred from the server to the browser.

To verify its functionality, run `npm run dev:ssr` to start the SSR application and use the steps described in the *Integrating Angular Universal* section to simulate a slow network. If you try to click on any link while the application is loading, you will notice that your browser will navigate to the selected link after the application has been fully loaded in the browser.

Summary

In this project, we build a portfolio application for our GitHub profile. Initially, we learned how to interact with the GitHub API in a new Angular application. We also used Bootstrap CSS and Bootstrap Icons to provide a beautiful user interface for our portfolio application.

We then saw how to convert our Angular application into an SSR application using Angular Universal. We learned how to benefit from prerendering content when users have low-end and slow-performant devices and some of the potential pitfalls of this technique.

We used some of the available SEO techniques that the Angular framework offers to improve the discoverability of our application. Finally, we installed the preboot library to improve the user experience of our application during loading.

In the next chapter, we will learn about the monorepo architecture and how we can manage the state of an Angular application.

Practice questions

Let's take a look at a few practice questions:

1. What is the purpose of environment files in an Angular application?
2. How do we subscribe to an observable in the template of a component?
3. Which command do we use for installing Angular Universal?
4. How can we differentiate programmatically between browser and server platforms?
5. Which command generates a prerendered version of an SSR application?
6. Which Angular module do we use to transfer the state from the server to the browser?
7. Which Angular service do we use to set the title of an Angular application?
8. Which Angular service do we use to set meta tags in an Angular application?
9. What is the purpose of the preboot library?
10. How do we enable preboot in an SSR application?

Further reading

Here are some links to build upon what we learned in the chapter:

- Angular Univeral guide: `https://angular.io/guide/universal`
- GitHub REST API: `https://docs.github.com/en/rest`
- Bootstrap CSS: `https://getbootstrap.com/`
- Bootstrap Icons: `https://icons.getbootstrap.com/`
- Angular HTTP guide: `https://angular.io/guide/http`
- TransferHttpCacheModule: `https://github.com/angular/universal/blob/master/docs/transfer-http.md`
- preboot: `https://github.com/angular/preboot`

8
Building an Enterprise Portal Using Nx Monorepo Tools and NgRx

Typical enterprise applications usually consist of a backend and a frontend system. The backend is responsible for interacting with a database for data persistence and exposes a REST API. The frontend communicates with the backend system via the REST interface to exchange data. In some cases, the frontend system can consist of more than one application, including a web interface or a mobile application. Keeping all these applications and systems in separate source control repositories does not scale well, and it is not easy to maintain and build. Alternatively, we can follow **monorepo** architecture for such large enterprise applications, where each application resides in a separate location inside the same repository.

A popular tool in the Angular ecosystem that embraces monorepo architecture is **Nx Dev Tools**. Combining an Nx monorepo application with a state management library can significantly level up your application. **NgRx**, a popular state management library for Angular applications, can help us keep a consistent and manageable state globally.

In this chapter, we will investigate both technologies by building an enterprise portal application for visiting **points of interest** (**POIs**). We will cover the following topics:

- Creating a monorepo application using Nx
- Creating user-specific portals
- Managing application state with NgRx
- Visualizing data with graphs

Essential background theory and context

Nx Dev Tools is a suite of development tools and libraries for building web applications based on monorepo architecture. A typical Nx application can contain many applications and shared libraries inside a single workspace. The flexibility of monorepo architecture allows for any type of application, backend or frontend, to use the same libraries inside the workspace.

> **Important note**
> In this project, we will consider *only* frontend applications built with the Angular framework.

Nx Dev Tools provides developers with the following features:

- **Centralized management of application dependencies**: Each application has the same version of the Angular framework so that it is easy to update all at once.
- **Fast builds**: The build process of an Nx application involves only those artifacts that have been changed and does not do a complete rebuild of the entire monorepo.
- **Distributed caching**: Each build of the application can be cached locally or to the cloud, using **Nx Cloud**, to improve the build process of other developers that build similar artifacts.

In a large Angular enterprise application, maintaining a consistent global state is a tedious process. The use of `@Input` and `@Output` decorators to communicate between Angular components is not always viable, especially when there are many levels of components that need to share the same state.

NgRx is a library that provides efficient management of the global application state powered by the **RxJS** library. The main building blocks of NgRx are the following:

- **Store**: The central storage that keeps the global state of the application.

- **Reducer**: A function that listens to a specific event and interacts directly with the store. Reducers derive a new state of the application based on the existing one from the store.

- **Action**: A unique event that is dispatched from components and services and triggers a reducer. Actions can be any type of such interaction initiated by the user or an external source such as an HTTP call.

- **Effect**: Handles interaction with external sources such as making an HTTP call or exchanging data with the local storage. Effects take care of side effects in an application by hiding the business logic from components.

- **Selector**: A function that selects the application state or a specific part of it (slice) from the store. Selectors support **memoization**, a technique where they can return the same state if called with the same parameters, greatly enhancing the performance of an application.

Project overview

In this project, we will build an Angular enterprise application for managing POI visits on a map. The application will consist of two portals where one will allow a visitor to select a POI from a list and view its location on a map. Another portal will allow an administrator to view the traffic of each POI.

First, we will build an Angular application from scratch using Nx Dev Tools. We will then create the skeleton of each portal by adding the essential components of our application. After we have scaffolded our application, we will start adding the functionality of the visitor portal using NgRx. Finally, we will implement the administrator portal and learn how to use an Angular library for visualizing data in a graph.

Build time: 3 hours

Getting started

The following software tools are required for completing this project:

- **Nx Console**: A **VSCode** extension that provides a graphical interface for working with Nx Dev Tools. You can find out more about installing it in *Chapter 1, Creating Your First Web Application in Angular*.

- **GitHub material**: The code related to this chapter can be found in the `Chapter08` folder at `https://github.com/PacktPublishing/Angular-Projects-Second-Edition`.

Creating a monorepo application using Nx

Nx Dev Tools provides developers with tools for working with monorepos, including the following:

- **create-nx-workspace**: An npm package that scaffolds a new Nx monorepo application.

- **Nx CLI**: A command-line interface that runs commands against a monorepo application. Nx CLI extends the Angular CLI to provide more commands, and it is faster due to the distributed caching mechanism.

> **Tip**
>
> It is recommended to use the *Quick Open* feature of VSCode when working with Nx monorepos. The number of generated folders and files will significantly increase, and it will be challenging to navigate through them. You can find out more at `https://code.visualstudio.com/docs/editor/editingevolved#_quick-file-navigation`.

When we use the preceding npm package to create a new Nx monorepo workspace, it will check whether Nx CLI has already been installed. To install Nx CLI, run the following command in a terminal:

```
npm install -g nx
```

The preceding command will install the nx npm package globally on our system. We can now scaffold a new Nx monorepo workspace using the following command:

```
npx create-nx-workspace packt --appName=tour --preset=angular
--style=css --linter=eslint --nx-cloud=false --routing
```

The preceding command uses npx, an npm command-line tool that allows us to execute an npm package without installing it first. It executes the `create-nx-workspace` package passing the following options:

- `packt`: The name of the Nx monorepo workspace. In large enterprise environments, we typically use the organization name.

- `--appName=tour`: The name of the application.

- `--preset=angular`: Nx supports applications built with various JavaScript frameworks. The `preset` option defines what type of application we want to build.

- `--style=css`: Indicates that our application will use the CSS stylesheet format.
- `--linter=eslint`: Configures our application to use **ESLint** as the default linter.
- `--nx-cloud=false`: Disables Nx Cloud for our application.
- `--routing`: Enables Angular routing in the application.

> **Important note**
>
> Creating a new Nx workspace may take some time to complete, as it installs all the necessary packages for an enterprise environment.

After the creation of the workspace has been completed, we can run it to verify that everything has been set up correctly:

1. Open the project in the VSCode editor and click on the **Nx Console** menu in the VSCode sidebar.

2. Select the **Serve** option from the **GENERATE & RUN TARGET** pane:

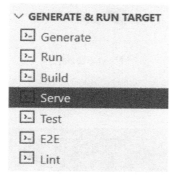

Figure 8.1 – Serve option

3. In the dialog that appears, select the application that we created:

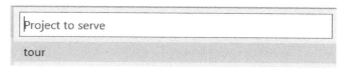

Figure 8.2 – Application selection

4. Click on the **Run** button of the **Serve** tab to build the application and open your browser at `http://localhost:4200`:

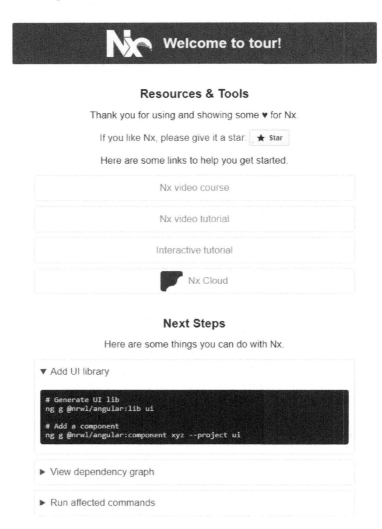

Figure 8.3 – Minimal Nx application

Congratulations! Your new application has been configured correctly! Nx creates a minimal skeleton application just like Angular CLI does for our convenience so that we can build our features on top of that.

In the next section, we will dive deeper into Nx Dev Tools by creating the administrator and visitor portals in our workspace.

Creating user-specific portals

Our application will consist of two portals that different users will use. Visitors will be able to view a list of POIs and select them on a map. Administrators will be able to view statistics for each POI. We will learn more about how to use Nx Dev Tools in the following sections:

- Building the visitor portal
- Building the administrator portal

Each portal will be a separate Nx library that will be loaded according to the URL entered in the address bar of the browser. Organizing our code in libraries allows us to reuse it between different applications and build and test it individually. We will start building the visitor portal in the following section.

Building the visitor portal

The visitor portal will be a library inside the Nx workspace that will be loaded by default. Let's see how we can build that library with Nx Console:

1. Run Nx Console from the VSCode sidebar and select the **Generate** option from the **GENERATE & RUN TARGET** pane:

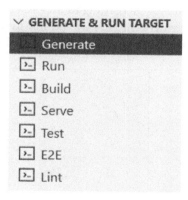

Figure 8.4 – Generate option

2. Select the **@nrwl/angular – library** option from the dialog that appears. The **@nrwl/angular** namespace contains schematics that we can execute in an Nx monorepo for Angular applications.

> **Important note**
> If you do not see the option in the dialog, restart VSCode.

3. Enter `visitor` as the name of the library and click the **Run** button in the **Generate** tab:

name

Library name

> visitor

Figure 8.5 – Library name

> **Tip**
> When you were typing the name of the library, you may have noticed that Nx was running the `generate` command in the terminal. Well, it did not run it actually. Instead, it was mimicking the effect of running the command in your system; a technique called **dry run**.

Nx will create the `visitor` library inside the `libs` folder of our workspace. The library does not contain any components yet. According to the project specifications, the visitor portal will contain a list of POIs where the user will be able to select them and view their location on a map. Thus, we need to create an Angular component with the following layout:

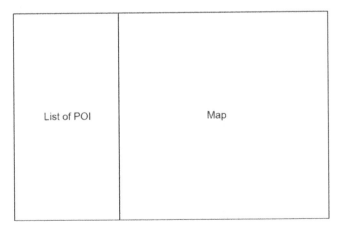

List of POI   Map

Figure 8.6 – Visitor portal layout

In the previous diagram, the portal consists of the sidebar that displays a POI list and the main content area for displaying the map. Instead of creating the layout from scratch, we will use Angular Material, which contains a handful of ready-made layouts, including one with a sidebar.

Before working with Angular Material, we need to install it in our application with the following command:

```
ng add @angular/material --theme=deeppurple-amber
--typography=true --animations=true
```

We use the `ng add` command of the Angular CLI to install the `@angular/material` npm package, passing additional options. You can learn more about the installation of Angular Material and its available options in *Chapter 4, Building a PWA Weather Application Using Angular Service Worker.*

Installing Angular Material in our application will also install the `@angular/cdk` npm package. `@angular/cdk` is called the **Component Dev Kit (CDK)** and contains specific behaviors and interactions used to build Angular Material.

> **Important note**
> The CDK can be used to build custom UI libraries without the need to rely on Angular Material. We will learn how to build such libraries in *Chapter 9, Building a Component UI Library Using Angular CLI and Angular CDK.*

The Angular Material library contains the following component templates that we can use:

- **address-form**: It uses Angular Material form controls for entering information about addresses.
- **navigation**: It contains a side navigation component along with a content placeholder and a title bar.
- **dashboard**: It consists of multiple Angular Material card and menu components that are organized in a grid layout.
- **table**: It displays an Angular Material table with sorting and filtering enabled.
- **tree**: It represents a visual folder structure in a tree view.

In our case, we will use the `navigation` component because we need a sidebar. Let's see how we can generate that component:

1. Open Nx Console from the VSCode sidebar and select the **Generate** option.

2. Select the **@angular/material – navigation** option from the dialog that appears. The **@angular/material** namespace contains schematics that we can run to create Angular Material components.

3. Enter the name of the component:

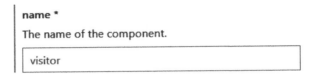

Figure 8.7 – Component name

4. Select the **visitor** library from the **project** dropdown that we created earlier:

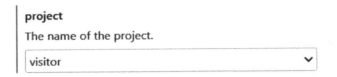

Figure 8.8 – Project selection

> **Important note**
> If the library does not appear in the dropdown, restart VSCode.

5. Check the **flat** option so that the component will not be generated in a separate folder:

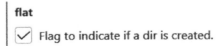

Figure 8.9 – The flat option

The component will be the main one of the library, so we want to have it in the same folder with its related module file.

6. Enter the folder where the component will be created:

> **path**
>
> The path to create the component.
>
> libs/visitor/src/lib

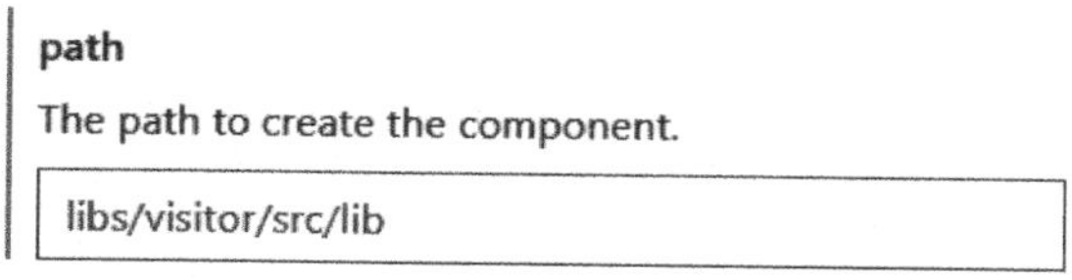

Figure 8.10 – Component folder

> **Tip**
> There is no need to define the module where the component will be created because the Angular CLI can deduce it directly from the **path** option.

7. Click the **Run** button to generate the component.

Nx Console will create the `visitor` component in the `visitor` library of the Nx workspace. We now need to connect it with the main application of the workspace:

1. Open the `app.component.css` file and remove all CSS styles because our application will be styled using the Angular Material library.

2. Open the `app.component.html` file and replace its content with the following HTML template:

```
<router-outlet></router-outlet>
```

The `router-outlet` component is part of the Angular router and is a placeholder where we will load our portals.

3. Open the `app.module.ts` file and add a route configuration that will load the visitor portal when the URL contains the `tour` path:

```
import { RouterModule } from '@angular/router';


@NgModule({
    declarations: [AppComponent],
    imports: [BrowserModule, BrowserAnimationsModule,
        RouterModule.forRoot([
            { path: 'tour', loadChildren: () =>
                import('@packt/visitor').then(m =>
                    m.VisitorModule) },
```

```
    { path: '', pathMatch: 'full', redirectTo:
      'tour' }
   ])
  ],
  providers: [],
  bootstrap: [AppComponent],
})
```

The route configuration contains two paths. The *default* path, denoted by the empty string, redirects to the `tour` path. The `tour` path lazily loads the module of the `visitor` library.

The `@packt` prefix in the `import` method is the organization name that we configured when creating the Nx workspace. When we want to import an artifact of our project, we will import it directly from the `@packt` namespace. It behaves as a path alias in our project.

4. Open the `visitor.module.ts` file and add a route configuration to load the `visitor` component that we created:

```
import { RouterModule } from '@angular/router';


@NgModule({
  imports: [CommonModule, LayoutModule,
    MatToolbarModule, MatButtonModule,
     MatSidenavModule, MatIconModule, MatListModule,
    RouterModule.forChild([
      { path: '', component: VisitorComponent }
    ])
  ],
  declarations: [VisitorComponent],
})
```

The route configuration will activate `VisitorComponent` by default as soon as `VisitorModule` is loaded using the `tour` path in *step 3*.

If we now run the **Serve** command from Nx Console and navigate to `http://localhost:4200`, we should see the following output:

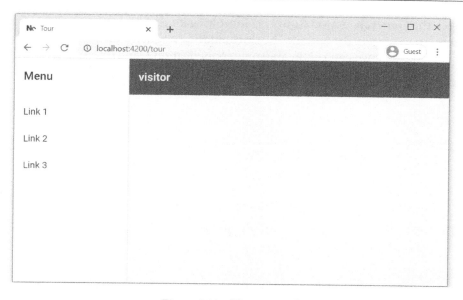

Figure 8.11 – Visitor portal

The Angular router will redirect us to `http://localhost:4200/tour`, and it will display the visitor portal. It currently contains some demo data that Angular Material entered when we generated the navigation component. We will revisit it in the *Managing application state with NgRx* section to implement the full functionality using NgRx. For the time being, we will continue by building the administrator portal in the next section.

Building the administrator portal

The administrator portal will be an Nx library with a single component, just like the visitor portal, except that it will not be based on an Angular Material template. Let's start scaffolding the structure of the library using Nx Console:

1. Run Nx Console from the VSCode sidebar and select the **Generate** option.

2. In the dialog that appears, select the **@nrwl/angular – library** option.

3. Enter `admin` as the name of the library and click the **Run** button:

name
Library name

    admin

Figure 8.12 – Library name

4. Click the **Generate** option from Nx Console again and select the **@schematics/ angular – component** option. The **@schematics/angular** namespace contains schematics that we can run in an Angular application using the Angular CLI.

5. Enter the same name for the component as that of the library:

name *

The name of the component.

admin

Figure 8.13 – Component name

6. Select the library that we created in the **project** drop-down list:

project

The name of the project.

admin

Figure 8.14 – Project selection

> **Important note**
> If the library does not appear in the dropdown, restart VSCode.

7. Check the **flat** option so that the component will be created in the same folder with the module file of the library:

flat

Create the new files at the top level of the current project.

Figure 8.15 – The flat option

8. Enter the folder where the component will be created and click the **Run** button:

path

The path at which to create the component file, relative to the current workspace. Default is a folder with the same name as the component in the project root.

libs/admin/src/lib

Figure 8.16 – Component folder

The Angular CLI will create the admin component inside the folder of the admin library. We now need to wire up the admin library to the monorepo application:

1. Open the app.module.ts file and add a new route configuration object for the admin library:

```
RouterModule.forRoot([
  { path: 'admin', loadChildren: () =>
  import('@packt/admin').then(m => m.AdminModule) },
  { path: 'tour', loadChildren: () =>
  import('@packt/visitor').then(m => m.VisitorModule)
    },
  { path: '', pathMatch: 'full', redirectTo: 'tour' }
])
```

2. Open the admin.module.ts file and add a route configuration to activate AdminComponent by default:

```
import { NgModule } from '@angular/core';
import { CommonModule } from '@angular/common';
import { AdminComponent } from './admin.component';
import { RouterModule } from '@angular/router';

@NgModule({
  imports: [
    CommonModule,
    RouterModule.forChild([
      { path: '', component: AdminComponent }
    ])
  ],
  declarations: [
    AdminComponent
  ],
})
export class AdminModule {}
```

3. Use the **Serve** option of Nx Console to run the application and navigate to http://localhost:4200.

4. Edit the URL address of the browser and change it to
    `http://localhost:4200/admin`:

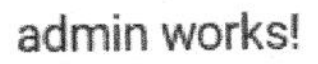

admin works!

Figure 8.17 – Administrator portal

The page will display the default template of the main component of the administrator library.

We have now completed the scaffolding of our enterprise application. First, we created the Nx monorepo workspace that will host the portals of the application. Then, we used Nx Console to generate our portals along with their main components. We also installed Angular Material to use its UI elements in our components.

In the next section, we will implement the functionality of the visitor portal using NgRx.

Managing application state with NgRx

The visitor portal will allow the user to see a list of available POIs and select one to view its location on a map. The list of available POIs and the selection of a POI is the global state of our application. We will integrate NgRx for managing the application state in the visitor portal by completing the following tasks:

- Configuring the state
- Interacting with the store

Let's begin by configuring the state of our application in the following section.

Configuring the state

Our application will consist of a root state for the whole application and a feature state for the visitor portal. We will start by executing the following command to create the root state:

```
nx generate ngrx app --root --no-interactive --project=tour
--module=apps/tour/src/app/app.module.ts
```

The preceding command uses the `generate` command of Nx CLI, passing the following options:

- `ngrx`: Indicates that we want to set up an NgRx state
- `app`: The name of the state
- `--root`: Indicates that we want to configure a root state

- `--no-interactive`: Disables interactive input prompts

- `--project=tour`: The name of the application in our workspace

- `--module=apps/tour/src/app/app.module.ts`: Registers the state with the main Angular module of our application

The previous command will add all necessary NgRx npm packages in the `package.json` file and install them. It will also modify the `app.module.ts` file to configure all NgRx-related artifacts such as the store, effects, and **Store DevTools**.

> **Tip**
>
> Store DevTools is an npm package of the NgRx library that provides debugging, monitoring, and instrumentation capabilities to the state of an NgRx application. It must be used in conjunction with the **Redux DevTools** browser extension, which can be found at `https://github.com/zalmoxisus/redux-devtools-extension`.

The `visitor` library itself will not manage the data for the state of the visitor portal. Instead, we will create a new library in our Nx workspace that will fetch and store data in the feature state. Execute the following command of Nx CLI to create a new library:

```
nx generate lib poi
```

The preceding command will generate the `poi` library in our Nx monorepo.

> **Tip**
>
> The `generate` command of Nx CLI that we used has the same effect as creating the library using Nx Console.

Now that we have created the library, we can set up the feature state using the following command:

```
nx generate ngrx poi --project=poi --no-interactive
--module=libs/poi/src/lib/poi.module.ts --barrels
```

The preceding command uses the `generate` command of Nx CLI to register a feature state passing additional options:

- `ngrx`: Indicates that we want to set up an NgRx state.

- `poi`: The name of the state.

- `--project=poi`: The name of the library in our workspace.

- `--no-interactive`: Disables interactive input prompts.
- `--module=libs/poi/src/lib/poi.module.ts`: Registers the state with the Angular module of our library.
- `--barrels`: Indicates to use barrel files to re-export NgRx artifacts such as selectors and state. The name of a barrel file is usually `index.ts` by convention.

The preceding command will create a folder, named `+state` by convention, inside our library that contains the following files:

- `poi.actions.ts`: Defines NgRx actions for the feature state
- `poi.effects.ts`: Defines NgRx effects for the feature state
- `poi.models.ts`: Defines an entity interface for POI data
- `poi.reducer.ts`: Defines NgRx reducers for the feature state
- `poi.selectors.ts`: Defines NgRx selectors for the feature state

Nx CLI has done most of the job by adding the necessary content in the previous files, eliminating the boilerplate code for us. We now need to create an Angular service in the library that will fetch the POI data:

1. Open the `poi.models.ts` file and add the following properties to the `PoiEntity` interface:

   ```
   export interface PoiEntity {
       id: string | number; // Primary ID
       name: string;
       lat: number;
       lng: number;
       description: string;
       imgUrl: string;
   }
   ```

2. Execute the following command to generate the Angular service:

   ```
   nx generate service poi --project=poi
   ```

   The preceding command will create an Angular service called `poi` in the `poi` library.

3. Open the `poi.service.ts` file and add the following `import` statements:

```
import { HttpClient } from '@angular/common/http';
import { Observable } from 'rxjs';
import { PoiEntity } from '..';
```

4. Inject `HttpClient` in the constructor of the `PoiService` class and create a method to get POI data from the `assets/poi.json` file:

```
export class PoiService {

  constructor(private http: HttpClient) {}

  getAll(): Observable<PoiEntity[]> {
    return
      this.http.get<PoiEntity[]>('assets/poi.json');
  }
}
```

We use the built-in HTTP client of the Angular framework to get POI data by initiating a GET HTTP request.

> **Important note**
>
> You can get the `poi.json` file from the GitHub repository of the *Getting started* section and copy it to the `apps\tour\src\assets` folder of your workspace.

5. Open the `poi.effects.ts` file and add the following `import` statements:

```
import { map } from 'rxjs/operators';
import { PoiService } from '../poi.service';
```

6. Inject `PoiService` in the constructor of the `PoiEffects` class:

```
constructor(private actions$: Actions, private
poiService: PoiService) {}
```

7. Modify the `init$` property to use the `poiService` variable:

```
init$ = createEffect(() =>
  this.actions$.pipe(
    ofType(PoiActions.init),
    fetch({
      run: (action) => {
        return this.poiService.getAll().pipe(
          map(pois => PoiActions.loadPoiSuccess({ poi:
            pois }))
        )
      },

      onError: (action, error) => {
        console.error('Error', error);
        return PoiActions.loadPoiFailure({ error });
      },
    })
  )
);
```

The effect is responsible for listening to all actions that are dispatched in the store. As soon as a `PoiActions.init` action is dispatched, the `init$` property is triggered and calls the `getAll` method of the `poiService` variable. The `init$` property knows which action to listen for by the parameters in the `ofType` operator.

> **Tip**
> The `ofType` operator can accept more than one action.

If the data is fetched successfully, the effect will dispatch a new action in the store, `PoiActions.loadPoiSuccess`, with POI data as the payload. If there is a failure getting the data, it will dispatch a `PoiActions.loadPoiFailure` action in the store.

8. Open the `app.module.ts` file and import `HttpClientModule` from the `@angular/common/http` namespace:

```
import { HttpClientModule } from
  '@angular/common/http';
```

Add the `HttpClientModule` class also in the `imports` array of the `@NgModule` decorator.

The global state of our application is now configured and ready to be used. In the following section, we will create additional Angular components in the `visitor` library that will interact with the feature state of our application.

Interacting with the store

The visitor portal will interact with the feature state of our application through two Angular components. One component will display the list of POIs and allow the user to select one. The other component will display a **Google Maps** map and display the selected POI on it.

Initially, we will build the component that displays the list of POIs:

1. Open the `visitor.module.ts` file and add the following `import` statement:

```
import { PoiModule } from '@packt/poi';
```

2. Add `PoiModule` in the `imports` array of the `@NgModule` decorator:

```
@NgModule({
    imports: [CommonModule, LayoutModule,
      MatToolbarModule, MatButtonModule,
       MatSidenavModule, MatIconModule, MatListModule,
      RouterModule.forChild([
        { path: '', component: VisitorComponent }
      ]),
      PoiModule
    ],
    declarations: [VisitorComponent],
})
```

We import `PoiModule` so that the `poi` feature state is registered in the store as soon as the visitor portal is loaded.

3. Execute the following command of Nx CLI to create the Angular component:

```
nx generate component poi-list --project=visitor
```

4. Open the `poi-list.component.ts` file and add the following `import` statements:

```
import { Store } from '@ngrx/store';
import { PoiActions, PoiSelectors } from '@packt/poi';
```

5. Inject the `Store` service in the constructor of the `PoiListComponent` class:

```
constructor(private store: Store) { }
```

6. Dispatch the `PoiActions.init` action in the store to fetch POI data when the component is initialized:

```
ngOnInit(): void {
    this.store.dispatch(PoiActions.init());
}
```

We execute the action as a method and pass its result to the `dispatch` method of the `store` variable.

7. Create a component property that invokes the `PoiSelectors.getAllPoi` selector to list POI data from the store:

```
pois$ = this.store.select(PoiSelectors.getAllPoi);
```

We use the `select` method of the `store` variable to execute the selector.

> **Important note**
>
> We did not create the `PoiSelectors.getAllPoi` selector. NgRx did it for us when we generated the feature state in the `poi` library.

8. Open the `poi-list.component.html` file and replace its content with the following HTML template:

```
<mat-action-list *ngFor="let poi of pois$ | async">
    <button mat-list-item>{{poi.name}}</button>
</mat-action-list>
```

We use the `mat-action-list` component of the Angular Material library to display each POI as a single action item. We subscribe to the `pois$` property using the `async` pipe and create a `button` element with the `mat-list-item` directive for each POI.

9. Open the `visitor.component.html` file and replace the `mat-nav-list` component with the selector of the Angular component that we created:

```
<mat-sidenav #drawer class="sidenav" fixedInViewport
    [attr.role]="(isHandset$ | async) ? 'dialog' :
        'navigation'"
```

```
    [mode]="(isHandset$ | async) ? 'over' : 'side'"
    [opened]="(isHandset$ | async) === false">
  <mat-toolbar>Menu</mat-toolbar>
  <packt-poi-list></packt-poi-list>
</mat-sidenav>
```

Use Nx Console to start the application, and you should see the following output in the menu sidebar:

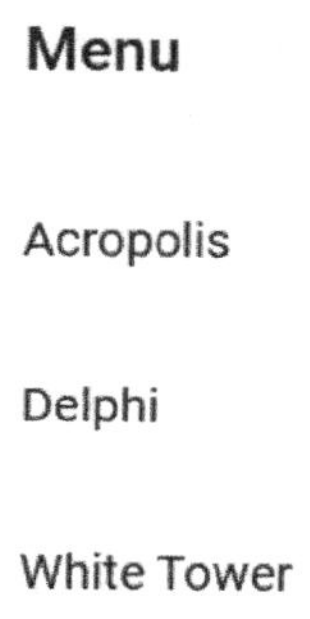

Menu

Acropolis

Delphi

White Tower

Figure 8.18 – List of POIs

We have already created the Angular component that will display the list of available POIs. Let's see now how to create the component to display a POI on the map using Google Maps.

The Angular Material library contains a component for Google Maps that we can use in our application:

1. Run the following command of the npm client to install the Google Maps component:

    ```
    npm install @angular/google-maps
    ```

2. Open the `visitor.module.ts` file and add the following `import` statement:

    ```
    import { GoogleMapsModule } from '@angular/google-maps';
    ```

3. Add `GoogleMapsModule` into the `imports` array of the `@NgModule` decorator:

    ```
    @NgModule({
      imports: [CommonModule, LayoutModule,
        MatToolbarModule, MatButtonModule,
        MatSidenavModule, MatIconModule, MatListModule,
        RouterModule.forChild([
    ```

```
      { path: '', component: VisitorComponent }
    ]),
    PoiModule,
    GoogleMapsModule
  ],
  declarations: [VisitorComponent, PoiListComponent],
})
```

4. Open the index.html file of the application and include the **Google Maps JavaScript API** inside the head element:

```
<script src="https://maps.googleapis.com/maps/api/js">
  </script>
```

Now that we have installed and registered Google Maps in our application, let's create the Angular component that will host it:

1. Execute the following command of Nx CLI to create a new Angular component:

```
nx generate component map --project=visitor
```

2. Open the map.component.ts file and add the following import statements:

```
import { Store } from '@ngrx/store';
import { PoiSelectors } from '@packt/poi';
```

3. Inject the Store service in the constructor of the MapComponent class and declare a property to get the selected POI from the store:

```
export class MapComponent implements OnInit {

  poi$ = this.store.select(PoiSelectors.getSelected);

  constructor(private store: Store) { }

  ngOnInit(): void {
  }

}
```

4. Open the `map.component.html` file and replace its content with the following HTML template:

```html
<google-map height="100%" width="auto" *ngIf="poi$ |
  async as poi" [center]="poi">
  <map-marker [position]="poi"></map-marker>
</google-map>
```

In the preceding template, we subscribe to the `poi$` property using the `async` pipe. As soon as we get a selected POI from the store, we display a `google-map` component and set the center of the map to the POI coordinates. Furthermore, we add a marker on the map in the specified POI coordinates.

5. Open the `visitor.component.html` file and replace the contents of the `mat-sidenav-content` component with the selector of `MapComponent`:

```html
<mat-sidenav-content>
  <mat-toolbar color="primary">
    <button
      type="button"
      aria-label="Toggle sidenav"
      mat-icon-button
      (click)="drawer.toggle()"
      *ngIf="isHandset$ | async">
      <mat-icon aria-label="Side nav toggle icon">
        menu</mat-icon>
    </button>
    <span>visitor</span>
  </mat-toolbar>
  <packt-map></packt-map>
</mat-sidenav-content>
```

The Angular component that we created will show the location of a POI on the map as soon as we select it from the list. If you try to select a POI from the list, you will notice that nothing happens. Why is that?

The global state of the application does not currently know when a POI has been selected. We need to add the necessary code for setting the selected POI and interacting with the store:

1. Open the `poi.actions.ts` file and add a new action for passing the ID of the selected POI:

```
export const selectPoi = createAction(
  '[Poi/API] Select Poi',
  props<{ poiId: string | number }>()
);
```

2. Open the `poi.reducer.ts` file and add a new statement in the `poiReducer` property that will listen to the `selectPoi` action and save the selected POI in the store:

```
const poiReducer = createReducer(
  initialState,
  on(PoiActions.init, (state) => ({ ...state, loaded:
    false, error: null })),
  on(PoiActions.loadPoiSuccess, (state, { poi }) =>
    poiAdapter.setAll(poi, { ...state, loaded: true })
  ),
  on(PoiActions.loadPoiFailure, (state, { error }) =>
    ({ ...state, error })),
  on(PoiActions.selectPoi, (state, { poiId }) => ({
    ...state, selectedId: poiId }))
);
```

3. Open the `poi-list.component.ts` file and import the `PoiEntity` interface:

```
import { Component, OnInit } from '@angular/core';
import { Store } from '@ngrx/store';
import { PoiActions, PoiEntity, PoiSelectors } from
  '@packt/poi';
```

4. Create a new method to dispatch the `selectPoi` action to the store along with the selected `PoiEntity`:

```
selectPoi(poi: PoiEntity) {
    this.store.dispatch(PoiActions.selectPoi({poiId:
      poi.id}));
}
```

5. Open the `poi-list.component.html` file and bind the `selectPoi` method to the `click` event of the `button` element:

```
<mat-action-list *ngFor="let poi of pois$ | async">
    <button mat-list-item
      (click)=»selectPoi(poi)»>{{poi.name}}</button>
</mat-action-list>
```

To see the new functionality in action, run the application using the **Serve** option from Nx Console and select a POI from the list. The output of the application should look like the following:

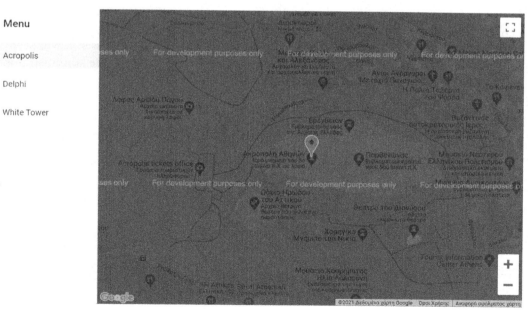

Figure 8.19 – POI selection

> **Important note**
>
> We are using Google Maps in development mode in this project. For production environments, you should get an API key at `https://developers.google.com/maps/gmp-get-started` and include it in the Google Maps JavaScript API script that you load in the `index.html` file such as `<script src="https://maps.googleapis.com/maps/api/js?key=YOUR_API_KEY"></script>`.

We have now completed all the required features for the portal of our visitors. Well done! Implementing the basic functionality of the visitor portal required interacting with NgRx for managing the global state of our application. The global state was separated into the root state for the application and the feature state for the visitor portal. The latter was used in the `visitor` library to create Angular components for displaying a POI list and selecting one to view in Google Maps.

In the next section, we will build the administrator portal to get visit statistics for each POI.

Visualizing data with graphs

The administrator portal will be responsible for displaying traffic visits for each POI using a chart. Traffic will be generated when a visitor visits a POI by clicking its marker on the map. The application will persist visit data in the local storage of the browser. It will keep a record for each visit containing the ID of the POI and the total visits. The administrator portal will consist of the following features:

- Persisting visit data in the store
- Displaying visit statistics

We will start building the administrator portal by implementing the mechanism of keeping track of visits in the following section.

Persisting visit data in the store

Our application does not record traffic statistics for POIs yet. Let's see how we can accomplish this task:

1. Open the `map.component.html` file and add a `map-info-window` component:

```
<google-map height="100%" width="auto" *ngIf="poi$ |
  async as poi" [center]="poi">
  <map-marker [position]="poi"></map-marker>
```

```
<map-info-window>
  <mat-card>
    <mat-card-header>
      <mat-card-title>{{poi.name}}</mat-card-title>
    </mat-card-header>
    <img mat-card-image [src]="poi.imgUrl">
    <mat-card-content>
      <p>{{poi.description}}</p>
    </mat-card-content>
  </mat-card>
</map-info-window>
</google-map>
```

The `map-info-window` component is a pop-up window that displays additional information about the current map marker. It displays the title, image, and description of a POI as an Angular Material card component.

The `mat-card` component contains a header denoted by the `mat-card-header` component and an image denoted by the `img` element with the `mat-card-image` directive. The `mat-card-content` component indicates the main content of the card.

2. Open the `visitor.module.ts` file and import `MatCardModule`:

```
import { MatCardModule } from
  '@angular/material/card';

@NgModule({
  imports: [CommonModule, LayoutModule,
    MatToolbarModule, MatButtonModule,
    MatSidenavModule, MatIconModule, MatListModule,
    RouterModule.forChild([
      { path: '', component: VisitorComponent }
    ]),
    PoiModule,
    GoogleMapsModule,
    MatCardModule
  ],
  declarations: [VisitorComponent, PoiListComponent,
    MapComponent],
})
```

The MatCardModule class is an Angular Material module that exposes all components that we need for creating a card component.

3. Open the map.component.ts file and add the following import statements:

```
import { Component, OnInit, ViewChild } from
  '@angular/core';
import { Store } from '@ngrx/store';
import { PoiSelectors } from '@packt/poi';
import { MapInfoWindow, MapMarker } from
  '@angular/google-maps';
```

4. Declare a component property to get a reference to the information window using the @ViewChild decorator:

```
@ViewChild(MapInfoWindow) info: MapInfoWindow |
  undefined;
```

5. Create a method for opening the information window:

```
showInfo(marker: MapMarker) {
  this.info?.open(marker);
}
```

In the preceding code, we call the open method of the information window reference, passing the associated map marker as a parameter.

6. Open the map.component.html file and bind the showInfo component method to the mapClick event of the map-marker component:

```
<map-marker #marker="mapMarker" [position]="poi"
(mapClick)="showInfo(marker)"></map-marker>
```

We create the marker template reference variable to get a reference to the mapMarker object and pass it as a parameter in the showInfo method.

7. Run the application using the **Serve** option of Nx Console and select a POI from the list.

8. Click on the POI marker on the map, and you should get an output similar to the following:

Figure 8.20 – Map information window

We consider that a POI is visited when the visitor clicks on the map marker and the information window appears. Our application will then notify the store of that action to save it in the local storage. Let's create the logic for interacting with the store:

1. Open the `poi.actions.ts` file and create a new action indicating that a POI has been visited:

```
export const visitPoi = createAction(
  '[Poi/API] Visit Poi',
  props<{ poiId: string | number }>()
)
```

2. Open the `poi.effects.ts` file and add the following `import` statement:

```
import { EMPTY } from 'rxjs';
```

3. Create a new effect that listens to the `visitPoi` action and increases the total visits of the specified `poiId` by *one*:

```
visit$ = createEffect(() =>
  this.actions$.pipe(
    ofType(PoiActions.visitPoi),
    fetch({
      run: action => {
        const stat = localStorage.getItem('tour-' +
          action.poiId);
        const total = stat ? Number(stat) + 1 : 1;
        localStorage.setItem('tour-' + action.poiId,
          total.toString());
        return EMPTY;
      }
    })
  )
);
```

In the preceding code, we fetch the local storage key that begins with the word `tour-` followed by the POI ID. If there is one, we increment it by *one* and update the local storage. Otherwise, we initialize it to *one*.

> **Tip**
>
> In a real case, it would be better to abstract the logic of `localStorage` in an Angular service that would act as a wrapper over the global `localStorage` object. We encourage you to create such a service while building this project.

The `run` method of the effect returns the `EMPTY` RxJS operator, which causes the observable to complete with no value.

4. Open the `map.component.ts` file and import `PoiActions` from the `@packt/poi` namespace:

```
import { PoiActions, PoiSelectors } from '@packt/poi';
```

5. Modify the `showInfo` component method so that it dispatches a `visitPoi` action to the store:

```
showInfo(marker: MapMarker, poiId: string | number) {
    this.store.dispatch(PoiActions.visitPoi({ poiId }));
    this.info?.open(marker);
}
```

6. Finally, open the `map.component.html` file and pass the selected POI ID into the `showInfo` method:

```
<map-marker #marker="mapMarker" [position]="poi"
    (mapClick)="showInfo(marker, poi.id)"></map-marker>
```

Our application can now record the visits of each POI and keep them in the local storage of the browser. In the following section, we will create the main component of the administrator portal that leverages visit data.

Displaying visit statistics

The administrator portal will display visit statistics on its main component with a graph. We will use the **ng2-charts** library for visualizing data on a pie chart. Let's see how to add the required functionality in that component:

1. Install the `ng2-charts` library using the following command:

```
npm install ng2-charts chart.js@2.9.3
```

The preceding command will also install the `chart.js` library, which is at the core of the `ng2-charts` library.

2. Open the `admin.module.ts` file and import `PoiModule` from the `@packt/poi` namespace and `ChartsModule` from the `ng2-charts` npm package:

```
import { NgModule } from '@angular/core';
import { CommonModule } from '@angular/common';
import { AdminComponent } from './admin.component';
import { RouterModule } from '@angular/router';
import { PoiModule } from '@packt/poi';
import { ChartsModule } from 'ng2-charts';
```

```
@NgModule({
  imports: [
    CommonModule,
    RouterModule.forChild([
      { path: '', component: AdminComponent }
    ]),
    PoiModule,
    ChartsModule
  ],
  declarations: [
    AdminComponent
  ],
})
export class AdminModule {}
```

3. Open the `angular.json` file and add the following property in the `options` property of the `build` section:

```
"options": {
  "outputPath": "dist/apps/tour",
  "index": "apps/tour/src/index.html",
  "main": "apps/tour/src/main.ts",
  "polyfills": "apps/tour/src/polyfills.ts",
  "tsConfig": "apps/tour/tsconfig.app.json",
  "assets": ["apps/tour/src/favicon.ico",
    "apps/tour/src/assets"],
  "styles": [
    "./node_modules/@angular/material/prebuilt-
      themes/deeppurple-amber.css",
    "apps/tour/src/styles.css"
  ],
  "scripts": [],
  "allowedCommonJsDependencies": ["chart.js"]
}
```

The chart.js npm package is a **CommonJS** module. The Angular CLI displays a warning when using a CommonJS module because it can prevent it from optimizing your application, resulting in large bundle sizes. Setting the allowedCommonJsDependencies option will not display the warning while building the application.

4. Open the admin.component.ts file and add the following import statements:

```
import { Component, OnDestroy, OnInit } from '@angular/
core';
import { Store } from '@ngrx/store';
import { PoiActions, PoiEntity, PoiSelectors } from
  '@packt/poi';
import { Subscription } from 'rxjs';
```

5. Modify the AdminComponent class so that it interacts with the application store for getting POI data:

```
export class AdminComponent implements OnInit,
  OnDestroy {

  private subscription: Subscription | undefined;

  constructor(private store: Store) { }

  ngOnInit(): void {
    this.subscription = this.store.select(
      PoiSelectors.getAllPoi).subscribe();
    this.store.dispatch(PoiActions.init());
  }

  ngOnDestroy() {
    this.subscription?.unsubscribe();
  }
}
```

In the preceding code, we subscribe to the `getAllPoi` selector manually using a `subscription` property instead of using an `async` pipe. In this case, we must also unsubscribe manually in the `ngOnDestroy` life cycle hook of the component, using the `unsubscribe` method. If we fail to do so, we may introduce a memory leak in our application.

Now that we have set up the interaction with the store, we can get statistics from the local storage and create our pie chart:

1. Execute the following command of Nx CLI to create a service in the `admin` library:

    ```
    nx generate service admin --project=admin
    ```

2. Open the `admin.service.ts` file and add the following `import` statement:

    ```
    import { PoiEntity } from '@packt/poi';
    ```

3. Create a method to get all saved traffic statistics from the local storage of the browser:

    ```
    getStatistics(pois: PoiEntity[]): number[] {
      return pois.map(poi => {
        const stat = localStorage.getItem('tour-' +
          poi.id) ?? 0;
        return +stat;
      });
    }
    ```

    In the preceding method, we get the traffic of each POI based on its `id` property. We convert the `stat` property to a number by adding the + prefix.

4. Open the `admin.component.ts` file and add the following `import` statements:

    ```
    import { Label } from 'ng2-charts';
    import { AdminService } from './admin.service';
    ```

5. Declare component properties for the labels and the actual data that we will display on the pie graph and inject `AdminService` in the constructor of the `AdminComponent` class:

    ```
    data: number[] = [];
    labels: Label[] = [];
    ```

```
constructor(private store: Store, private
    adminService: AdminService) { }
```

6. Create a component method to set the labels and the data of the graph:

```
private buildChart(pois: PoiEntity[]) {
  this.labels = pois.map(poi => poi.name);
  this.data = this.adminService.getStatistics(pois);
}
```

The graph labels are the titles of the POI, and the data is coming from the `getStatistics` method of the `adminService` variable.

7. Call the `buildChart` method inside the `subscribe` method of the `getAllPoi` selector:

```
ngOnInit(): void {
  this.subscription = this.store.select(
    PoiSelectors.getAllPoi).subscribe(pois => {
      this.buildChart(pois);
  });
  this.store.dispatch(PoiActions.init());
}
```

8. Finally, open the `admin.component.html` file and replace its content with the following HTML template:

```
<div class="chart" *ngIf="data.length">
  <canvas height="100" baseChart
    [data]="data"
    [labels]="labels"
    chartType="pie">
  </canvas>
</div>
```

In the preceding template, we use the `baseChart` directive to convert the `canvas` element to a graph. The graph is set to `pie` using the `chartType` property and the `data` and `labels` properties from the respective component properties.

If we now run our application using Nx Console, visit some POI from the map, and switch to the `http://localhost:4200/admin` URL, we should see the following output:

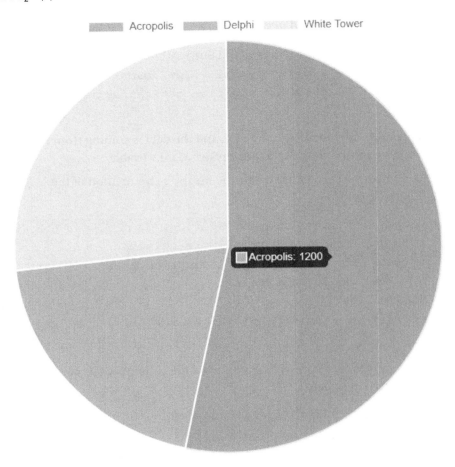

Figure 8.21 – POI statistics

An administrator can now have a complete overview of how each POI is doing from a visit perspective. Our administrator portal has now been completed. The visitor portal can interact with the store and save visit statistics for each POI in the local storage of the browser. The administrator portal can then fetch that data and display it on a pie chart using the `ng2-charts` library.

Summary

In this project, we built an enterprise portal application for visiting POIs on a map and displaying visit statistics for each one. First, we saw how to use Nx Dev Tools to scaffold a new Nx monorepo application. Then, we created two different portals for our application, a visitor and an administrator one. We learned how to use the NgRx library in the visitor portal to maintain and manage the state of our application. Finally, we saw how to use a chart library in the administrator portal for displaying statistics for each POI.

In the next chapter, we will use the Angular CLI to build a UI component library using the Angular CDK.

Practice questions

Let's take a look at a few practice questions:

1. Which npm package creates an Nx monorepo application?
2. What are the differences between the Angular CLI and Nx CLI?
3. How can we enable NgRx in the library of a monorepo?
4. How do we select data from the store?
5. How do we interact with HTTP in NgRx?
6. Where do we modify the state of an NgRx store?
7. What is the difference between a root and a feature state?
8. Which npm package can we use for Google Maps in an Angular application?
9. How can we subscribe to an NgRx selector manually?
10. Which component do we use for displaying additional information on Google Maps?

Further reading

Here are some links to build upon what we learned in the chapter:

- Nx Dev Tools: `https://nx.dev/`
- Nx CLI: `https://nx.dev/latest/angular/getting-started/cli-overview`
- NgRx: `https://ngrx.io/`
- NgRx store guide: `https://ngrx.io/guide/store`

- Angular Material card component: `https://material.angular.io/components/card/overview`

- Angular Google Maps: `https://github.com/angular/components/tree/master/src/google-maps`

- `ng2-charts`: `https://valor-software.com/ng2-charts/`

- `create-nx-workspace`: `https://www.npmjs.com/package/create-nx-workspace`

9
Building a Component UI Library Using Angular CLI and Angular CDK

An Angular application consists of Angular components that are organized into modules. When components need to share a similar appearance or behavior across modules, we extract their functionality into reusable components and group them in a shared module. Reusable components may vary from complex **user interface** (**UI**) structures with many controls (such as forms) up to single native **HyperText Markup Language** (**HTML**) elements (such as buttons).

A component UI library is a collection of reusable components that can be used outside of a specific application domain. A large enterprise application built with a monorepo architecture can use these components across all its applications. A project outside of an organization can also use the same component library as an external dependency.

The Angular **command-line interface (CLI)** includes all the necessary tooling for creating libraries with Angular. The **Angular Component Dev Kit (CDK)** provides a broad range of functionalities for creating accessible and high-performant UI components. In this chapter, we will combine them with **Bulma**, a modern **Cascading Style Sheets (CSS)** framework, to create a simple component UI library from scratch.

In this chapter, we will cover the following topics in more detail:

- Creating a library with the Angular CLI
- Building a draggable card list
- Interacting with the clipboard
- Publishing an Angular library to npm
- Using components as Angular elements

Essential background theory and context

The Angular CDK contains a collection of common interactions and behaviors that we can apply to Angular components. It is at the heart of the Angular Material library, but can be used with any CSS framework in an Angular application. The Angular CDK is available from the @angular/cdk npm package.

The Angular CLI supports creating Angular libraries out of the box. The functionality of an Angular library can be used only in Angular applications, and it is decoupled from specific business logic. If we want to use an Angular library in a non-Angular application, we need to convert it into Angular elements.

Custom elements are a web standard that allows the creation of HTML elements, independent of any JavaScript framework. It works by declaring a custom HTML tag and associating it with a JavaScript class. The browser can identify the HTML tag and execute the JavaScript code that is defined inside the class.

Angular elements are Angular components converted to custom elements using the @angular/elements npm package. Packaging an Angular component as a custom element connects the Angular framework to the **Document Object Model (DOM)**, enriching the native HTML element with data binding, component life cycle, and change detection features.

Project overview

In this project, we will build a component UI library for our Angular projects. Initially, we will use the Angular CLI to scaffold a new Angular workspace for our library. We will then use the Angular CDK and the Bulma CSS framework to create the following components:

- A list of cards that we can rearrange using drag-and-drop features
- A button that will allow us to copy arbitrary content to the clipboard

We will learn how to deploy the library into a package registry such as npm. Finally, we will convert one of our components into an Angular element for sharing it with non-Angular applications, using the ngx-build-plus library.

Build time: 1½ hours

Getting started

The following prerequisites and software tools are required for completing this project:

- Angular CLI: A CLI for Angular that you can find at https://angular.io/cli.
- GitHub material: The related code for this chapter can be found in the Chapter09 folder at https://github.com/PacktPublishing/Angular-Projects-Second-Edition.

Creating a library with the Angular CLI

Before we can start working with Angular libraries using the Angular CLI, we need to create an Angular CLI workspace. The Angular CLI workspace will contain our Angular library and an Angular application for testing the library.

Use the following command to generate a new Angular CLI workspace:

```
ng new my-components --defaults
```

The preceding command will create a new Angular CLI workspace that contains an Angular application named my-components. Navigate to the my-components folder and execute the following command to generate a new Angular library:

```
ng generate library ui-controls
```

The preceding command will create a `ui-controls` library inside the `projects` folder of the workspace. It will contain various files similar to those when creating an Angular application, including the following:

- `src\lib`: This contains the source code of the library, such as modules, components, and services.
- `src\public-api.ts`: This exports artifacts from the library that we want to make publicly available in other Angular applications.
- `ng-package.json`: This contains a configuration for the `ng-packagr` library that the Angular CLI uses under the hood for building libraries.
- `tsconfig.lib.json`: The TypeScript configuration file for our library that also contains several Angular compiler options.
- `tsconfig.lib.prod.json`: The TypeScript configuration file that is used when building our library in production mode.

The Angular CLI will generate a module, a component, and a service in the `src\lib` folder for us by default. It will also export them so that they can be used by any Angular application that will use the library. You can see an example of this here:

public-api.ts

```
/*
 * Public API Surface of ui-controls
 */

export * from './lib/ui-controls.service';
export * from './lib/ui-controls.component';
export * from './lib/ui-controls.module';
```

Now that we have set up our Angular CLI workspace, we can go ahead and install the Bulma and the Angular CDK libraries, as follows:

1. Execute the following npm command to install the Angular CDK:

   ```
   npm install @angular/cdk
   ```

2. Run the following command to install the bulma CSS framework:

   ```
   npm install bulma
   ```

3. Open the `angular.json` configuration file and add the CSS style sheet file of the `bulma` library in the `styles` section of the `build` architect entry, as follows:

```
"options": {
  "outputPath": "dist/my-components",
  "index": "src/index.html",
  "main": "src/main.ts",
  "polyfills": "src/polyfills.ts",
  "tsConfig": "tsconfig.app.json",
  "assets": [
    "src/favicon.ico",
    "src/assets"
  ],
  "styles": [
    "src/styles.css",
    "./node_modules/bulma/css/bulma.css"
  ],
  "scripts": []
}
```

4. Open the `package.json` file of the `projects\ui-controls` folder and add the following packages to the `peerDependencies` section:

```
{
  "name": "ui-controls",
  "version": "0.0.1",
  "peerDependencies": {
    "@angular/common": "^12.0.2",
    "@angular/core": "^12.0.2",
    "@angular/cdk": "^12.0.2",
    "bulma": "^0.9.2"
  },
  "dependencies": {
    "tslib": "^2.1.0"
  }
}
```

We add the Angular CDK and the Bulma library to the `peerDependencies` section to ensure that any consuming application has a specific version of the packages to run our library.

> **Important note**
>
> The version numbers of each package may vary if you follow along with this project. To make sure that you have the correct versions, copy them from the `package.json` file of the root folder of the workspace.

We have now completed the basic setup of our UI components library. We have also configured the Angular application that comes with the Angular CLI workspace to preview and test the library. In the following section, we will build the first component of our library—a card list that can be re-ordered.

Building a draggable card list

The first component of our UI library will be a list of Bulma card elements. Each card will display a title, a description, and an anchor link element. We will also be able to drag a card and change the order of the card list using the Angular CDK. Building our component will consist of the following tasks:

- Displaying card data
- Adding drag-and-drop functionality

In the following section, we will first see how to display data on the card list.

Displaying card data

Our Angular application should pass a list of cards as an input property to the component for displaying them. Let's see how we can create a draggable card component, as follows:

1. Execute the following Angular CLI command to create an Angular component:

```
ng generate component card-list --project=ui-controls
--export
```

The preceding command will create a `card-list` component in the `ui-controls` project of our Angular CLI workspace. The `--export` option will also export the component from `UiControlsModule`.

The `UiControlsModule` class is already exported from the `public-api.ts` file. So, when our Angular application imports `UiControlsModule`, it will also have our component available to use.

2. Use the `generate` command of the Angular CLI to create an interface for the structure of card data, as follows:

```
ng generate interface card --project=ui-controls
```

The preceding command will create a `card.ts` file in the `ui-controls` project of our workspace.

3. Open the `card.ts` file and add the following properties to the `Card` interface:

```
export interface Card {
    title: string;
    description: string;
    link: string;
}
```

4. Open the `public-api.ts` file and add the following `export` statements to make the component and the interface available to the library consumers:

```
export * from './lib/card-list/card-list.component';
export * from './lib/card';
```

5. Open the `card-list.component.ts` file and use the `@Input` decorator to define an Input property, as follows:

```
import { Component, Input, OnInit } from '@angular/core';
import { Card } from '../card';

@Component({
    selector: 'lib-card-list',
    templateUrl: './card-list.component.html',
    styleUrls: ['./card-list.component.css']
})
export class CardListComponent implements OnInit {
    @Input() cards: Card[] = [];

    constructor() { }
```

```
ngOnInit(): void {
}

}
```

The `cards` property will be set later from the Angular application with the card data that we want to display.

6. Open the `card-list.component.html` file and replace its content with the following HTML template:

```html
<div>
  <div class="card m-4" *ngFor="let card of cards">
    <header class="card-header">
      <p class="card-header-title">{{card.title}}</p>
    </header>
    <div class="card-content">
      <div class="content">{{card.description}}</div>
    </div>
    <footer class="card-footer">
      <a [href]="card.link" class=
        "card-footer-item">View on Wikipedia</a>
    </footer>
  </div>
</div>
```

The preceding template uses the Bulma library card component and iterates over the `cards` component property to display each one, using the `*ngFor` directive.

7. Open the `card-list.component.css` file and add the following CSS styles:

```css
:host > div {
  display: grid;
  grid-auto-flow: column;
  overflow: auto;
}

.card {
  width: 200px;
}
```

In the preceding styles, we use the `:host` selector to target the `div` element in the host element of our component and apply a **CSS Grid** style to display all cards in a single row.

8. Open the `ui-controls.module.ts` file and add `CommonModule` to the `imports` array of the `@NgModule` decorator, as follows:

```
import { NgModule } from '@angular/core';
import { UiControlsComponent } from './ui-controls.
component';
import { CardListComponent } from './card-list/card-list.
component';
import { CommonModule } from '@angular/common';

@NgModule({
  declarations: [
    UiControlsComponent,
    CardListComponent
  ],
  imports: [CommonModule],
  exports: [
    UiControlsComponent,
    CardListComponent
  ]
})
export class UiControlsModule { }
```

The `CommonModule` class is needed for the `*ngFor` directive we use in the card list component template.

Our component is now ready to accept data and display it in a card list representation. Let's see how to consume it from the Angular application, as follows:

1. First, execute the following command to build the component UI library:

```
ng build ui-controls
```

The Angular CLI will start building the library, and it will have been completed as soon as you see the following output on the terminal:

```
------------------------------------------------
Building entry point 'ui-controls'
------------------------------------------------
✓ Compiling TypeScript sources through NGC
✓ Bundling to FESM2015
✓ Bundling to UMD
✓ Writing package metadata
✓ Built ui-controls
```

Figure 9.1 – Library build output

2. Open the app.module.ts file and add the UiControlsModule class to the imports array of the @NgModule decorator, as follows:

```typescript
import { NgModule } from '@angular/core';
import { BrowserModule } from '@angular/platform-browser';
import { UiControlsModule } from 'ui-controls';

import { AppComponent } from './app.component';

@NgModule({
  declarations: [
    AppComponent
  ],
  imports: [
    BrowserModule,
    UiControlsModule
  ],
  providers: [],
  bootstrap: [AppComponent]
})
export class AppModule { }
```

Important note

We import `UiControlsModule` from the `ui-controls` namespace, which is the library name, and not from the full absolute path in our workspace.

---

3. Open the `app.component.ts` file and declare a component property of the `Card[]` type, as follows:

```
import { Component } from '@angular/core';
import { Card } from 'ui-controls';
import { assassins } from './assassins';

@Component({
  selector: 'app-root',
  templateUrl: './app.component.html',
  styleUrls: ['./app.component.css']
})
export class AppComponent {
  title = 'my-components';
  cards: Card[] = assassins;
}
```

We initialize the `cards` component property using demo data from the `assassins.ts` file, which you can find in the GitHub repository of the *Getting started* section.

4. Open the `app.component.html` file and replace its content with the following HTML template:

```
<div class="container is-fluid">
  <h1 class="title">Assassins Creed Series</h1>
  <lib-card-list [cards]="cards"></lib-card-list>
</div>
```

5. To preview the application, run `ng serve` and open your browser at `http://localhost:4200`. You should then see something like this:

Assassins Creed Series

Assassins Creed	Assassins Creed II	Assassins Creed Black Flag	Assassins Creed Rogue
Altaïr Ibn-La Ahad	Ezio Auditore da Firenze	Edward Kenway	Shay Patrick Cormac
View on Wikipedia	View on Wikipedia	View on Wikipedia	View on Wikipedia

Figure 9.2 – Card list component

The card list component displays data that a consumer application passed using the `cards` input property. In the following section, we will take our component a step further and make our cards able to change their location in the list.

Adding drag-and-drop functionality

A feature of the card list component is that we will be able to change the location of a card by dragging and dropping it inside the list. The order of the card list should be emitted back to the consumer application using an output property binding.

The Angular CDK contains a drag-and-drop module that we can use for this purpose. To do so, follow these steps:

1. Open the `ui-controls.module.ts` file and import `DragDropModule` from the `@angular/cdk/drag-drop` namespace, like this:

```
import { DragDropModule } from '@angular/cdk/drag-drop';
```

2. Add the `DragDropModule` class to the `imports` array of the `@NgModule` decorator, like this:

```
@NgModule({
  declarations: [
    UiControlsComponent,
    CardListComponent
  ],
```

```
  imports: [
    CommonModule,
    DragDropModule
  ],
  exports: [
    UiControlsComponent,
    CardListComponent
  ]
})
```

3. Open the `card-list.component.html` file and modify the template as follows:

```
<div cdkDropListOrientation="horizontal" cdkDropList
(cdkDropListDropped)="sortCards($event)">
  <div cdkDrag class="card m-4" *ngFor="let card of
    cards">
    <header class="card-header">
      <p class="card-header-title">{{card.title}}</p>
    </header>
    <div class="card-content">
      <div class="content">{{card.description}}</div>
    </div>
    <footer class="card-footer">
      <a [href]="card.link" class=
        "card-footer-item">View on Wikipedia</a>
    </footer>
  </div>
</div>
```

First, we add the `cdkDrag` directive to each card element to be able to move it by dragging it. Then, we add the `cdkDropList` directive to the container element to mark it as a drop list. A drop list in the Angular CDK indicates that its contents can be re-ordered using drag-and-drop actions. We set the drag-and-drop orientation to `horizontal` because our card list is rendered in a single row, and we also bind a `sortCards` component method to the `cdkDropListDropped` event of the drop list.

4. Open the `card-list.component.ts` file and add the following
    `import` statements:

```
import { Component, Input, Output, OnInit, EventEmitter }
from '@angular/core';
import { Card } from '../card';
import { CdkDragDrop, moveItemInArray } from '@angular/
cdk/drag-drop';
```

5. Create an output property using the `@Output` decorator and use it in the
    `sortCards` component method to emit the re-ordered list to the consumer of the
    component, as follows:

```
export class CardListComponent implements OnInit {
  @Input() cards: Card[] = [];
  @Output() cardChange = new EventEmitter<Card[]>();

  constructor() { }

  ngOnInit(): void {
  }

  sortCards(event: CdkDragDrop<string[]>): void {
    moveItemInArray(this.cards, event.previousIndex,
      event.currentIndex);
    this.cardChange.emit(this.cards);
  }
}
```

In the previous code snippet, we use the `moveItemInArray` built-in method of
`DragDropModule` to change the order of the `cards` property. We pass the `event`
parameter to the `moveItemInArray` method containing the previous and current
index of the moved card. We also use the `emit` method of the `cardChange`
property to propagate the change back to the Angular application.

The card list component has now acquired drag-and-drop superpowers. Let's give it a try, as follows:

1. Open the `app.component.html` file and add an event binding to the `cardChange` event of the `lib-card-list` component, as follows:

    ```
    <div class="container is-fluid">
      <h1 class="title">Assassins Creed Series</h1>
      <lib-card-list [cards]="cards"
        (cardChange)="onCardChange($event)">
      </lib-card-list>
    </div>
    ```

2. Open the `app.component.ts` file and create an `onCardChange` method to log the new card list, as follows:

    ```
    onCardChange(cards: Card[]) {
      console.log(cards);
    }
    ```

3. Run the following command to build the library:

    ```
    ng build ui-controls
    ```

4. Execute the `serve` command of the Angular CLI to start your application, like this:

    ```
    ng serve
    ```

5. Try to drag and drop some of the cards from the list and notice the output in the **Console** window of your browser.

The first component of our UI library is now packed with all the functionality to make it a drag-and-drop list. It can display a list passed from our Angular application in a Bulma card format. It can also change the order of each item in the list using the Angular CDK drag-and-drop module, and propagate the change back to our application.

In the following section, we will create a second component of our library for copying data to the clipboard.

Interacting with the clipboard

The Angular CDK library contains a collection of Angular artifacts that we can use to interact with the system clipboard. Specifically, it includes a directive for copying data to the clipboard and an event binding for taking additional action when the content has been copied. Let's see how we can integrate both in our component library, as follows:

1. Execute the following command of the Angular CLI to create a new Angular component in the library:

```
ng generate component copy-button --project=ui-controls
--export
```

2. Export the newly generated component from the `public-api.ts` file, as follows:

```
export * from './lib/ui-controls.service';
export * from './lib/ui-controls.component';
export * from './lib/ui-controls.module';
export * from './lib/card-list/card-list.component';
export * from './lib/card';
export * from './lib/copy-button/copy-button.component';
```

3. Open the `ui-controls.module.ts` file and import `ClipboardModule` from the `@angular/cdk/clipboard` namespace, like this:

```
import { ClipboardModule } from '@angular/cdk/clipboard';
```

4. Add the `ClipboardModule` class to the `imports` array of the `@NgModule` decorator, like this:

```
@NgModule({
  declarations: [
    UiControlsComponent,
    CardListComponent,
    CopyButtonComponent
  ],
  imports: [
    CommonModule,
    DragDropModule,
    ClipboardModule
  ],
```

```
    exports: [
      UiControlsComponent,
      CardListComponent,
      CopyButtonComponent
    ]
  })
```

5. Open the `copy-button.component.ts` file and declare the following component properties:

```
import { Component, EventEmitter, Input, OnInit, Output }
from '@angular/core';

@Component({
  selector: 'lib-copy-button',
  templateUrl: './copy-button.component.html',
  styleUrls: ['./copy-button.component.css']
})
export class CopyButtonComponent implements OnInit {

  @Input() data = '';
  @Output() copied = new EventEmitter();

  constructor() { }

  ngOnInit(): void {
  }

}
```

The `data` property will be used to set clipboard data, and the `copied` event will fire when the data is successfully copied to the clipboard.

6. Create a component method to trigger a `copied` output event, as follows:

```
onCopy() {
  this.copied.next();
}
```

7. Open the `copy-button.component.html` file and replace its content with the following HTML template:

```html
<button
  class="button is-light is-primary"
  [cdkCopyToClipboard]="data"
  (cdkCopyToClipboardCopied)="onCopy()">
    Copy
</button>
```

In the preceding template, we use a Bulma `button` element and attach two Angular CDK bindings to it. The `cdkCopyToClipboard` property binding indicates that the `data` component property will be copied to the clipboard when the button is clicked. The `cdkCopyToClipboardCopied` event binding will call the `onCopy` component method as soon as data has been copied to the clipboard successfully.

Now that we have set up our component, let's find out how to use it in our Angular application, as follows:

1. Open the `app.component.html` file and add a `div` element that consists of an `input` HTML element and a `lib-copy-button` component, as follows:

```html
<div class="container is-fluid">
  <h1 class="title">Assassins Creed Series</h1>
  <lib-card-list [cards]="cards"
    (cardChange)="onCardChange($event)">
  </lib-card-list>
  <h1 class="title mt-5">Clipboard interaction</h1>
  <div class="field has-addons">
    <div class="control">
      <input class="input" type="text"
        [(ngModel)]="title">
    </div>
    <div class="control">
      <lib-copy-button [data]="title"
        (copied)="log()"></lib-copy-button>
    </div>
  </div>
</div>
```

In the previous template, we bind the `title` property of the component to the `input` element using the `ngModel` directive. We also bind it to the `data` property of the `lib-copy-button` component to copy the contents of the `input` element to the clipboard. We also bind the `copied` event to the `log` component method.

2. Open the `app.component.ts` file and create a `log` method for displaying an information message when data is copied to the clipboard, as follows:

```
log() {
    alert(this.title + ' copied to the clipboard');
}
```

3. Open the `app.module.ts` file and import `FormsModule`, like this:

```
import { FormsModule } from '@angular/forms';

@NgModule({
    declarations: [
        AppComponent
    ],
    imports: [
        BrowserModule,
        UiControlsModule,
        FormsModule
    ],
    providers: [],
    bootstrap: [AppComponent]
})
```

The `FormsModule` class is part of the `@angular/forms` npm package and is required when we want to use `ngModel` in our application.

4. Execute the following command to build the library so that our application can recognize the new component:

```
ng build ui-controls
```

5. Run the application using the `serve` command of the Angular CLI, and you should get the following output:

Figure 9.3 – Clipboard interaction

6. Enter `my awesome library` into the textbox and click on the **Copy** button, as illustrated in the following screenshot:

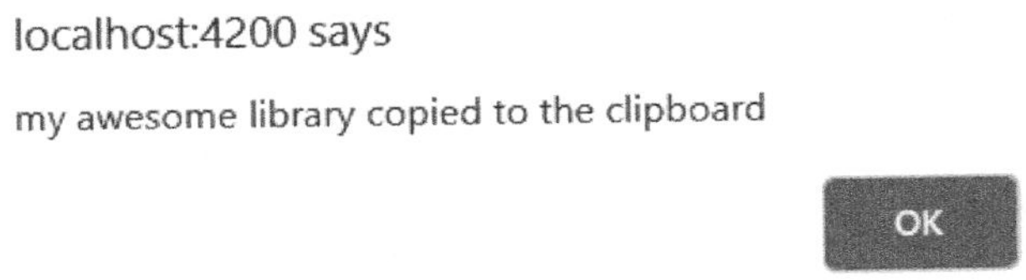

localhost:4200 says

my awesome library copied to the clipboard

OK

Figure 9.4 – Alert message

We have successfully created a button that we can attach to an Angular application and interact with the clipboard directly!

The Angular CDK contains various other components and behaviors that we can use in our Angular applications. When combined with a highly customizable CSS framework such as Bulma, it can create compelling and unique interfaces. Try them in your Angular projects and build a library with a rich set of components. In the following section, we will learn how to publish a library in the npm package registry.

Publishing an Angular library to npm

We have already seen how to build an Angular library and consume it in an Angular application when both exist in the same repository or organization. However, there are cases where you may want to make your library available to Angular projects outside your infrastructure via a public package registry such as npm. A usual case is when you want to make your library open source so that other members in the development community can benefit from this. Let's see how to publish our `ui-controls` library to npm, as follows:

1. If you do not have an npm account, navigate to `https://www.npmjs.com/signup` to create one. Otherwise, continue to *Step 3*.

2. Enter the following details and click the **Create an Account** button:

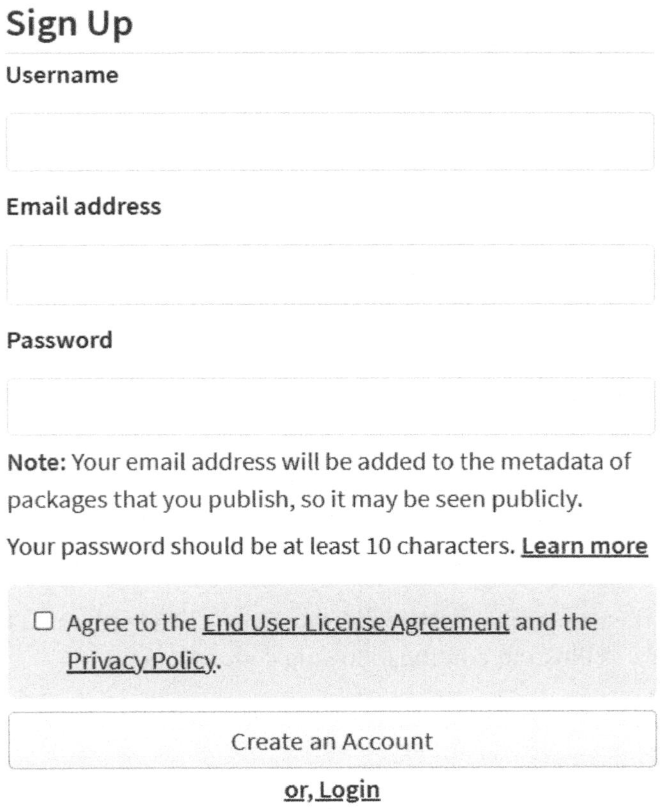

Sign Up

Username

Email address

Password

Note: Your email address will be added to the metadata of packages that you publish, so it may be seen publicly.

Your password should be at least 10 characters. **Learn more**

☐ Agree to the End User License Agreement and the Privacy Policy.

Create an Account

or, Login

Figure 9.5 – Creating an npm account

After your account has been created, you will be redirected to your profile page in npm.

3. Open the `package.json` file that exists in the `projects\ui-controls` folder of the Angular CLI workspace and change the version of your library accordingly, as follows:

```
{
    "name": "ui-controls",
    "version": "1.0.0",
    "peerDependencies": {
        "@angular/common": "^12.0.2",
        "@angular/core": "^12.0.2",
```

```
     "@angular/cdk": "^12.0.2",
     "bulma": "^0.9.2"
  },
  "dependencies": {
     "tslib": "^2.1.0"
  }
}
```

> **Tip**
>
> It is considered a good practice to follow **semantic versioning** in your library and publish it as version `1.0.0` for the first time. Angular also follows semantic versioning, and you can learn more about this at `https://semver.org/`.

4. Open a terminal window and run the following Angular CLI command to build your library:

```
ng build ui-controls
```

5. Navigate to the `dist` folder where the Angular CLI has generated the final bundle of our library, as illustrated in the following code snippet:

```
cd dist\ui-controls
```

6. Execute the following npm command to log in to the npm registry from the terminal:

```
npm login
```

The preceding command will ask you to fill in your **Username**, **Password**, and **Email** values.

7. After you have successfully authenticated with npm, run the following command to publish your library:

```
npm publish
```

> **Important note**
>
> Running the preceding command will throw an error because the npm package registry already contains a `ui-controls` package. If you want to preview the result of the previous command, make sure that you change the `name` field in the `package.json` file of the library.

Well done! Your library is now on the public npm registry and can be used by other developers in their Angular applications.

> **Important note**
>
> Always remember to change the version number in the `package.json` file of your library before publishing it. Otherwise, the npm registry will throw an error, stating that the version you are trying to publish already exists. There are also some npm packages such as `standard-version` that can automate this for you.

In the following section, we will learn how to use our library in non-Angular applications using Angular elements.

Using components as Angular elements

We have already learned how to use the Angular CLI for creating an Angular library. We also saw how to publish our library to the npm registry so that other Angular projects can use it and benefit from it. In this section, we will go the extra mile and learn how to build our Angular library to be used in non-Angular environments.

As we have already pointed out, the Angular framework is a cross-platform JavaScript framework in many ways. It can run on the server using **Angular Universal**, and on mobile platforms. It can also run on a native desktop environment. In addition to those platforms, it can even run on web applications that are not built with Angular, using Angular elements.

Let's see how we can convert our clipboard component to an Angular element, as follows:

1. Execute the following Angular CLI command to generate a new Angular application in our workspace:

```
ng generate application ui-elements --defaults
```

The preceding command will generate the `ui-elements` Angular application in the `projects` folder using default options.

> **Important note**
>
> The Angular CLI does not currently support the use of Angular elements directly on an Angular library. Thus, we need to create an Angular application whose only purpose will be to export our components as Angular elements.

2. Run the following `add` schematic of the Angular CLI to install the Angular Elements package in the `ui-elements` application:

```
ng add @angular/elements --project=ui-elements
```

The `@angular/elements` npm package contains all the necessary artifacts for working with Angular elements. The installation will update the `package.json` file of our workspace with the latest version. It will also import the `document-register-element` library into the `polyfills.ts` file of the `ui-elements` application for browsers that do not support custom elements.

3. Open the `app.module.ts` file of the `ui-elements` application and remove any references to the `AppComponent` class.

4. Add the following `import` statements at the top of the `app.module.ts` file:

```
import { Injector, NgModule } from '@angular/core';
import { createCustomElement } from '@angular/elements';
import { BrowserModule } from '@angular/platform-browser';
import { UiControlsModule, CopyButtonComponent } from 'ui-controls';
```

5. Add the `UiControlsModule` class to the `imports` array of the `@NgModule` decorator, as follows:

```
@NgModule({
  declarations: [],
  imports: [
    BrowserModule,
    UiControlsModule
  ],
  providers: [],
  bootstrap: []
})
```

6. Add a constructor to the `AppModule` class and inject the `Injector` service, as follows:

```
constructor(private injector: Injector) {}
```

7. Implement an ngDoBootstrap hook method to create the custom element for the CopyButtonComponent class, as follows:

```
export class AppModule {

  constructor(private injector: Injector) {}

  ngDoBootstrap() {
    const el =
      createCustomElement(CopyButtonComponent,
        { injector: this.injector });
    customElements.define('copy-button', el);
  }
}
```

The ngDoBootstrap method is used to hook in the manual bootstrap process of the Angular application. We use the createCustomElement method from the @angular/elements npm package to create a custom element, passing the class of the component and the injector. Finally, we use the define method of the customElements object to declare the custom element, passing the HTML selector that we want to use and the custom element as parameters.

Now that we have put into practice all the workings for converting an Angular component into an Angular element, it's time to build it so that we can use it in a web application.

Building an Angular element differs from a standard build of an Angular application. When we build an Angular application, the Angular CLI generates different JavaScript bundles that contain the application source code, the Angular framework, and any third-party libraries. In an Angular element scenario, we only want to generate one bundle file containing our component. For this purpose, we will use the ngx-build-plus library, which can generate a single bundle, among other things. Let's see how to install it and use it in our application, as follows:

1. Execute the following command of the Angular CLI to install the ngx-build-plus package:

```
ng add ngx-build-plus --project=ui-elements
```

The preceding command will modify the angular.json file of the Angular CLI workspace to use the ngx-build-plus library for building the ui-elements application.

2. Run the following `build` command of the Angular CLI to build the application:

```
ng build ui-elements --single-bundle
```

The previous command will build the `ui-elements` application and produce a single bundle for all application code.

3. Copy the `dist\ui-elements` folder to another location of your choice in your hard disk and open the `index.html` file, using your **integrated development environment (IDE)**.

4. Remove the `<base>` tag from the `head` element and add the Bulma CSS minified file using a **content delivery network (CDN)**, as follows:

```
<link rel="stylesheet" href="https://cdn.jsdelivr.net/
npm/bulma@0.9.2/css/bulma.min.css">
```

5. Replace the `app-root` selector with the following HTML snippet in the `body` element:

```
<div class="container is-fluid">
  <h1 class="title">My Angular Element</h1>
  <copy-button></copy-button>
</div>
```

In the preceding snippet, we added a `div` element styled with Bulma CSS classes, and the selector of the Angular element that we defined in `AppModule`.

6. Insert the following JavaScript code after the `div` element:

```
<script>
  const el = document.getElementsByTagName(
    'copy-button')[0];
  el.setAttribute('data', 'Some data');
  el.addEventListener('copied', () => alert('Copied to
    clipboard'));
</script>
```

In the preceding script, we communicate with the component that is hidden behind the Angular element using vanilla JavaScript. First, we query the global `document` object to get a reference to the Angular element. Then, we set the `data` input property using the `setAttribute` method of the element. Finally, we listen for the `copied` output event by attaching an event listener using the `addEventListener` method.

7. Open the `index.html` file using your browser, and you should see the following output:

My Angular Element

Figure 9.6 – Angular element

8. Click on the **Copy** button, and you should see the following alert dialog:

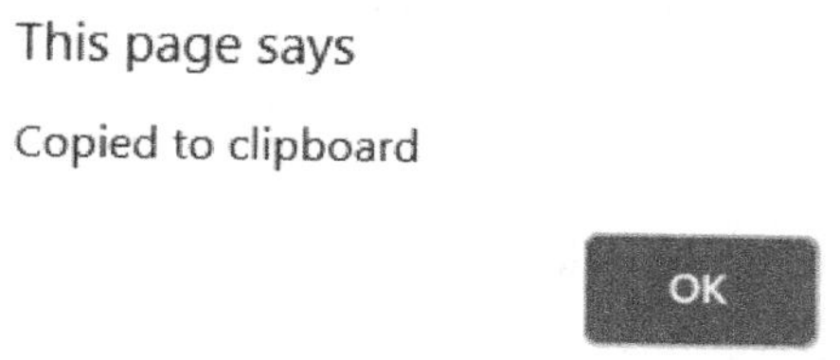

This page says

Copied to clipboard

OK

Figure 9.7 – Alert dialog

We have managed to use an Angular component from our UI component library as a native HTML element in a web application that has nothing to do with Angular! The custom element looks and behaves the same as its Angular counterpart. The only difference is how we set up and configure the custom element in our web application using plain JavaScript.

Summary

In this project, we built a component UI library that we can use in our Angular applications. Initially, we learned how to use the Angular CLI to create an Angular library. We scaffolded a new Angular CLI workspace that contained our Angular library, along with an Angular application for testing it.

We then used the Angular CDK with the Bulma CSS framework to build the UI components of our library. We created a card list that can be re-ordered using drag-and-drop features and a button for copying content to the clipboard.

We also saw how to publish our library in the npm registry to use it in other Angular projects. Finally, we converted it into custom elements using Angular elements for distribution to non-Angular applications.

In the next project, which will be the final project in the book, we will learn how to customize the Angular CLI to create our generation schematics.

Practice questions

Let's take a look at a few practice questions:

1. How do we generate a new Angular library using the Angular CLI?
2. How do we make an Angular artifact of our library public?
3. Which CSS selector do we use for targeting the host element of an Angular component?
4. How do we mark an element as draggable in the Angular CDK?
5. Which method do we use for re-ordering a draggable list of items?
6. Which Angular CDK directive is responsible for passing data to the clipboard?
7. In which mode do we build an Angular library for publishing it?
8. How do we create a single bundle using the `ngx-build-plus` library?
9. How do we pass data to and from an Angular element?
10. Why do we need polyfills when working with Angular elements?

Further reading

Here are some links to build upon what we learned in the chapter:

- Angular libraries overview: `https://angular.io/guide/libraries`
- Creating Angular libraries: `https://angular.io/guide/creating-libraries`
- Bulma CSS: `https://bulma.io/`
- Angular CDK: `https://material.angular.io/cdk/categories`
- Drag-and-drop module: `https://material.angular.io/cdk/drag-drop/overview`
- Clipboard module: `https://material.angular.io/cdk/clipboard/overview`
- Angular elements overview: `https://angular.io/guide/elements`
- ngx-build-plus: `https://github.com/manfredsteyer/ngx-build-plus#advanced-example-externals-and-angular-elements`
- Standard Version: `https://github.com/conventional-changelog/standard-version`

10
Customizing Angular CLI Commands Using Schematics

The Angular CLI is a very powerful tool and the de facto solution for working with Angular applications. It eliminates most of the boilerplate code and configuration from the developer and allows them to focus on the fun stuff, which is building awesome Angular applications. Apart from enhancing the Angular development experience, it can be easily customized to the needs of each developer.

The Angular CLI contains a set of useful commands for building, bundling, and testing Angular applications. It also provides a collection of special commands, called **schematics**, that are used to generate various Angular artifacts such as components, modules, and services. Schematics expose a public API that developers can use to create their own Angular CLI commands or extend the existing ones.

In this chapter, we will cover the following details about schematics:

- Installing the **schematics CLI**

- Creating a **Tailwind** component

- Creating an HTTP service

Essential background theory and context

Angular schematics are libraries that can be installed using npm. They are used in various situations, including creating components that share a standard user interface or even enforcing conventions and coding guidelines inside an organization. A schematic can be used standalone or as a companion for an existing Angular library.

Angular schematics are packaged into collections, and they reside in the **@schematics/ angular** npm package. When we use the Angular CLI to run the `ng add` or the `ng build` command, it runs the appropriate schematic from that package. The Angular CLI currently supports the following types of schematics:

- **Add schematic**: This is used to install an Angular library in an Angular CLI workspace using the `ng add` command.

- **Update schematic**: This is used to update an Angular library using the `ng update` command.

- **Generate schematic**: This is used to generate Angular artifacts in an Angular CLI workspace using the `ng generate` command.

In this project, we will focus on generate schematics, but the same rules apply to all the other commands.

Project overview

In this project, we will learn how to use the schematics API to build custom Angular CLI generate schematics for creating components and services. First, we will build a schematic for creating an Angular component that uses the Tailwind CSS framework in its template. Then, we will create a schematic to generate an Angular service that injects the built-in HTTP client by default and creates one method for each HTTP request in a CRUD operation.

Build time: 1 hour

Getting started

The following prerequisites and software tools are required to complete this project:

- Angular CLI: A command-line interface for Angular that you can find at `https://angular.io/cli`.

- GitHub material: The code for this chapter can be found in the `Chapter10` folder at `https://github.com/PacktPublishing/Angular-Projects-Second-Edition`.

Installing the schematics CLI

The schematics CLI is a command-line interface that we can use to interact with the schematics API. To install it, run the following npm command:

```
npm install -g @angular-devkit/schematics-cli
```

The preceding command will install the `@angular-devkit/schematics-cli` npm package globally on our system. We can then use the schematics executable to create a new schematics collection:

```
schematics blank my-schematics
```

The previous command will generate a schematics project called `my-schematics`. It contains a schematic with the same name by default inside the `src` folder. A schematic contains the following files:

- `collection.json`: A JSON schema that describes the schematics that belong to the `my-schematics` collection
- `my-schematics\index.ts`: The main entry point of the `my-schematics` schematic
- `my-schematics\index_spec.ts`: The unit test file of the main entry point of the `my-schematics` schematic

The JSON schema file of the collection contains one entry for each schematic associated with that collection:

collection.json

```json
{
  "$schema": "../node_modules/@angular-
    devkit/schematics/collection-schema.json",
  "schematics": {
    "my-schematics": {
      "description": "A blank schematic.",
      "factory": "./my-schematics/index#mySchematics"
    }
  }
}
```

Each schematic in the collection contains a short description, as indicated by the `description` property, and a `factory` property that points to the main entry point of the schematic using a special syntax. It contains the filename `./my-schematics/index`, followed by the `#` character, and the name of the function exported by that file, named `mySchematics`.

The main entry point of a schematic contains a rule factory method that is exported by default and returns a `Rule` object:

index.ts

```ts
import { Rule, SchematicContext, Tree } from '@angular-devkit/
schematics';


// You don't have to export the function as default.
// You can also have more than one rule factory
// per file.
export function mySchematics(_options: any): Rule {
  return (tree: Tree, _context: SchematicContext) => {
    return tree;
  };
}
```

A schematic does not interact directly with the filesystem. Instead, it creates a virtual filesystem that is represented by a `Tree` object. The virtual filesystem contains a *staging* area where all transformations from schematics happen. This area aims to make sure that any transformations that are not valid will not propagate to the actual filesystem. As soon as the schematic is valid to execute, the virtual filesystem will apply the changes to the real one. All transformations of a schematic operate in a `SchematicContext` object.

In the following section, we will learn how to use the schematics CLI and create a component generation schematic.

Creating a Tailwind component

Tailwind is a very popular CSS framework that enforces a utility-first core principle. It contains classes and styles that can be used in Angular applications to create easily composable user interfaces.

We will use the schematics API of the Angular CLI to build a generation schematic for Angular components. The schematic will generate a new Angular component that is styled with a Tailwind container layout.

> **Important note**
>
> The schematic that we will build does not need to have Tailwind CSS installed by default. However, the application in which we will use the schematic does require it.

Let's see how we can accomplish that:

1. Execute the following schematics CLI command to add a new schematic to our collection:

    ```
    schematics blank tailwind-container
    ```

    The preceding command will update the `collection.json` file to contain a new entry for the `tailwind-container` schematic. It will also create a `tailwind-container` folder in the `src` folder of our workspace.

2. Create a `schema.json` file inside the `tailwind-container` folder and add the following content:

    ```json
    {
        "$schema": "http://json-schema.org/schema",
        "id": "TailwindContainerSchema",
        "title": "My Tailwind Container Schema",
        "type": "object",
        "properties": {
          "name": {
            "description": "The name of the component.",
            "type": "string"
          },
           "path": {
            "type": "string",
            "format": "path",
            "description": "The path to create the
              component.",
            "visible": false
          }
    ```

```
    },
    "required": ["name"]
}
```

Each schematic can have a JSON schema file that defines the options that are available when running the schematic. Since we want to create a component generation schematic, we need a `name` and a `path` property for our component. Each of these properties has metadata associated with it, such as the `type` and the `description`. The name of the component is required when invoking the schematic as indicated by the `required` array property.

3. Open the `collection.json` file and set the properties of the `tailwind-container` schematic as follows:

```
{
    "$schema": "../node_modules/@angular-
      devkit/schematics/collection-schema.json",
    "schematics": {
      "my-schematics": {
        "description": "A blank schematic.",
        "factory": "./my-schematics/index#mySchematics"
      },
      "tailwind-container": {
        "description": "Generate a Tailwind container
          component",
        "factory": "./tailwind-
          container/index#tailwindContainer",
        "schema": "./tailwind-container/schema.json"
      }
    }
}
```

In the preceding file, we set a proper `description` for our schematic. We also add the `schema` property that points to the absolute path of the `schema.json` file we created in *step 3*.

4. Create a `schema.ts` file inside the `tailwind-container` folder and add the following content:

```
export interface Schema {
    name: string;
    path: string;
}
```

The preceding file defines the `Schema` interface that contains mapping properties to those defined in the `schema.json` file.

We have now created all the underlying infrastructure that we will use to create our schematic. Let's see how to write the actual code that will run our schematic:

1. Create a folder named `files` inside the `tailwind-container` folder.

2. Create a file called `__name@dasherize__.component.html.template` inside the `files` folder and add the following contents:

```
<div class="container mx-auto">
</div>
```

The preceding file denotes the template of the component that our schematic will generate. The `__name` prefix will be replaced by the name of the component that we will pass as an option in the schematic. The `@dasherize__` syntax indicates that the name will be separated with dashes and converted to lowercase if passed in camel case.

3. Create a file called `__name@dasherize__.component.ts.template` and add the following contents:

```
import { Component } from '@angular/core';

@Component({
    selector: 'my-<%= dasherize(name) %>',
    templateUrl: './<%= dasherize(name)
        %>.component.html'
})
export class My<%= classify(name) %>Component {}
```

The preceding file contains the TypeScript class of the component that will be generated. The `selector` and the `templateUrl` properties of the `@Component` decorator are built using the `dasherize` method and the `name` of the component. The name of the class contains a different method called `classify` that takes the name of the component as a parameter and converts it to title case.

4. Open the `index.ts` file of the `tailwind-container` folder, set the type of options to `Schema` and remove the `return` statement:

```
import { Rule, SchematicContext, Tree } from '@angular-
devkit/schematics';
import { Schema } from './schema';


// You don't have to export the function as default.
// You can also have more than one rule factory
// per file.
export function tailwindContainer(_options: Schema): Rule
{
  return (_tree: Tree, _context: SchematicContext) => {};
}
```

5. Add the following `import` statements at the top of the file:

```
import { normalize, strings } from '@angular-devkit/
core';
import { apply, applyTemplates, chain, mergeWith, move,
Rule, SchematicContext, Tree, url } from '@angular-
devkit/schematics';
import { Schema } from './schema';
```

6. Insert the following code inside the `tailwindContainer` function:

```
_options.path = _options.path ?? normalize('src/app/' +
_options.name as string);

  const templateSource = apply(url('./files'), [
    applyTemplates({
      classify: strings.classify,
      dasherize: strings.dasherize,
      name: _options.name
```

```
        }),
        move(normalize(_options.path as string))
    ]);
```

In the preceding code, first, we set the `path` property of the component in case one is not passed in the schematic. By default, we create a folder inside the `src\app` folder that has the same name as the component. We then use the `apply` method to read the template files from the `files` folder and pass the `dasherize`, `classify`, and `name` properties using the `applyTemplates` function. Finally, we call the `move` method to create the generated component files in the provided path.

7. Add the following statement at the end of the factory function:

```
return chain([
    mergeWith(templateSource)
]);
```

In the preceding snippet, we call the `chain` method to execute our schematic, passing the result of the `mergeWith` function that uses the `templateSource` variable we created in *step 6*.

Now we can go ahead and test our new component schematic:

1. Execute the following npm command to build the schematic:

```
npm run build
```

The preceding command will invoke the TypeScript compiler and transpile the TypeScript source files into JavaScript. It will generate the JavaScript output files into the same folders, side by side, with the TypeScript ones.

2. Run the following command to install the schematics library into our global npm cache:

```
npm link
```

The preceding command is used so that we can install the schematics later without querying the public npm registry.

3. Execute the following Angular CLI command in a folder of your choice outside the workspace to scaffold a new Angular application with default options:

```
ng new my-app --defaults
```

4. Navigate to the my-app folder and run the following command to install our schematics:

```
npm link my-schematics
```

The previous npm command will install the my-schematics library into the current Angular CLI workspace.

> **Tip**
>
> The link command is like running npm install my-schematics, except that it downloads the npm package from the global npm cache of our machine and does not add it to the package.json file.

5. Use the generate command of the Angular CLI to create a dashboard component:

```
ng generate my-schematics:tailwind-container
--name=dashboard
```

In the preceding command, we use our custom schematic by passing the name of our collection, my-schematics, followed by the specific schematic name, tailwind-container, separated by a colon. We also pass a name for our component using the --name option of the schematic.

We can verify that our schematic worked correctly by observing the output in the terminal:

```
CREATE src/app/dashboard/dashboard.component.html (39 bytes)
CREATE src/app/dashboard/dashboard.component.ts (178 bytes)
```

Figure 10.1 – Generate Angular component

We have successfully created a new schematic that we can use for crafting custom Angular components according to our needs. The schematic that we built generates a new Angular component from scratch. Angular CLI is so extensible that we can use it to hook into the execution of built-in Angular schematics and modify them accordingly.

In the following section, we will investigate this by building a schematic for Angular HTTP services.

Creating an HTTP service

For our schematics library, we will create a schematic that scaffolds an Angular service. It will generate a service that imports the built-in HTTP client. It will also contain one method for each HTTP request that is involved in a CRUD operation.

The generation schematic that we are going to build will not stand on its own. Instead, we will combine it with the existing generation schematic of the Angular CLI for services. Thus, we do not need a separate JSON schema.

Let's get started by creating the schematic:

1.   Execute the following command to add a new schematic to our collection:

```
schematics blank crud-service
```

2.   Open the `collection.json` file and provide an explanatory description for the schematic:

```
"crud-service": {
  "description": "Generate a CRUD HTTP service",
  "factory": "./crud-service/index#crudService"
}
```

3.   Create a folder named `files` inside the `crud-service` folder of the workspace.

4.   Create a file named `__name@dasherize__.service.ts.template` inside the `files` folder and add the following code:

```
import { Injectable } from '@angular/core';
import { HttpClient } from '@angular/common/http';
import { Observable } from 'rxjs';

@Injectable({
  providedIn: 'root'
})
export class <%= classify(name) %>Service {
  constructor(private http: HttpClient) { }
}
```

The preceding file is the template of the Angular service file that our schematic will generate. It injects the `HttpClient` service in the constructor of the class by default.

5. Define a service property that will represent the URL of the API with which we want to communicate:

```
apiUrl = '/api';
```

6. Add the following methods for each HTTP request of a CRUD operation:

```
create(obj) {
  return this.http.post(this.apiUrl, obj);
}


read() {
  return this.http.get(this.apiUrl);
}


update(obj) {
  return this.http.put(this.apiUrl, obj);
}


delete(id) {
  return this.http.delete(this.apiUrl + id);
}
```

Creating all the methods beforehand eliminates much of the boilerplate code. The developer that uses the schematic will only need to modify these methods and add the actual implementation for each one.

We have almost finished our schematic except for creating the factory function that will invoke the generation of the service:

1. Open the `index.ts` file of the `crud-service` folder and add the following `import` statements:

```
import { normalize, strings } from '@angular-devkit/
core';
import { apply, applyTemplates, chain, externalSchematic,
MergeStrategy, mergeWith, move, Rule, SchematicContext,
Tree, url } from '@angular-devkit/schematics';
```

2. Rename the `tree` parameter and remove it from the `return` statement because we will not use it. The resulting factory function should look like the following:

```
export function crudService(_options: any): Rule {
  return (_tree: Tree, _context: SchematicContext) =>
    {};
}
```

3. Add the following snippet in the `crudService` function:

```
const templateSource = apply(url('./files'), [
    applyTemplates({
      ..._options,
      classify: strings.classify,
      dasherize: strings.dasherize
    }),
    move(normalize(_options.path ??
      normalize('src/app/')))
  ]);
```

The previous snippet looks identical to the one that we used for our component schematic. The main differences are that the default path is the `src\app` folder and that we pass all available options using the `_options` parameter to the schematic.

> **Important note**
>
> It is not possible to know which options will be used to generate the Angular service beforehand. Thus, we use the *spread* operator to pass all available options to the `templateSource` method. That is also the reason that the `_options` parameter is of type `any`.

4. Add the following `return` statement at the end of the function:

```
return chain([
  externalSchematic('@schematics/angular', 'service',
    _options),
  mergeWith(templateSource, MergeStrategy.Overwrite)
]);
```

In the preceding statement, we first use the `externalSchematic` method to call the built-in generation schematic for creating Angular services. Then, we merge the result from executing that schematic with our `templateSource` variable. We also define the strategy of the merge operation using `MergeStrategy.Overwrite` so that any changes made by our schematic will overwrite the default ones.

Our schematic for creating CRUD services is now complete. Let's use it in our sample application:

1. Execute the following command to build the schematics library:

    ```
    npm run build
    ```

    > **Tip**
    > We do not need to link the schematics library again. Our application will be automatically updated as soon as we make a new build of our schematics.

2. Navigate to the `my-app` folder in which our application resides.

3. Execute the following command to generate an Angular service using our new schematic:

    ```
    ng generate my-schematics:crud-service --name=customers
    ```

    We use the `generate` command of the Angular CLI, passing the name of our schematics collection again but targeting the `crud-service` schematic this time.

4. The new Angular service is created in the `src\app` folder as indicated by the output in the terminal window:

    ```
    CREATE src/app/customers.service.spec.ts (372 bytes)
    CREATE src/app/customers.service.ts (545 bytes)
    ```

    Figure 10.2 – Generating an Angular service

    Notice that the schematic has generated a unit test file for us automatically. How is this possible? Well, recall that we merged our schematic with the built-in generate schematic of the Angular CLI. So, whatever the default schematic does, it reflects directly to the execution of the custom schematic.

We have just added a new helpful command to our schematics collection. We can generate an Angular service that interacts with HTTP endpoints. Moreover, we have added the fundamental methods that will be needed for communicating with the endpoint.

Summary

In this project, we used the schematics API of the Angular CLI to create custom schematics for our needs. We built a schematic for generating Angular components that contain Tailwind CSS styles in their template. We also built another schematic that creates an Angular service to interact with the built-in HTTP client. The service contains all the necessary artifacts for working with an HTTP CRUD application.

The Angular CLI is a flexible and extensible tool that enhances the development experience dramatically. The imagination of each developer is all that limits what can be done with such an asset in their toolchain. The CLI, along with the Angular framework, allows developers to create excellent web applications.

As we have learned throughout this book, the popularity of the Angular framework in the web developer world is so great that it is straightforward to integrate it today with any technology and create fast and scalable Angular applications. So, we encourage you to get the latest version of Angular and create amazing applications today.

Exercise

Create a template for the unit test file that is generated when running the **crud-service** schematic. The file should be placed in the `files` folder of the related schematic. It should configure the testing module to use `HttpClientTestingModule` and `HttpTestingController`. It should also contain one unit test for each method of the service.

You can find the solution to the exercise in the GitHub repository indicated in the *Getting started* section.

Further reading

- Schematics overview: `https://angular.io/guide/schematics`
- Authoring schematics: `https://angular.io/guide/schematics-authoring`
- Schematics for libraries: `https://angular.io/guide/schematics-for-libraries`
- Angular CLI built-in schematics: `https://github.com/angular/angular-cli/tree/master/packages/schematics/angular`

Packt.com

Subscribe to our online digital library for full access to over 7,000 books and videos, as well as industry leading tools to help you plan your personal development and advance your career. For more information, please visit our website.

Why subscribe?

- Spend less time learning and more time coding with practical eBooks and Videos from over 4,000 industry professionals

- Improve your learning with Skill Plans built especially for you

- Get a free eBook or video every month

- Fully searchable for easy access to vital information

- Copy and paste, print, and bookmark content

Did you know that Packt offers eBook versions of every book published, with PDF and ePub files available? You can upgrade to the eBook version at packt.com and as a print book customer, you are entitled to a discount on the eBook copy. Get in touch with us at customercare@packtpub.com for more details.

At www.packt.com, you can also read a collection of free technical articles, sign up for a range of free newsletters, and receive exclusive discounts and offers on Packt books and eBooks.

Other Books You May Enjoy

If you enjoyed this book, you may be interested in these other books by Packt:

Angular for Enterprise-Ready Web Applications - Second Edition
Doguhan Uluca
ISBN: 978-1-83864-880-0

- Adopt a minimalist, value-first approach to delivering web apps
- Master Angular development fundamentals, RxJS, CLI tools, GitHub, and Docker
- Discover the flux pattern and NgRx
- Implement a RESTful APIs using Node.js, Express.js, and MongoDB
- Create secure and efficient web apps for any cloud provider or your own servers
- Deploy your app on highly available cloud infrastructure using DevOps, CircleCI, and AWS

Learning Angular - Third Edition

Aristeidis Bampakos, Pablo Deeleman

ISBN: 978-1-83921-066-2

- Use the Angular CLI to scaffold, build, and deploy a new Angular application
- Build components, the basic building blocks of an Angular application
- Discover techniques to make Angular components interact with each other
- Understand the different types of templates supported by Angular
- Create HTTP data services to access APIs and provide data to components
- Enhance your application's UX with Angular Material
- Apply best practices and coding conventions to your large-scale web development projects

Packt is searching for authors like you

If you're interested in becoming an author for Packt, please visit `authors.packtpub.com` and apply today. We have worked with thousands of developers and tech professionals, just like you, to help them share their insight with the global tech community. You can make a general application, apply for a specific hot topic that we are recruiting an author for, or submit your own idea.

Share Your Thoughts

Hi!

I am Aristeidis Bampakos, author of *Angular Projects Second Edition*. I really hope you enjoyed reading this book and found it useful for increasing your productivity and efficiency in Angular.

It would really help me (and other potential readers!) if you could leave a review on Amazon sharing your thoughts on *Angular Projects Second Edition*. Go to the link below or scan the QR code to leave your review:

`https://packt.link/r/1800205260`

Your review will help me to understand what's worked well in this book, and what could be improved upon for future editions, so it really is appreciated.

Best Wishes,

Index

Made in the USA
Monee, IL
11 August 2022

11379533R00190